Alabama Bill and the Bowery

Whitney Snow

OXFORD SOUTHERN

an imprint of Sunbury Press, Inc.
Mechanicsburg, PA USA

OXFORD SOUTHERN

an imprint of Sunbury Press, Inc.
Mechanicsburg, PA USA

For information about special discounts for bulk purchases, please contact Sunbury Press Orders Dept. at (855) 338-8359 or orders@sunburypress.com.

To request one of our authors for speaking engagements or book signings, please contact Sunbury Press Publicity Dept. at publicity@sunburypress.com.

FIRST OXFORD SOUTHERN EDITION: November 2020

Set in Adobe Garamond | Interior design by Crystal Devine | Cover by Madeleine Norris | Edited by Lawrence Knorr.

Publisher's Cataloging-in-Publication Data
Names: Snow, Whitney Adrienne, editor.
Title: Alabama bill & the bowery : letters from a genteel hobo, 1925–141 / edited by Whitney Adrienne Snow.
Description: First trade paperback edition. | Mechanicsburg, PA : Oxford Southern, 2020.
Summary: World traveler and socialite William Monroe Nabors recorded his journeys and famous encounters in letters to his hometown newspaper. After falling on hard times, Nabors's later years were as a hobo dealing with mental illness.
Identifiers: ISBN 978-1-620064-09-2 (softcover).
Subjects: HISTORY / United States / State & Local / South | HISTORY / United States / State & Local / Middle Atlantic | LANGUAGE ARTS & DISCIPLINES / Journalism | LITERARY COLLECTIONS / Letters | PSYCHOLOGY / Mental Health.

Product of the United States of America
0 1 1 2 3 5 8 13 21 34 55

Continue the Enlightenment!

CONTENTS

Editorial Decisions

When assembling this collection of letters, the editor made very few alterations so as to preserve the voice of William Nabors. First, when transcribing, Microsoft Word flagged many words as misspelled. Nabors had a profound vocabulary, and while these items may be antiquated, they are words, nonetheless. Second, Nabors attempted to write in southern dialect, and with rare exception, the editor did not change the style. One instance was modifying one title, "Uncle Bim F'rm Geogha" to "Uncle Bim From Georgia." Third, Nabors was prone to use run-on sentences, and the editor did not attempt to correct this. Doing so would have required rewriting virtually every one of his letters. Fourth, Nabors had his own style of punctuation, which the editor did not modify so as to retain his inflections.

The editor attempted to identify all the historical figures Nabors claimed to have met. Sometimes, however, he provided only a surname or no name, just a description. In those cases, it was not always possible to discern their identities. The editor did not provide descriptions of well-known political figures like Franklin D. Roosevelt or renowned authors like Gertrude Stein and Erskine Caldwell.

C H A P T E R   1

The Life and Times of William Nabors

"Father calls me William
Sister calls me Will
Mother calls me Willie
But the fellas call me Bill"
—*Jest 'Fore Christmas* by Eugene Field

Journalist, poet, short-story author, and philosopher, William Monroe Nabors led a life fraught with adventure, reflection, and sorrow. While traveling the world and the United States multiple times in his 58 years, he made either the acquaintance or friendship of many historical figures like Hobo King Dan O'Brien, novelist Maxwell Bodenheim, and Arizona Governor George W.P. Hunt.[1] He recorded his experiences in letters to his hometown newspaper, the *Guntersville Advertiser and Democrat.* These letters contain his observations on historical figures like Zane Grey and Harry Houdini as well as events like the

---

1. Dan O'Brien (1859–1949) was often referred to as the King of Hobos or as the Hobo Philosopher. In O'Brien's words, "The hobo is merely a migratory worker, willing to swap work anywhere for the privilege of travel and freedom from the annoyance of possessions. The tramp, on the contrary, is a passive misanthrope, too lazy to work, and the bum is definitely anti-social." "A Man to Envy," *Times Record* (New York), November 7, 1949. Maxwell Bodenheim (1892–1954) wrote over a dozen novels and eight poetry books in addition to writing for magazines like the *New Yorker.* Originally from Mississippi, Bodenheim grew up in Chicago where he entered the literary scene. He later moved to New York City where he became widely known as King of the Bohemians. Bodenheim often pretended to be blind when panhandling. See, for example, Jack B. Moore, *Maxwell Bodenheim* (New York City: Twayne Publishers, 1970); and Maxwell Bodenheim, *My Life and Loves in Greenwich Village* (New York City: Belmont, 1961). George W.P. Hunt (1859–1934) was Arizona's first governor and had a soft spot for the poor and downtrodden. See, David R. Berman, *George Hunt: Arizona's Crusading Seven-Term Governor* (Tucson: University of Arizona Press, 2015).

fire of the SS *Morro Castle*.[2] Nabors's correspondence began in the late 1920s and tapered off in the early 1940s. The reason for the silencing of so passionate and addictive a voice was progressive mental illness, which culminated in his eventual suicide. Born to a farming family in north Alabama, Nabors died indigent in New York City's Bowery.

It is only fitting to begin this treatise with his profoundly touching description of the hometown newspaper within which Nabors wrote his joys, troubles, hopes, and above all else, wonderment at the changing world:

> The home paper is not only a faithful chronicle of our desires, aspirations, achievements, pleasures, tragedies, comedies, successes, and failures, it is in somewhat a record of our lives here, and often the only testament to our existence. And its (the paper's) files shall sooner or later become the repository in which shall repose in transcript the remains of many of us who otherwise shall have ceased to be. And, who knows? Perhaps fifty years hence, when some enterprising researcher is perusing this column, he will wonder what matter of person this quaint individual was who signed himself Wm. Nabors!

Nabors claimed to be psychic, but his 1937 prophecy came to fruition more than 80 years later. In 2016 at the Marshall County, Alabama, Archives, I discovered Nabors's articles. His foresight envisioned an avid scholar; little did he realize the researcher to be a great-niece. While the Marshall County Archives, Arab Historical Society, and one of his nieces, Annette (Snow) Haislip, accumulated an array of his publications, I diligently collected every scrap, essays, poems, and stories, published by the local newspaper under Nabors's byline. Fortunately, I also found references to him in other newspapers, including the *New York World*, the *Columbia Spectator*, the *Birmingham Age-Herald*, and the *Bowery News*.

---

2. Novelist Zane Grey (1872–1939) wrote almost eighty books like *Riders of the Purple Sage*, becoming an icon in western literature. See, Stephen J. May, *Zane Grey: Romancing the West* (Athens: Ohio University Press, 1997); and Thomas H. Pauly, *Zane Grey: His Life, His Adventures, His Women* (Chicago: University of Illinois Press, 2005). Harry Houdini (1874–1926) won fame for his skills as a magician/illusionist. See, Brooke Kamin Rapaport, *Houdini: Art and Magic* (New Haven: Yale University Press, 2010). On September 8, 1934, a fire broke out on the SS *Morro Castle*, ultimately killing 137 people. The ship later beached close to Asbury Park on the Jersey Shore. See, for example, Hal Burton, *The Morro Castle: Tragedy at Sea* (New York: Viking, 1973); and Thomas Gallagher, *Fire at Sea: The Mysterious Tragedy of the Morro Castle* (Guilford, CT: Lyons Press, 2003).

Nabors's prediction certainly hit home about one thing. From the first moment of reading one of his letters, I became mesmerized. Wanting to understand more about this mysterious great-uncle, I began a crusade of collecting to understand his life. Family lore remembered him as gifted with many talents but fraught with wanderlust and various addictions. Unsatisfied with hearsay, I sought mention of Nabors in online newspaper repositories. A college professor, I have a knack for researching obscure topics and find it something of a treasure hunt.

Based on remarks made by Nabors, I doubt that he had any respect for academia. He reviled college professors, especially after a debate with an austere Harvard University professor who had offended by asking if there were still "wild Indians" in Alabama. Nabors once said:

> There is not one professor out of a hundred who could even describe
> a dogfight. They can only repeat what somebody else, usually some
> writer, has written. The average professor is apt to be too preoccupied,
> pedagogue like, with the correctness of the speech to ever say anything
> worth listening to.

I hope this project has the merit to disprove his assessment.

A volunteer at the Marshall County Archives, I read old bound newspapers in a quest for topics/stories to write for the *Advertiser-Gleam* as community service. Along the way, I also record anything pertinent to family genealogy. Some four years ago, I started reading serialized articles written by a man whose surname was Nabors. Using a digital camera, I snapped photographs while pursuing the more immediate task of seeking stories on celebrities who had visited Guntersville. As I progressed in chronology, I found more and more articles and eventually felt compelled to read one. Doing so broke one of my cardinal rules—never get sidetracked—but I have no regrets. Hooked, I devoured his writings. The more I read, the more I wanted to learn about this journalist who traveled not only the country but the world and concluded, "most of it was merely wasted time!" By sleuthing, I slowly pieced together his life and transitioned from calling him Nabors to William, Will, or Uncle Will. Because I did not like part of what I discovered, this process became a difficult, challenging journey.

As a historian, remaining objective remains a constant goal but, I must confess, finding a relative, albeit a distant one, with an amazing journalistic anthology fueled my passion for the project. As I started researching, I had

3

little to go on except a non-too-complimentary description by my late father: "He was a drunken bum and Hemingway wannabe." Giving people the benefit of the doubt, I dismissed the assessment since my dad never actually met his uncle. For good or bad, shards of truth can be found in family gossip. Although Nabors professed to be a teetotaler, I discerned hints or innuendo referencing a drinking problem. Alcoholism was merely one of his foibles.

Over time, I found some of Nabors's writings included Anti-Semitic, nativist, and racist statements. This greatly dismayed me, for I find such attitudes reprehensible. Although these remarks, however cringe-worthy, appear to reflect common sentiments from that era, there is no excuse or justification for bigotry. One example of Nabors's intolerance can be found in the article "More Foreigners Coming," which was written in the summer of 1938:

> Justice Cardozo, one of the two members of the Jewish faith on the bench of the U.S. Supreme Court, has passed away. And this is to be regretted indeed, for Mr. Justice Cardozo, whom I knew personally, was a great jurist, a profoundly learned scholar, and a gracious and humane man. And if we had more Jews like him and fewer of the rabble-rousing lunatic types our country would be better off.[3]

I regret to say that this is one of his milder commentaries.

In Nabors's letters, I also found that he believed in the paranormal and thought himself psychic. He confessed, rather proudly, to having visions and hearing voices. Thinking he may have been pulling the proverbial leg of his readers, I first questioned his convictions. Eventually, I granted that he seemed to believe that which he professed. As Nabors explained, "I, like many another poet, am much preoccupied with thoughts of the mystery and meaning of life here on earth, and the (probable) continuation of it in that other, and eternal, life to come." In his article "Children of the Shadows," he argued that "genius and insanity are very closely related."

Perplexed by his talk of hearing voices, I asked several older relatives who had met Nabors. One niece assessed his behavior as bi-polar while another judged it schizophrenic. Intrigued, I consulted a colleague, Dr. Michael Vandehey, a professor of psychology at Midwestern State University. After reading a sampling of

---

3. Benjamin N. Cardozo (1870–1938), a progressive liberal, served as an Associate Justice on the U.S. Supreme Court from 1932 until his death. See, Richard A. Posner, *Cardozo: A Study in Reputation* (Chicago: University of Illinois Press, 1990).

Nabors's letters, he speculated the disorder to be "schizophrenia, schizoaffective disorder, depression with psychotic features, or Bipolar I or II with psychotic features." Though hesitant, given that he had never met Nabors, Vandehey's personal opinion was late-onset schizophrenia, which may have been caused or exacerbated by a head injury sustained during an automobile collision and worsened by alcohol consumption. Realizing that my great uncle had more layers than imagined, I often thought of my grandmother and wanted to ask her myriad questions. Alas, that opportunity had been long lost.

My paternal grandmother Gladys (Nabors) Snow, whom I called "Granny," was a younger sister of William Nabors.[4] I remember little about Granny except that she loved to paint, sew, make dolls, write poetry, and study genealogy. I also recall that she always spoke of herself in the third person. She often talked of her four sisters, Dura, Zola, Tempie, and Lou, and her brother Riley.[5] She never mentioned William when regaling me with stories. I never met any of her siblings, so the names blurred in my mind. Being a child, far more focused on Granny's teacakes than family lore, I asked no questions; something I deeply regret. Granny passed away in 2005, and, oh, what I would ask about William if she were still alive today!

---

4. Gladys Odell Nabors (1908–2005) married Roy Snow on December 25, 1928. Gladys and Roy farmed until the latter took a job with the Tennessee Valley Authority. Throughout her life, Gladys enjoyed participating in social clubs and church activities. As hobbies, she painted and wrote poetry. She and Roy had two children, Donald and Annette. U.S., Find a Grave, 1600s-Current, Alabama, County Marriages, 1805–1967; and Snow Private Collection.

5. Dura Nabors (1902–1974) married cotton broker Millard F. Elrod on May 10, 1923. She later worked as a nurse. After Elrod's death in 1960, she married William H. McGaughey. Alabama, Deaths and Burials Index, 1881–1974; Alabama, Marriage Collection, 1800–1969; and *Advertiser-Gleam*, November 28, 1974. Zola Carolyn Nabors (1914–1979) married Ralph Hough and had one son, Charles. She moved from Alabama to Arkansas and then to Miami, Florida. She later married Charles Vandenburg whom she predeceased. Alabama, County Marriages, 1805–1867; U.S. City Directories, 1822–1995; and U.S., Find a Grave Index, 1600s-Current. Tempie Jean Nabors (1912–2002) preferred to go by "Jean." She married Louie Irwin Lumpkin on November 22, 1932. They had three children: Jerry, Betty, and Steve. Louie worked at the Soil Conservation Service while she was a housewife. Like her brother William, Tempie enjoyed writing poetry. U.S., Find a Grave Index, 1600s-Current; Alabama County Marriages, 1805–1967; and Nabors Private Collection. Lula Mae Nabors (1906–1976) attended college to become a teacher. An automobile accident left her confined to a wheelchair, but she insisted on doing her own housework. In 1940, she married Norman Vaughn and later had a daughter named Jane. The Vaughns eventually divorced. U.S., Find a Grave Index, 1600s-Current; Alabama Marriage Index, 1800–1969; U.S., WWII Draft Cards Young Men, 1940–1947; and Nabors Private Collection. Riley Nabors (1903–1966) married Grace Bunch in 1922 and had a son named Ray. After they divorced, Riley wed Bonnie Nunn in 1931. The couple had five children: June, Robert, Billy, James, and Sammy. Riley worked for the Tennessee Valley Authority. U.S., Find a Grave Index, 1600s-Current; Alabama, Deaths and Burials Index, 1881–1974; Alabama County Marriages, 1805–1967; and *Advertiser Gleam*, July 22, 1966.

Then again, when I do the math, Granny was only eleven in 1919, the year when William fled the state after being arrested for bootlegging. From that time until he died in 1958, he made only three visits to Guntersville, so while Granny professed a strong relationship, one she likely felt due to an exchange of letters, brother and sister spent very little time together. Indeed, I have often wondered if Granny thought him as big a mystery as I do. There is an old saying that those closest to us elude our comprehension. I do not doubt that Granny spent much of her life thinking of her brother. Apparently, William took his own life ten days after she signed a form to commit him to Bryce, Alabama's state mental hospital.

When one of his nieces mentioned that William had undergone electroshock treatment, I tried to find evidence. To my mind, it made sense that the location would have been Bellevue since he spent most of his life in New York City. Due to HIPPA laws, however, I was unable to confirm or disprove if he had ever been institutionalized. I then looked to Bryce and was thwarted again by current regulations on medical records. I almost gave up until I was informed by Betty Taylor, the head of the Marshall County Archives, about a filing cabinet which contained commitment forms. I vividly remember the day I approached that cabinet. Looking through the alphabetical files, I felt a mixture of excitement and sadness as I saw the name William Nabors. My heart immediately sank as I read the signature at the bottom of the page—Mrs. Roy Snow. Although my grandmother was trying to help her brother, a little over a week later, he was dead.

William Nabors was born on January 2, 1900, in Marshall County, Alabama, near Guntersville. While his parents Richard and Lucinda (Hulsey) Nabors owned acreage plus a cotton gin and grist mill, William wanted to escape provincial life.[6] The eldest of seven children, his siblings were Dura, Riley, Lula, Gladys, Tempie, and Zola. The blue-eyed William had a mop of brown hair and could often be seen with his nose in a book. Dabbling in writing, he fancied becoming a great poet. On December 23, 1915, "War Times,"

---

6. The son of Joseph Riley Nabors and Amanda Stephens, Richard Monroe Nabors (1876–1963) had a head of bright red hair and a personality to match. In addition to farming, Richard and his wife Lucinda Caroline Hulsey (1882–1961) operated a sawmill, gin, and grist mill on Shoal Creek at a place called Nabors Mill. Based on census records, their already large household was enhanced with farm hands and mill workers. Richard memorized the Bible and often corrected ministers who misquoted passages. He also loved to preach to anyone willing to listen. Even so, he enjoyed drinking and carried around a hollow Bible in which he kept a flask. A short man, his grandchildren called him "Little Daddy." Alabama County Marriages, 1805–1967; U.S., Find a Grave Index, 1600s-Current; and Nabors Private Collection.

a Civil War-themed poem, was published in a local newspaper. For a family focused on putting food on the table, William's preoccupation with writing was deemed extraordinarily odd. His parents expected him to become a farmer and one day run the family business. To their dismay, their eldest son appeared to have his head in the clouds, always talking of distant places and his ambition to become a famous author. William became the black sheep of the family at an early age. Even so, he grew into a jovial, albeit intellectually vain young man.

William's education began with his father Richard, who, though lacking formal schooling, constantly read and memorized passages from the Bible. From the age of six to eight, William attended a one-room schoolhouse at a community named Frogpond. Under the tutelage of teacher Campbell Leach, he learned the basics. William then advanced to a two-room school at the Union Grove community. While there, he had two teachers—J.O. Johnston and Walker Shumate. At fifteen, William attended the Marshall County High School, where he studied with Oscar Horton, teacher and principal. Because there were no buses in his rural community, he boarded with the Dr. David C. Jordan family.[7] In remarkable time, William graduated in 1916 and moved back home. Much of his later writings look back on this period with deep nostalgia.

By his late teens, William had become more convinced than ever that his fate lay elsewhere. His discontent manifested into troublemaking. On April 30, 1919, William and his Uncle Jud Nabors were arrested for "manufacturing prohibited liquor."[8] While a similar case had taken place when William was fourteen, due to his youth, he was only made to spend a night in jail. This time, given his age and the preponderance of the evidence, a court date had been scheduled. Both he and his uncle jumped bail and fled the area. Thus, began William's life as a wanderer.

Wherever he went, by late July, William was back in Guntersville, albeit briefly, because on July 8, 1919, the local newspaper reported that he and Phocian Shipp left the day before to travel to Akron, Ohio, to seek work in a tire factory. It can be deduced that no employment was found, at least for William,

---

7. Dr. David Carnes Jordan (1868–1951) was a physician, health officer, bank director, and drugstore owner in Guntersville. He was married to Sophia Timmons. U.S., Find a Grave Index, 1600s- Current; and County Marriage Records, 1805–1967, Marshall County Archives, Guntersville, Alabama.

8. Jud Nabors (1890–1984), Richard's brother, worked in the Texas oilfields as a young man and played baseball. He returned to Marshall County, Alabama, where he married Mamie Graves. The couple reared four sons—Ronald, Donald, Max, and Franklin—and three daughters—Shirley, Sarah Ann, and Gaynell. The family farmed. Unlike Richard, Jud was rather tall. Friends and family teased them about being Mutt and Jeff. U.S., Find a Grave Index, 1600s-Current; Alabama, County Marriages, 1805–1967; and Nabors Private Collection.

because he soon returned. Then, on July 22, 1919, the newspaper reported that he and Calvin Bolding left the day before with the intent of moving to South Dakota to work in the upcoming harvest. In late November, William once again visited Guntersville, and according to the newspaper, he was late from the "woolly west." From a note in the paper in April 1920, William was living in Hull, Texas, and by December, he was residing in Humble, Texas. In May 1921, Guntersville boy Raymond Gilley, who was living in Norphlet, Arkansas, claimed William was residing in or at least passing through El Dorado, Arkansas. However, that October, William renewed his subscription to the Guntersville newspaper and listed Mexia, Texas, as his address.

According to family legend, William moved to Tyler, Texas, sometime in 1922. This location was chosen in part because his Uncle Johnnie Nabors lived there.[9] William must not have stayed long because his later writings place him in Tyronza, Arkansas, that same year. While in Tyronza, relatives provided him housing. After a short but sweet romance with a planter's daughter, William joined a Texas barber on a trek from De Queen, Arkansas, to Seminole Territory, Oklahoma. Seemingly caught up in oil-fever, he worked as a derrickman throughout Oklahoma and Texas. When the border called in 1922, he explored Mexico and fell in love with a young woman named Carmelita, the daughter of a Castilian general. The general did not approve of their relationship. Once back in the U.S., William could have returned to his parents. Goodness knows they certainly needed him as the family's cotton gin/grist mill burned in October, and there was no insurance. Since his parents could not afford to rebuild, the family fell on hard times, forced to rely solely on farm income. William never mentioned this tragedy in his writings, so his sentiments are unknown on the subject. While he no doubt pitied his parents, he sought something besides a hardscrabble life on the farm. That said, he resumed his attempt to see as much of the world as possible.

At Skull Valley, Arizona, in 1923, William had a harrowing experience when he and a companion were trapped in a railroad refrigerator car. After surviving this close call, he traveled to San Francisco, where he became the victim of a robbery. From there, he went to Alaska, where he met a Captain Allen whom he referred to as the "famous English globetrotter."[10] He had a brief stint

---

9. John Riley Nabors (1880–1957), the brother of Richard and Jud, married Belle Fielding and had eight children. In 1920, the couple resided in Tyronza, Arkansas. By 1930s, they had moved to Tyler, Texas. 1920, 1930 U.S. Federal Census; Alabama County Marriages, 1805–1967; and U.S., Find a Grave Index, 1600s-Current.

10. The editor was unable to definitively discern the identity of Captain Allen.

as a fisherman but returned to California and became a reporter for Cornelius Vanderbilt IV's *Los Angeles Illustrated Daily News*.[11] This position allowed him to hone his writing skills while learning about L.A. Though he seemed to enjoy his time in southern California, William concluded that "writing, instead of being a short or an easy way to riches, is too often apt to be only a slow way of starving to death!"

More often than not, William was assigned stories that failed to spark his interest. For example, he was sent to cover a séance which, at that time, he found ridiculous. There were, however, exceptions, namely his coverage of the 1926 Rose Bowl in which the University of Alabama competed. Living in L.A. also afforded unexpected treats like meeting actress Marie Dressler and seeing Harry Houdini perform.[12] Unable to resist the glitz and glamour of Hollywood, William wrote a screenplay, but its plot, about the hardships would-be actresses faced, was so depressing that it failed to sell. For whatever reason, in 1925, he journeyed to Astoria, Oregon, where he boarded the *Admiral Peary Smith*.[13] Over the following year, he spent time in Denver, Colorado; Dallas, Texas, which he called "The New York of the South;" St. Louis, Missouri; and various parts of Arizona.

William, it seemed, enjoyed Arizona even though the *Los Angeles Illustrated Daily News* assigned him to cover that particular beat. In 1925, William traveled from Yuma to Phoenix with a psychology lecturer named Dr. Moffet.[14] While in Arizona, he claimed that he became well acquainted with Governor George W.P. Hunt. I tried to verify this relationship through the George Hunt Collection but found the 1925 diary had entries only for January and February, a period before William arrived in Arizona.

When the *Los Angeles Illustrated Daily News* went bankrupt in 1926, William found himself without employment. He said that Hunt gave him a job as a commissary clerk at the "Mesa Canyon Dam." According to Rob Spindler, the

---

11. The *Los Angeles Illustrated Daily News* (1923–1926) stood out because it used a lot of photographs, almost like a tabloid but without sensationalism. The paper went bankrupt in 1926, but after being acquired by Manchester Boddy, became the *Los Angeles Daily News*. Online Archives of California, https://oac.cdlib.org/findaid/ark:/13030/kt9b69q98h/

12. Marie Dressler (1868–1934) segued from Vaudeville to Broadway and then to films. A versatile actress, she was primarily known as a comic and singer. She won an Academy Award in 1931 for her role in the dramedy *Min and Bill*. See, Betty Lee, *Marie Dressler: The Unlikeliest Star* (Lexington: University Press of Kentucky, 1997).

13. The editor found few references on the *Admiral Peary Smith*. See, for example, "Ship Wireless Reports," *San Francisco Examiner*, April 1, 1926; and "Ship Wireless Reports," *San Francisco Examiner*, July 30, 1928.

14. The editor was unable to discern the identity of Dr. Moffet.

University Archivist at Arizona State University Libraries, "This could refer to a series of dams on the Salt River near Mesa, Arizona, possibly Horse Mesa Dam or Mormon Flat Dam, both of which were completed between 1925–1927." Unhappy, William asked for another option, so Hunt offered him a position as a concrete shooter on the Gila Canal, part of the Wellton-Mohawk Irrigation District close to Yuma. William accepted and much preferred it to the previous job, but he only stayed a brief time as wanderlust struck again.

Throughout the late 1920s, William worked in lumber camps in Washington. While traveling to Vancouver, British Columbia, he was mugged by a white man, described as having the air of an old cowboy. At some point, William worked as a traveling salesman. In February 1927, he journeyed on the SS *Montana* from Antwerp and Hamburg to New York City.[15] That May, he visited Montreal, Canada. While there, he was asked by a working man's club to participate in a debate on contemporary literature. He also spoke on Keats at a poetry club. In Montreal, William met Hobo King Dan O'Brien at a coffee shop on Rue Saint Antoine. Later that year, he tramped with painter Simeon H. Pickering through the Adirondack Mountains, Quebec, and Nova Scotia.[16] At some point, he also visited Milwaukee, Chicago, and Detroit. Around that time, William claimed to have declined a Phoenix job offered by Governor Hunt. In September 1927, he traveled from London to New York City and then took a train to Washington, D.C. While in Virginia, he did journalistic work. The following year, William finally decided to find a permanent home.

In April 1928, William sailed from Cuba to New York City on a ship called *Moon Dance*.[17] While in New York City, he ran into future literary critic Ralph Adimari who convinced him to remain in the Big Apple.[18] William and Adimari partnered in the ownership of a bookstore, the Columbia Book

---

15. Likely the cargo steamer SS *Wheatland Montana*, commissioned in 1919 and sunk in 1942. "Wheatland Montana SS," Wreck Site, https://www.wrecksite.eu/wreck.aspx?183001 (Accessed April 2, 2020).

16. Originally from Utah, Simeon Horace Pickering (1894–1987) served in World War I. He studied at the Art Institute of Chicago and did post-graduate work in New York City where he later worked as a guide at the Statue of Liberty. "Centerville Chats," *Davis County Clipper* (Bountiful, UT), September 12, 1919; "To Study Commercial Art," *Salt Lake Tribune*, September 14, 1919; "Plan for Liberty," *Miami News*, March 7, 1948; and "Simeon H. Pickering," *Salt Lake Tribune*, July 8, 1987.

17. The editor was unable to discover any information on the *Moon Dance*.

18. Ralph T. Adimari (1902–1970) was a bibliophile who worked as an editor and historian of the novel. His papers are currently housed in the Fales Library and Special Collections at the Elmer Holmes Bobst Library in New York. The Fales Library Special Collections, http://dlib.nyu.edu/findingaids/html/fales/adimari/ (Accessed April 4, 2020). For a time, Adimari and Nabors co-owned the Columbia Book Service on West 23rd Street in New York City. "William Nabors Slowly Improving," *Guntersville Advertiser*, August 28, 1935.

Service, at 131 West 23rd Street in Manhattan. It was there that William met Edgar Lee Masters, who patronized the shop.[19] As a favor to a friend, William briefly managed a hotel on 33rd Street near 5th Avenue. On April 12, 1932, he met poets Edwin Markham and Vachel Lindsay.[20] The Great Depression likely curtailed the success of the bookstore because, in 1933, William became an Associate Editor at an unnamed New York City publishing firm. That year held an array of vivid experiences.

By then, William had firmly settled into life in the Big Apple. One weekend, he visited with an unnamed Japanese diplomat, who owned an impressive apartment. At one point, William attended a speech by George Bernard Shaw.[21] In December, he bumped into Hobo King Dan O'Brien at the 5th Avenue Play House. With O'Brien was Anna Denisevich, the widow of playwright/novelist Leonid Andreyev.[22] Also, in1933, William expressed his belief in the supernatural, namely spirits. While apartment sitting in the Lower East Side near Brooklyn Bridge, he felt a ghostly presence. This was the first of many such claims.

The year 1934 resulted in a slew of letters from William to the *Guntersville Advertiser*. In June, he wrote of seeing President Franklin D. Roosevelt give a speech for the U.S. Navy at the New York harbor. In August, he had lunch with sculptor Homer Bevans.[23] On September 10, 1934, William drove to the New Jersey coast to see the remains of the SS *Morro Castle*. This letter is particularly

---

19. Author Edgar Lee Masters (1868–1950) wrote numerous poetry collections and novels. He also wrote biographies on figures ranging from Abraham Lincoln to Vachel Lindsay. See, Herbert K. Russell, *Edgar Lee Masters: A Biography* (Chicago: University of Illinois Press, 2001).

20. Edwin Markham (1852–1940) was an Oregon-born poet and speaker who published several collections of verse like *The Man with the Hoe and Other Poems* (1899) and *Gates of Paradise* (1920). See, Louis Filler, *The Unknown Edwin Markham: His Mystery and Its Significance* (Kent, OH: Kent State University Press, 1966). Born in Springfield, Illinois, Vachel Lindsay (1879–1931) was a famous poet who published works like *Rhymes to be Traded for Bread* (1912). He spent much of his youth tramping the country. When his career declined, he committed suicide. See, Mark Harris, *City of Discontent: An Interpretive Biography of Vachel Lindsay, Being also the Story of Springfield for that City, that State, and that Nation* (Second Chance Press, 1990).

21. George Bernard Shaw (1856–1950) was a famous Irish playwright known for works like *Pygmalion* (1912). See, for example, Michael Holroyd, *Bernard Shaw: The One-Volume Definitive Edition* (New York: Random House, 1998).

22. Leonid Andreyev (1871–1919) married Anna Ilyinishna Denisevich in April 1908. Based on his diary entries, the widowed Russian playwright was absolutely besotted with his new wife. See, Alexander Kaun, *Leonid Andreyev: A Critical Study* (New York: B.W. Huebsch, Inc., 1924), 86; and Josephine Newcombe, *Leonid Andreyev* (Ungar, 1973).

23. Homer Bevans, Jr. (-1934), the son of Homer Bevans Sr and Jane Murray, worked as a sculptor in New York City. He died there on November 19, 1934, leaving behind wife Gladys and son Michael. "Death Notices," *Chicago Tribune*, November 23, 1934.

descriptive and shows his appreciation for history and his sympathy for its victims.

On August 14, 1935, William endured the pain of an array of broken bones when hit by a taxi-cab. In the aftermath, the *New York World-Telegram* printed the following: "William Nabors, Southern poet and writer, who with Ralph Adimari, owned the Columbia Book Service on W. 23rd St., was run down last week by a speeding auto and very badly broken up. He is at St. Vincent's Hospital." Of the accident, the *Guntersville Advertiser* reported, "We are indeed sorry to learn that Wm. Nabors, of New York City, who has written so many interesting articles for the *Advertiser* is in St. Vincent's Hospital in New York, suffering from a crushed leg and other injuries he received in an automobile accident."[24] Hospitalized for almost a month, he wrote multiple letters and poems, some about the nurses and patients.

A little over a year later, William made news for public intoxication. This can be interpreted as either ironic or hypocritical because William professed to abhor drunks. In reflecting on this later event, one wonders if the accident mentioned above could be blamed on the taxi driver. According to the September 29, 1936, edition of the *Columbia Daily Spectator*, William made a spectacle of himself on the campus of Columbia University:

> William Nabors had a disappointed audience last night. That is, if he
> had an audience at all. He claimed, in the course of his wanderings about
> the campus yesterday, that he was to lecture on poetry. He also claimed
> that he was the greatest authority on poetry, . . . the greatest journalist in
> the country. Mr. Nabors, who said he was a graduate of Columbia in the
> class of 1921, spent his afternoon yesterday telling all who would stop
> and listen to his alcoholic words everything they wanted to know about
> the present state of Alma Mater. His words were slightly indistinct, and
> one could only determine that his college brethren were 'just a bunch
> of punks.' As if to demonstrate that he did not fall into this category, he
> showed his savoir faire, savoir vivre, and general worldliness by tipping
> his hat and uttering a sprightly 'hello, darling' to every incredulous
> Barnard and University undergrad student passing. 'Sure, I know poetry,'
> he said belligerently to a lawyer emerging from Kent. 'Why, I know
> Max Bodenheim too. He's a good friend of mine. Why he and I used

---

24. untitled, *Guntersville Advertiser*, August 14, 1935.

to . . .' Here he stopped to greet, in his courtly manner, a girl bound for University Hall. Somebody reminded him that Maxwell Bodenheim was working for the WPA. That raised Mr. Nabors' ire. 'Well, did you ever know a poet who (pause—business of greeting) . . . wasn't poor?—The only ones who aren't are those rich boys that pander to the tastes of . . .' He paused again with another 'Hello, darling.' Then, stepping jauntily, if somewhat uncertainly along, swinging a lacquered cane and twirling his moustache (which he wears pointed at the ends), he lapsed back into a heartfelt but mumbled condemnation. Mr. Nabors' love for his college was felt to be somewhat misplaced in the Registrar's office and in the Alumni office. The former claimed that no such gentleman was planning to speak on poetry that night. It was though in some circles that Mr. Nabors was referring to a mass meeting at the Sun Dial. At the Alumni office, a search of the files revealed a dearth of Mr. Nabors. However, he had already reeled his way off the campus and so was unavailable for a statement when news of his standing at Columbia was released.[25]

Just why he decided to visit the university is unclear because he never mentioned this embarrassing episode in his writings. What most struck me was his claim to be a college graduate when he had repeatedly maintained that "surprisingly few of the truly profound and learned minds whom it has been my privilege to encounter could boast a college education." Drinking likely contributed to his mental decline. Around that same time, William started having what he dubbed "visions." He believed he had predicted an elderly friend's stroke. Yet another, even more disturbing alteration to his personality occurred the following year.

On May 10, 1937, while walking on New York City's Houston Street, William was mugged and beaten by two men he perceived to be Italian. Having been punched so hard that he lost all of his teeth on the left side of his mouth, he feared the "muggers" intended to kill him. Afterward, William developed an even stronger aversion to immigrants. While some of his letters already had overt aspects of nativism, his xenophobic language intensified. He was conflicted, however, because several letters condemned intolerance. In a few writings, he made a point to describe his attempts to aid city newcomers, including a Black man.

---

25. "Tipsy 'Alumnus' Hellos Females, Forgets his 'Lecture' on Poetry," *Columbia Spectator*, September 29, 1936.

In 1938, William resided at 16 Rivington Street in Greenwich Village. That May, his comments about the passing of poet laureate Samuel Minturn Peck were published in the *Birmingham Age-Herald*.[26] Sometime that summer, he was employed "as associate editor on a big publication that employed no less than 400 writers." The following year, William was painted by the artist Clifford Addams.[27] In 1940, William worked at an unnamed newspaper in New York City. The only clue he provided was that he wrote on the twentieth floor of a skyscraper. During this year, William asserted that "one of our most gifted and respected Alabama writers wrote me not long ago and honored me by requesting permission to present my name for honorary membership in the Alabama Poetry Society." Then, in 1941, William slipped into a mental abyss when he spoke of having a "Guardian Angel," whom only he could see and hear.

Before delving into his later life, I would like to take a moment to discuss William's love for literature. He had a habit of inserting off-topic trivia tidbits about authors into his writings. His favorite American authors were Edgar Allan Poe, Washington Irving, Nathaniel Hawthorne, and Stephen Crane. French writers like Honoré de Balzac, Alexandre Dumas, Théophile Gautier, and Victor Hugo were greatly admired. He had a soft spot for Russian authors Fyodor Dostoyevsky, Maxim Gorky, and Leo Tolstoy. He called Dostoyevsky "the greatest novelist the world has ever seen." English writers like Thomas De Quincey, Charles Dickens, Henry Fielding, Oliver Goldsmith, William Thackeray, and Oscar Wilde were close to William's heart. While he loved Poe's poems, he believed that Geoffrey Chaucer, Edmund Spenser, and William Shakespeare, all Englishmen, were the greatest poets who ever lived. Much as he made clear his likes, so too did William voice his dislikes.

While he professed to disdain several authors, the three he often criticized were Gertrude Stein, William Faulkner, and Erskine Caldwell. In an article titled "Communism: A Racket," he wrote that Stein "goes in mostly for nasal

---

26. Samuel Minturn Peck (1854–1938) was the first poet laureate from Alabama. He was born in Tuscaloosa County and earned a master's degree from the University of Alabama in 1876. He earned a medical degree at New York's Bellevue Hospital Medical School, but his true passion lay with writing. He authored several poetry collections like *Rhymes and Roses* (1895) and *Maybloom and Myrtle* (1910). Benjamin Buford Williams, "Samuel Peck," *Encyclopedia of Alabama*, http://www.encyclopediaofalabama.org/article/h-2550 (Accessed April 4, 2020).

27. Clifford Addams (1876–1942) gained fame through his paintings and etchings. Born in New Jersey, he attended the Pennsylvania Academy of Fine Arts and later traveled to Paris where he studied at Whistler's Académie Carmen. Eventually, he became an apprentice to Whistler himself. "Clifford Addams," Campbell Fine Art, http://www.campbell-fine-art.com/artists.php?id=15 (Accessed April 4, 2020).

inarticulations and incoherent babblings that are supposed, by those who cannot understand it, to constitute this good lady a genius of a very lofty and world-shaking order." In that same article, he said Faulkner was "uncouth" and "mistakes vulgarity for daring smartness." As to Caldwell, William believed the author was prejudiced against the South. Indeed, William took great offense to Caldwell's February 21, 1935, *New York Post* article "Starving Babies Suckled by Dogs in Georgia Wastes." It should be noted, however, that the title of that article was chosen by the *Post*, not Caldwell. Even so, William referred to Caldwell as a "renegade southerner" and "anti-Southern ranter." It is safe to say that William was extremely passionate about the South and did not abide stereotypes. He felt just as zealously about politics.

William often gave opinions on politicians running for office at local, state, and national levels. In a 1938 letter titled "Stick with Starnes," he stated:

> I once asked H.G. Wells how best to judge the intelligence of a country, thinking that, being a famous historian and writer himself, he'd say something about literature and the fine arts.[28] But no! 'By the politicians they represent,' came his shrewd reply. And it is true that the world is apt to judge our level of intelligence by the type of people we select to represent us.

Years later, in an article titled "Our Limited Knowledge," which appeared in the September 17, 1941, edition of the *Guntersville Advertiser*, William wrote:

> In this year of our Lord 1941 the men of earth are destroying one another on a gigantic scale never dreamed of before in all history. And the really tragic and sad part is, that these myriads of perishing men know not for why or what purpose they are so quickly and so ruthlessly eliminated from the earth scene. For the dreadful holocaust is not of their making . . .

A similar letter, titled "Too Many Wars," included William's grim summation of wars in general: "And so shall it ever be—he who covets and runs after the things of this world will find upon attaining them, that they are but vain and

---

28. Herbert George Wells (1866–1946) was a famous English novelist known for works like *The Time Machine* (1895) and *The Island of Doctor Moreau* (1896). See, Adam Roberts, *H.G. Wells: A Literary Life* (New York: Palgrave Macmillan, 2019).

empty delusions, with no more substance than a shadow!" William often commented on World War II, but the last article he ever wrote for the *Guntersville Advertiser*, one dated December 3, 1941, was on the art of writing letters.

When his letters stopped, the poems continued until October 14, 1942. At first, I thought that William had simply taken a break, but the letters never resumed. Eventually, I granted he had stopped writing letters, at least to his hometown paper. Given his love for the written word and Guntersville, I could not fathom why he chose to sever this long-standing connection. I pondered as to whether his mental issues had deteriorated to the extent that he no longer wrote at all. He had long expressed dissatisfaction with the pay he received for each piece: $10 a letter, essay, or story and $5 a poem. Perhaps he requested a raise and was once more denied. Then, too, when editor Yancy Burke died on May 31, 1944, William may have, at long last, ended his relationship with the paper.[29] In the aftermath, R.H. Williams served as editor until late August 1944 when the Burke estate sold the *Guntersville Advertiser* to Porter Harvey, the editor of the *Guntersville Gleam*, a rival newspaper.[30] Harvey continued both newspapers for several years before eventually combining them into the *Advertiser-Gleam*. Harvey, whose style had little room for letters to the editor, may have either refused to print William's articles or did not want to pay for the privilege. Whatever the case, William's voice ceased appearing in the local newspaper, although he would, on occasion, be mentioned in either the society column or news articles.

Years passed before William was once more referenced in a Guntersville paper. On May 23, 1947, the *Guntersville Gleam* mentioned that Mrs. M.F. Elrod (Dura) had spent three months visiting her brother William in New York.[31] This was one of many trips she made to the Big Apple. However, three months is an exceptionally long visit, and she had responsibilities as a wife and worked as a nurse. Feasibly, William suffered a breakdown and needed a caretaker during his recovery. Conceivably, this experience strengthened their

---

29. Yancey Burke (1882–1944) purchased the *Democrat* and meshed it with the *Advertiser* in 1928. Burke edited Guntersville newspapers from 1914 until his death. U.S., Find a Grave Index, 1600s-Current; and Larry Smith, ed., *Guntersville Remembered* (Albertville, AL: Creative Publishers, 2001), 81, 86.

30. Robert Hamill Williams (1887–1961) was hired at the *Guntersville Advertiser* by Hugh Williams, part owner until his death in 1919. The younger Williams was elected probate judge of Marshall County in 1922. Smith, 77, 79. Porter Harvey published newspapers in Guntersville from 1940 until his death in 1995. For the longest time, the *Advertiser-Gleam* was edited by either Porter or his son Sam. The newspaper's current editor is Anthony Campbell. (Marshall County Archives).

31. "G'ville Personals," *Guntersville Gleam*, May 23, 1947.

relationship, for, in October 1950, William visited his parents and sisters.[32] Nothing is known of this visit aside from a brief reference in the society column of a local paper. More is known about the following visit. In the spring of 1951, Dura journeyed to New York City to bring William home by train. Sadly, it would not be a happy reunion.

When William arrived at his parents' house, in which Dura and her husband M.F. were also residing, several relatives found his eccentric behavior puzzling and disquieting. According to Gladys' daughter Annette, who would have been fourteen in 1951:

> By that time, he had been diagnosed as manic-depressive . . . I was
> interested in activities in high school and not in some withdrawn, quite
> displaced, depressed man. We never had a meaningful discussion. I
> knew very little about his life other than he was a writer and lived in
> NYC. I am sure he dismissed us all as ignorant, unread, Southern hicks,
> which we probably were.[33]

William made no better an impression on his first cousin Ronald Nabors, one of Jud's sons. The city slicker struck Ronald, then 24, as "uppity."[34] Ronald's teenage sister Ann also got a negative vibe from William. Ann thought him "scary" and said that during one lunch, William put down his silverware and wordlessly left the house only to sit in the garden with his hands raised in the air.[35] Lula's daughter Jane, then ten, remembered him as a "dear, sweet man," but even she had a strange encounter. One night, while pointing out constellations like the Little Dipper, William told Jane that he had a vision of her in a coffin. Though greatly unnerved, Jane maintained a great affection for her uncle.[36] Not too long afterward, a troubling event took place.

It started like any other day. Jane's father Norman had gone to work, so she and her mother Lula had the house all to themselves. Jane had busied herself dusting while Lula set about ironing. Lula, said to have been the sweetest and funniest of the sisters, had long since been confined to a wheelchair after being paralyzed in a car wreck. While mother and daughter worked, William barged

---

32. "Graves Center," *Advertiser-Gleam*, October 18, 1950.
33. Annette Haislip, article on William Nabors, Arab Historical Society, n.d.
34. Ronald Nabors, Oral Interview, July 26, 2017.
35. Ann (Nabors) Watson, Oral Interview, June 15, 2017.
36. Jane (Vaughn) Oddo, Oral Interview, July 9, 2017.

in. He was visibly intoxicated and demanded to know where Norman kept the whiskey. When Lula refused to divulge that information, he became angrier. He swept her out of her wheelchair, carried her into the bedroom, tossed her on the bed, and was about to strike her when their father Richard entered and intervened. Although Jane did not remember the aftermath, it could only have been harrowing. One can only think about how frightful and confusing this would have been for a child to witness. Even this, however, did not change Jane's mind about her uncle. To this day, she expresses great love and devotion to his memory.[37] Although William was adored by Jane and Dura, he tried the patience of most of his other relatives.

One day, William took it upon himself to play a practical joke on a teenage nephew, Jerry Lumpkin, a son of his sister Tempie. When Jerry went camping, his uncle, perhaps for sport, hid behind a tree and leaped out to frighten Jerry. After laughing off the scare and thinking William had gone on his way, Jerry went about setting up camp. Suddenly, out of nowhere, William attempted to spook him again. Visibly irked, Jerry demanded to be left alone. When William persisted, Jerry became outraged and threatened to shoot his uncle. William finally took the hint and departed, unscathed from this brush with a gun. He would not be so lucky next time.

On July 6, 1951, the *Advertiser-Gleam* reported that Dura's husband, M.F. Elrod, used a shotgun to shoot William at point-blank range.[38] The article depicted the affray as an argument, one of unknown origin, which quickly escalated. Evidently, William had struck M.F. in the head with the butt of the shotgun. The article's unnamed author queried as to whether this took place before or after the shooting because the shotgun's stock was broken almost in two pieces. Since the injuries were serious, William had a long convalescence at the Guntersville Hospital. No charges were lodged by either party. After being released, William was welcomed home by his parents and the Elrods. Jane described the incident as a drunken brawl. In her words, "All was forgiven and forgotten, and Willie stayed a good while before going back to New York."[39] He never returned to Guntersville.

While many of William's letters mentioned how deeply he missed Guntersville, this visit, one he had anticipated for ages, did not live up to expectations. He had longed for his family, his mother in particular, and his

---

37. Ibid.
38. "One Wounded, One Hit," *Advertiser-Gleam*, July 6, 1951.
39. Jane (Vaughn) Oddo, Oral Interview, July 9, 2017.

old schoolmates. One of his letters mentioned how, during his travels, he had desperately sought a familiar face. This is a sample excerpt: "I have not had the pleasure to meet a one of them in all my wanderings. But I only hope that their chosen paths have not been so solitary and so lonely as mine has been!" In another letter, he beautifully painted an image of his youth:

> The other children from around Nabors Mill sat gathering our lessons while in the towering hickory-nut trees outside the squirrels were chirruping and birds were singing, and our young hearts were so light and gay with the innocent laughter of childhood and the sheer joy of living. And though in the little churchyard there by our windows slept some of our friends and loved ones, our thoughts, like our young eyes, were mostly on the rosebushes and butterflies, beauty and life, and not sorrow and sadness and death. O gay, sweet youth! Where are those now? 'But where are the snows of yesteryear'?

On his trip, back to New York City, William may have brooded over the old adage that "you can't go home again."

I have thought a great deal about the tumult of this long visit to Guntersville. What must William have felt about being home after so long an absence? Did he feel out of place as if among strangers? Was he just as lonely as being in the big city? Perhaps more? What did he think of his family members? His letters reveal a man who likely came off as an intellectual elitist or in layman's terms, a snob. Extremely verbose, William may have had the air of a bore because he talked incessantly of himself. In his defense, he always said: "writing is a long-winded profession." William's advanced terminology and tales of obscure celebrities meant nothing to his parents, siblings, or cousins. It can be safely assumed that he thought himself more worldly and intelligent than his relatives. Likely, both William and his kinfolk came to the bittersweet conclusion that aside from blood, they had absolutely nothing in common. Then, too, as the shotgun calamity indicates, William's drinking had worsened. Whether he was self-medicating or simply boozing, the alcohol had an extremely negative impact on his normally pleasant personality. Something my father once said about another relative could easily be applied to William: "He was a really good guy as long as he was sober. The problem was he wasn't sober very often."

Sometime in the 1950s, William became indigent, a lowly resident of the Bowery. An empathetic man, he had often expressed profound concern for the homeless. As his niece, Annette, commented, "Many of his columns concerned the plight of the poor and downtrodden in New York and the lack of compassion of the wealthy." Plus, he had always admired the hobo life. In a December 6, 1933, article titled "Hoboes and Royalty," William argued that "there is a decided distinction between a hobo and a tramp." In his eyes, a hobo was not an idler looking to mooch off others and the government, but rather a respectable man who lived by his wits and answered to no one. It was a chosen lifestyle rather than a reflection of the inability to earn a living. While living in the Bowery, he may have written for the *Bowery News: The Voice of Society's Basement*, Harry Baronian's Lower East Side paper, which often paid the homeless for poems and stories.[40] In an article printed after his death, the *Associated Press* included a reflection of Alabama Bill as "a courtly panhandler."[41] This piece also mentioned that in addition to having been close to the late poet Maxwell Bodenheim, William had many noteworthy friends like Hobo King Dan O'Brien, Hobo Queen Boxcar Betty, and Pling Plong Prince Robert.[42] This article and others like it were tactful, and though they never used the word "suicide," it was certainly implied.

In another article titled "Alabama Bill Crosses the Ties," the *Bowery News* printed:

---

40. Originally from Illinois, Harry Baronian (1909–1965) moved to New York City in 1932. He thought of himself as the voice of "the lower depths." After working at Patrick Mulkern's the *Hobo News*, Baronian edited the *Bowery News* which published short stories, poems, cartoons, and general news. Baronian also published *Bowery Social Register*. It was considered quite the honor for a hobo be inducted into this register, "the blue book of society's basement." The last issue of the *Bowery News* was published on November 22, 1963, but the social register was published as late as 1965. "Obituary, Harry Baronian," *Daily News* (New York), August 4, 1965. Copies of the *Bowery News* are exceptionally rare. Occasionally, copies come up for sale on Amazon and Ebay. Some issues can be found at the Buffalo & Erie County Public Library and at the University of Virginia Libraries.

41. "Alabama Bill was of Bowery's Elite," *Birmingham News*, July 13, 1958.

42. Emma Link (1893–?) had hoboed through every state and most of Canada by the age of 66. Often seen puffing on a cigar, she was known as "Boxcar Betty" and as "Queen of the Hoboes." She claimed to have worked as a hula dancer, a snake charmer, and even as a coal miner. In 1952, she married Christopher Lubey, a ship's cook, but the marriage did not last. She was frequently invited to speak on radio programs and even appeared on television programs like *The Tonight Show*. She was active in raising money for underprivileged children and in seeing to it that hoboes received "a decent burial." She earned money working on farms and selling subscriptions to the *Bowery News*. She once said, "There is a big difference between hoboes and bums. Hoboes will work." Blaine Marz, "Boxcar Betty Fascinates Students with Talk; Stay in School, she says," *The Times* (Munster, IN), September 15, 1959. In her old age, she developed diabetes and heart problems. By 1970, she lived in San Francisco. untitled, *Algona Upper Des Moines*, July 16, 1970. Prince Robert de Rohan Courtenay, better known as Pling Plong Prince Robert, claimed to be descended from "three emperors of Byzantium." Though a hobo, he dressed in a suit, wore spats, and donned a silk hat while carrying a cane for added style. He wrote poems, and would often recite one in exchange for money or a beer. Prince Robert and Boxcar Betty both made the 1958 Bowery Social Register. Virginia Irwin, "Who's Who in the Bowery Social Register," *St. Louis Post-Dispatch*, May 21, 1958.

You read about it in the papers—the shabby old fellow with the beard
who apparently lay down in the middle of the street at 23rd and 4th
Ave in NYC some time ago. A taxi ran into him and that was curtains
for the old fellow. That was Alabama Bill, well known to the Bowery
News gang. He had come to our office about 12 years ago, always
getting a handout—Alabama Bill needed flop money, you see. Alabama
Bill had attended the University of Alabama. He was a cultured sort
of fellow; even though he was on the downgrade so many years, you
could still see the keen intellectual look in his eyes, the poise about
him when he wasn't mokus (drunk). Alabama Bill was never the same
after an auto crash years ago when his head was fractured. There was an
ugly scar on his side where a bullet from a railroad bull tore through.
He complained that his mind didn't work right anymore. He had run
a bookstore on West 23rd St. but after that crash years ago, the trail
led to the Bowery and the flophouses. He became a stem artist, or
panhandler. But he was invariably gracious about it, doffing his hat
and bowing and speaking in a charming Southern accent. "Pardon me
for this intrusion, kind sir, but may I humbly importune you for a bit
of temporary assistance? You see, I'm an old bum now, but there were
better days . . . university days, when there was music and laughter . . ."
Another character gone from the streets of New York, Alabama Bill has
crossed the ties. So long, old boy.[43]

As previously mentioned, on July 2, 1958, Gladys filed a request to have
William committed to Bryce. According to Jane, Dura wrote a letter informing
William that she planned to travel to New York City to escort him to Alabama
for treatment. While I have no way of confirming just what motivated him to
end his life, the timing speaks for itself. On July 12, 1958, William died in such
a way that he made nationwide headlines as an Associated Press release. This
July 13 sample appeared in the *Greenville News*:

A shabbily dressed man killed by a taxicab yesterday—while lying in
4th Ave—was tentatively identified last night as 'Alabama Bill Nabors,'
a scholarly habitue of the Bowery. The man, bewhiskered and about 55,

---

43. "Alabama Bill Crosses the Ties," *Bowery News* 69 (October 1958), 8.

stepped from the curb, witnesses said, and laid down in the roadway at
2 o'clock. Seconds later, a cab rolled over and killed him.[44]

According to a New York *Daily News* article titled "Beloved Bowery Bum
Killed," the cab was driven by Benjamin Goldstein of Queens.[45] It is unknown
whether William died at the scene or later at a hospital. When attempting to
secure a copy of his death certificate from New York, I have been denied because
I am neither his child nor his grandchild. I have long grappled with the events
of July 12, but fear I will never understand them.

After all, William was an adult living in New York, not Alabama. With that
in mind, I fail to understand how his sisters could have forced him to do anything
against his will. In addition, Gladys's commitment form was rather problematic.
When I first saw it, I wondered how on earth she had persuaded a physician,
one who had never seen William, to sign. Only later did I learn that Dr. W.R.
Huckaby was a family friend, distant relative, and county health officer.[46] One
wonders what other options the sisters considered, especially since Richard and
Lucinda were still living. It is particularly telling that in life, William preferred to
live as a hobo in the Bowery rather than with his parents in Guntersville, the city
he professed to love. For William, independence trumped nostalgia.

I have come up with two alternative explanations for William's death.
The first is that his inebriation may have caused him to collapse in the street.
Second, maybe hearing the voice of his "Guardian Angel" triggered his lying in
the thoroughfare. In one letter, William expressed a belief that people "do not
die when they fall asleep in the coma called death." Based on his history and the
timing of his demise, I maintain that my great uncle chose to die rather than
lose his independence and be forced into treatment, perhaps more electroshock
therapy or worse. It was the ultimate act of defiance and desperation for a man
who so passionately cleaved to the idea of living life to its fullest. Extremely
religious, William often expressed his belief in life after death, so he may have
thought the action the start of a new beginning. In a 1941 article titled "The
Purpose of Life," William argued that life's meaning was "progress, advancement, evaluation" and "the eternal struggle toward the infinite perfection which
only God possesses." Possibly, William believed he had fulfilled his purpose. It

44. "Educated Bum Dies While Lying in Road," *Greenville News* (Greenville, SC), July 13, 1958.
45. "Beloved Bowery Bum Killed," *Daily News* (New York), July 13, 1958.
46. In 1931, Dr. W.R. Huckaby and Dr. T.E. Martin opened the Tennessee Valley Infirmary in
Guntersville. Huckaby later served as health officer for Marshall County. Smith, 83.

can be assumed that his sisters thought it suicide because had he simply been hit by a car, they would have submitted a lengthy, ornate obituary to the local newspaper. William's death received no mention in Guntersville's then only newspaper, the *Advertiser-Gleam*.

When word arrived, Dura and Gladys traveled to New York City to handle William's affairs such as they were. According to my mother, Gladys said she went solely to "help Dura." Although I thought the statement bizarre, this may have reflected her closeness to Dura and respect for her elder sister's close relationship with William. According to Jane, the sisters visited the Bowery and spoke to several people who knew William. One individual handed Dura an article from the *Bowery News*. It was a tribute to the passing of "Alabama Bill."

Self-taught in history, philosophy, poetry, political science, and life in general, William Nabors was a brilliant but flawed man. Though many of his writings reflected bleakness; others exuded optimism. He once said, "We are living in a truly wonderful age; perhaps the most wonderful of all. I believe with Herbert Spencer that in the world, all things are possible."

To me, William Nabors was a mix of Henry Higgins and Edward Rochester, so it is often difficult to know when he was frank or facetious. Even his definition of truth is food for thought: "Truth, as I conceive it, is a relative term denoting an abstraction in logic. Logic has been defined as the science of thought. But more correctly speaking, logic is an exposition of the process involved in thinking." Phenomenal in his attention to detail, William had the knack of conveying a "mind picture," especially when it comes to people. In many ways, this collection is half diary and half autobiography. Though I collected 56 of his poems and 149 letters and short stories, William's loquacious nature meant I had to be selective as to which pieces to include. The articles I omitted dealt mainly with Marshall County, Alabama, and historiography; I also chose to leave out some of his more blatant nativist writings. Though I have pieced together his controversial and fascinating life, my great uncle will forever remain a sphinx, elusive, and inscrutable. He never married and, to my knowledge, had no offspring, so his words are his only legacy. Because he died indigent, he was buried in a pauper's grave, which, sadly, is lost to history. For a small memorial, my mother and I purchased a commemorative brick that was placed in the sidewalk in front of Guntersville's historic Gilbreath House.

CHAPTER 2

Lonely Wanderer, 1925-1929

"I suspect that cacoethes scribendi (the itch to write) is a sort of disease that afflicts only the weak and the feeble-minded, who, in turn, take it out on the public!" —William Nabors

---·•·---

Not Dead Yet
November 4, 1924

Correction of the statement that appeared in a recent issue of the *Advertiser* which reported that I had been drowned off the coast of Mexico. I want to state that I am alive, very much so, and have not been dead at any time to my knowledge. And furthermore, it is my urgent request that I not be dead in print.

Off the drowning subject, if allowed the space, I will comment in regards to the land of paradise and flowers. California this time of year is quite a state. However, there are thousands of tourists pouring in from the north and east to avoid the bad winters of those sections. Economically, industrially and otherwise, there tends to be a general slump throughout the state. Most of the [unclear] has been marketed. The oil [unclear] aren't operating at full capacity so a count of overproduction is claimed. However, it is believed by optimistic writers that things will pick up.

The motion picture movie industry is about the only one doing anything to speak of at present. Most of the big studios are running at full blast now, soon to be closed for [unclear] which will throw thousands out of work.

As for the climate, one can't wish for better. Socially, Los Angeles is still a haven for the world's distinguished characters as this is a playground all the way around.

The writer had the privilege of seeing Jack Dempsey in action a few nights ago at Doyle's Vernon in which there were several encounters, the proceeds of which went to charity.[1]

Miss Ruth Roland has been appearing at the Pantages Theatre in person of late, accompanied by her pianist.[2] The song "That Old Gang of Mine" made the hit of the season.

Well, not being a staff correspondent to the *Advertiser*, I won't attempt to write too much. With best wishes to the *Advertiser*, I thank you.

One Hundred Years Ago and Today
May 5, 1925

One hundred and four years ago today Napoleon died an exiled prisoner of war on that volcano island of St. Helena, which is located twelve hundred miles off the west coast of Africa. Today is different. Von Hindenburg, also a defeated general, is elected president of his country.[3] Time wreaks great changes does it not? Men may come and men may go, but wars shall always be. The Balkan states are again at their favorite pastime—war. While the pacifists are advocating peace and the League of Nations and World Courts are striving to eliminate international conflicts, the preparations for the destruction of humanity continue to go forward.

Today, Japan has over two hundred factories that are turning out fighting airplanes as fast as their highly skilled mechanics can do the work; France has the greatest air force in the world and also the largest standing army, while England has the largest navy in the world. The United States is the richest country in the world, and, according to our army and navy experts, our armament facilities are inadequate for our security. In other words, our coastal defense and military protection is insufficient to guard our vast stretches of open coast from

---

1. From 1919 to 1926, professional boxer Jack Dempsey (1895–1983) was Heavyweight Champion of the World. Jack Dempsey, *Dempsey* (New York: Harper & Row, 1977); and Randy Roberts, *Jack Dempsey, the Manassa Mauler* (Chicago: University of Illinois Press, 2003). Jack Doyle was a promoter who had an arena in Vernon, California. Cecilia Ramussen, "A Teetotaler's Bar and Boxing Mecca," *Los Angeles Times*, June 23, 1997.

2. Ruth Roland (1892–1937) was a Hollywood actress known as the "Queen of the Thriller Serials." "Ruth Roland Dies; Former Film Star," *New York Times*, September 23, 1937. The Hollywood Pantages Theatre, designed by Benjamin Priteca and built by Alexander Pantages, opened in 1930 and still stands at Hollywood and Vine. See, for example, Taso G. Lagos, *American Zeus: The Life of Alexander Pantages, Theater Mogul* (Jefferson, NC: McFarland, 2018).

3. Paul von Hindenburg (1879–1936) served as President of Germany from 1925 to 1934. See, for example, Anna von der Goltz, *Hindenburg: Power, Myth, and the Rise of the Nazis* (New York: Oxford University Press, 2009).

an attack, in case some of those powers should decide to pay us a visit in that capacity. While it isn't likely that such a thing should occur in the immediate future, it is highly probable. Nobody realizes Japan's alertness and resources at present more fully than does England and France. It is a known fact that Japan is overpopulated, and it is safe to say that she will, in time, seek new territories, and our islands of the Pacific will, in all probability, be her objective should the occasion arise. Now, I am not assuming the role of prophet neither am I advocating larger appropriations for army and naval defense, but on the other hand I think the people are already overburdened with excess and needless taxes which, if properly handled, would be appropriate to dispense with national protection. The recent aeronautic controversy at Washington disclosed some very startling facts, which are worthy of comment, especially one particular phrase and that is: Who got the four hundred million dollars the taxpayers appropriated for air service, when there are only sixteen fighting planes in service that are considered real fighting planes? General Mitchell admitted while being quizzed by the investigating committee that this country has only sixteen fighting planes that can be considered modern; the other hundreds are useless and obsolete according to General Mitchell of the United States Air Service.[4] Is it not enough to cause the cotton grower, the wheat grower, the cattle raiser, and the wage earner to wonder why things are so muddled?

There is nothing sensational or startling happening in Los Angeles that is out of the ordinary. Of course, there have been two new murder mysteries added to the crime calendar of the day, bringing the total to date to eighteen unsolved murders. Gloria Swanson has returned from abroad with her royal hubby. She is now a marchioness, if you know what that is. The outfit from the Lasky Studio greeted her at the station with a band and everything.[5] Hollywood today is enshrouded with a gorgeous display of flags to celebrate her homecoming. Although she has married into a noble family, she will resume work on the studio lot with the rest of the picture folk. Funny, isn't it, that people will go crazy over a picture star who only portrays the character of a story. The writer should get some of the credit?

4. William "Billy" Mitchell (1879–1936) was a general, often dubbed the father of the U.S. Air Force. See, for example, Ruth Mitchell, *My Brother Bill: A Biography of General "Billy" Mitchell* (New York City: Harcourt Brace, 1953).
5. While best known for her depiction of Norma Desmond in *Sunset Boulevard* (1950), Gloria Swanson (1899–1983) had a long, impressive film career. In 1925, she married her third husband—Henri de la Falaise, the Marquis de la Coudraye. Lasky Studio is in reference to the Famous Players-Lasky Corporation. See, Tricia Welsch, *Gloria Swanson: Ready for Her Close-Up* (Jackson: University Press of Mississippi, 2013).

Los Angeles, Calif.
June 30, 1925

Lost, somewhere between a breaking dawn and twilight's misty hue, twelve golden hours with lightning speed from you. And thus, it is with us. When the sun sets in the evening, we are poorer by a day, as destiny checks out the time we linger on the way. And thus, it seems we are doomed to lose in the long run. The first person who invents something that could cheat or redeem time will be a man or woman after my own heart. With all the surgical, medical, mechanical and astronomical sciences that the ingenuity of man has thus far been able to achieve, life still remains piteously in its infancy, as far as longevity is concerned. One New York author has advanced the theory that if the modern, hectic mode of living was removed or revised so as to do away with the unnecessary superfluous culture and assumed refinement that the longevity of the human subsistence would immediately increase. To substantiate or strengthen his proffered solution of the highly inconsistent and perplexing mode of living, the author has thoughtfully injected into his argument some facts pertaining to the longevity of certain tribes of humanity who inhabit some of the South Sea Islands. One tribe, in particular, the scientists have discovered surpassed everything hither to regarding longevity of the human race.

This island is called Pago Pago (pronounced Pango Pango), and by the way, on a neighboring island adjoining Pago Pago is where Mr. Frederick O'Brien wrote his immortal "White Shadows."[6] The average span of life on the island of Pago Pago is long past eighty years. Imagine that! Now, we will readily concede that the New Yorker's suggestion sounds highly plausible—on paper. But it is quite improbable to life. For, as the author should know, there are only two things (with the exception of evolution of custom) that can change the standards of social relations. And these two things are phenomenical calamity and war. It is a well-known fact that literally thousands of our people are annually eating themselves into premature graves. Overeating is the direct or indirect cause of seventy-five percent of the "natural" deaths, according to the American Medical Association. Mr. Henry Ford, the world's wealthiest man says that habit is responsible for a great number of afflictions. This genius does not have

---

6. Frederick O'Brien (1870–1932), a famous author and world traveler, wrote the books *White Shadows on the South Seas* (1919) and *Mystic Tales of the South Seas* (1921). "Frederick O'Brien, Author, Dies at 62," *New York Times*, January 10, 1932.

any regular time for eating. He says he only eats when he is hungry, and very little then. "Regular hours for eating," he says, "is nothing more than habit." Mr. Thomas A. Edison works away for two days at a time without eating. "To possess a clear mind," he says, "one should be very careful about loading the stomach." The food that goes into our stomachs is food for thought only a very few hours after having eaten it. If we overload the stomach with the wrong combinations of food, the result is reactionary on the mind. For instance, how many of us know that it isn't good to eat potatoes with meats? Still you cannot go into a restaurant and order meats (unless specified) that you don't get a side order of potatoes. Think it over.

———•••———

Los Angeles, Calif.
July 7, 1925

Say, but ain't this a funny old world. We find lots of things to criticize, few to approve and just lots of things to ignore or disregard. This aspiring writer had a rather unique experience this evening. It was around seven thirty o'clock. The window shoppers, theatre goers, and other frequenters of the gay, white way had just begun to throng the sidewalks for an evening's outing. Strolling leisurely down main street with the rest of the mob, I happened to be passing one of those help yourself cafeterias when the sound of a peppy jazz orchestra lured the writer into the garlic scented dive that is patronized by the lower strata of society. Once inside the dive and after have made negotiations for a slice of watermelon, a cut of strawberry shortcake and other little nick knacks, I maneuvered this anatomically subjected apparatus to a little table in an obscure corner of the "joint." I sat munching away at the delicacies and enjoying the orchestra, unaware of what was taking place around me. An old Jew and a young Jewish kid, whom I took to be the Old Jew's son, came over and parked at the table adjoining the one at which I sat. They were immediately followed to the table by a demure, sedate little slip of a girl, who looked to be an American. Hardly had she arrived at the table when the argument started. The Old Jew was using both his Yiddish tongue and his equally Jewish hands and adding emphasis to whatever it was that he was trying to drive home. The writer being able to talk a little Yiddish was quick to catch the drift of the argument. And, as usual, the argument was about "ze money." The little girl, it seemed, had ordered too much grub to suit the Jew. The argument seemed to gain momentum with the seconds, and the words were flying fast and furious. In defiance to a slur hurled at her, the little girl said, "That's a lie." Hardly had she uttered the words till the younger Jew jumped up and slammed the poor little girl to the floor. Two or three toughs were sitting at a nearby table, and as the little girl fell to the floor, the toughs proceeded to find merriment in the poor kid's plight and laughed aloud at her embarrassment. Being Southern, of course, I lost no time in going to the little lady's aid. I helped her back into the chair and as I did so, the young Jew became enraged at the kindness I displayed to his little spouse and pushed, or rather shoved me backward from her chair. I caught him with an upper cut to the chin (pardon my boasting) and sent him sprawling beneath a table. At that instance, the Old Jew jumped up: "For vy do you fight mit boy? Dis nadle is my boys visfe!" I begged their pardons for having butted in on a family affair. "I—was hungry and married him this morning," the poor girl sobbed. Poor, ignorant little thing had drifted in off the scorching desert, or ran away from a good family, perhaps, to get in the movies. If she had but been wise in the ways of the city, she would have gone to the police when she got so hungry instead of letting the little Hebrew talk her into spending the rest of her young life in an attic rooming house and having to take her meals at a cheap cafeteria. The moral is: Young ladies, unless you are capable of taking care of yourself, DON'T go to the big, wicked city looking for work.

The volcano Sierra Blanca, which lies about thirty miles south of the U.S. Mexican boundary line is now in activity.[7] Three thousand Americans and Mexicans are in great danger of being overcome by the intense heat, according to the afternoon papers. Scientists are rushing there from all the nearby cities to watch the maneuvers of the strange phenomena. A terrific heat wave has hit this city. Although the temperature is only ninety, that is about twenty-five degrees above the normal temperature of the average summers for Los Angeles. Two deaths and a score of prostrations. Needles, California, which is a little desert town has recorded a temperature of 128 degrees in the shade for the day. By the way, it is claimed that Needles is the hottest spot on earth inhabited by man. Bakersfield, Taft, and Death Valley Junction have recorded temperatures of 126, 125 and 125, respectively. That is almost like being in an inferno, isn't it? If it were to get that hot down in old Alabama, the people would be dying by the thousands, owing to the high humidity.

William Jennings Bryan, Jr., confirmed to the writer yesterday that he would assist his father in the prosecution of Prof. Scopes, as had been the

---

7. The Sierra Blanca is in southern New Mexico.

current report. Mr. Bryan is an attorney, with local offices in the Van Nuys Building of this city. He was reticent to talk, but hinted that the trial would be a quick and speedy one, and that states' rights would be upheld. He absolutely does not believe in evolution.[8]

Well, I must run along as I know you good readers are getting tired of this stuff. Night, everybody.

Wm. Nabors Writes from Sea Aboard the Admiral Peary Smith from Puget South[9] July 28, 1925

That the writer is a staff correspondent to the *Advertiser* is not to be doubted, but to abuse that honor is another thing. Anyway, since this is being written while far out at sea, perhaps the good editor will censure it okay and printable.

It is now 11:30 o'clock p.m. and all the crew are asleep except the engineer, firemen, pilot, and the seaman who is walking his watch on the bow of the ship. The old boat is rocking and swaying to and fro as though it were only a tiny leaf being tossed about by the gigantic waves. Midnight at sea, and especially when the moon and stars are glittering beautifully over the black, blue waves, somehow seems to have an awe-inspiring effect. The rolling, billowy sea is so beautiful, yet so wicked. When one sees how easily the powerful vessels of today are thrown and tossed about on the waters, it only evokes an admiration for our ancestors who braved these same waters in nothing more than a canoe, compared to the sea-going monsters of this hectic day and age.

The writer finds that living conditions aboard the freighters of the Pacific are ideal. Food is in abundance and of a variety and is excellently prepared and served with a "taste." Of the writer's observations of living conditions among the working classes, along the west coast from Tijuana, Mexico, to Vancouver, British Columbia, he finds nothing that can compare with the humane treatment which is accorded the sea-faring workers. The writer had half harbored and nurtured the belief, as gathered from cheap novels of sea life, that the seamen

---

8. William Jennings Bryan, Jr. (1889–1978) was the son of the famous populist and three-time presidential candidate William Jennings Bryan. The senior Bryan served as prosecutor in the Scopes Trial or Scopes Monkey Trial. Between 1915 and 1920, the junior Bryan served as assistant U.S. attorney in Arizona. "William Jennings Bryan Jr., Only Son of the Famed Orator," *New York Times*, March 28, 1978.

9. The editor found few references relating to the *Admiral Peary Smith*. See, for example, "Ship Wireless Reports," *San Francisco Examiner*, April 1, 1926; and "Ship Wireless Reports," *San Francisco Examiner*, July 30, 1928.

led a hard, miserable life and that what little food they got was doled out to them as though they were slaves. That, however, has been completely dispelled.

The writer shipped from Astoria as an ordinary seaman, and after being at sea a couple of days the chief engineer, in some mysterious way, discovered that among the seamen was a newspaper correspondent, and of course the writer was prevailed upon to accept officer's quarters for the rest of the trip.[10] There are different nationalities upon the waters same as on the land. The captain of the *Peary* is an Icelander, the chief engineer is a Scotchman, the first engineer is an American, and by the way, the "wench operator" is an American who hails from Mobile, Alabama.

We are due to dock in port San Pedro, Calif., tomorrow night at 9:30, so these lines will probably be mailed from that port. There are fifty men and officers aboard the Peary, and the writer has yet to see a crew of workmen, regardless of the place or job, get along as well and all around as genial as this bunch of men. If such concord and unison as this were attained along other lines of endeavor and industry there would never be such a thing as a strike.

Well, we're sailing through some more rough sea and I guess I'll have to rewrite this when I get ashore and, as I hate rewriting, I will make it short. The wireless operator is coming down to the galley to get a cup of coffee and I think I'll join him.

———·•·———

Wm. Nabors Writes from California
September 29, 1925

Back again in the old haunts—Broadway, Hell Street, Spring and Main— which are the most dignified thoroughfares, so far as traffic and pedestrians are concerned of the city. Ah, how quickly things change in these Western cities. But, then, one can expect changes and contemplate them with maddening regularity when one lives in a city of a transient population. Even a few months bring about the most amazing transformations. The night life of old Broadway isn't what it was a year or so ago. The milling throngs have vanished, to a notable extent.

Of course, in the afternoon, between the hours of four and six there are thousands of commuters—those who ride to and from work—running hither and yon, each trying to be the first in the street car, stage double-decked bus,

---

10. Astoria, Oregon.

train, or whatnot. They push and shove one another about as though they were but so many cattle being permitted to new pasture; old ladies with little baskets swinging from their arms, little flappers with their vanity cases, tired looking old men; youthful mechanics of every description mingle with the counter jumpers, pen pushers, bank clerks, soda jerks and the toilers of the hundred and one different shops.

We board a street car and ride through the congested streets for a few minutes' diversion. And in the street cars we have the best chance to study old Miss Humanity. Here sits an elaborately and coquettishly gotten up little flapper, who is holding her little mirror up to her pretty eyes and powdering her little sneezer; a wrinkled and tired looking old lady is hanging on to a strap, no one seems to notice her or to offer her a seat; an empty-headed blank-faced youth of around sixteen is smoking a cigarette and reading a "Whiz-bang"; a tired-looking business man is scanning over the stock exchange of the "Evening Herald"; a young woman is quarreling with the conductor for failing to call her street—the street car stops and we get off.

We're now on East Fifth Street, which the agnostics have impudently dubbed "Mission Row." We stroll along Fifth St. and have begun to count the different missions: The Midnight Mission, the Holy Mission, the Latter-day Saints' Mission, the Holy Union Mission, the Salvation Army headquarters, the Welfare Workers' Mission and others of less importance to mention here. The missions are, in reality, nothing more or less than subsidiaries of the various churches which they attempt to represent. One will hear about the same old raving and see about the same frothing at the mouth in one as in the other. In fact, some of their own churches do not recognize them, as every straggling person who is religiously inclined drifts into the missions; some go there merely to get the stale bread and pale coffee which are doled out in the name of the Lord. The mission business is rapidly becoming a fad, and is bringing no little pressure of a depraved nature down upon the heads of the innocent churches. For instance, one mission became so bold as to erect a huge electric sign over its door, advertising its seemingly angelic hospitality. They might have gotten by with their nefarious scheme had not an evangelist, whose intentions were good, donated a hundred thousand dollars to help carry on the good work. The officers of the law discovered the two prime factors of the mission were ex-convicts. An investigation into their activities ensued which brought out some startling revelations.

The two "deacons," it developed, were canvassing the various restaurants and bakeries and getting what food they came into possession of free gratis instead of using the generous endowment which the big-hearted evangelist had placed at their disposal. The really sincere and legitimate churches, have let it be known that they aren't sponsoring any "missions."

The writer is recipient of a KKK membership application blank, which was given him by a former Texan, who is now on the L.A. police force.[11] That the fundamental principles of the Klan are wholly American is not to be questioned, but unlike some of our older institutions, the Klan, from what I have gleaned of its activities in and around Los Angeles, is given over to propaganda propagating machines, which are more detrimental than beneficial to the American commonwealth. No, I'm not writing exclusively for the Jews, the Catholics, Negroes, agnostics, or any other particular creed or sect. To the hotel and to bed.

Those Hollywood Divorces
October 13, 1925

Up bright and early this morning to finish a story that I have been trying to do for weeks. It is just now six o'clock and the big, red sun is peeping over snow-clad peaks to the eastward although winter is beginning to demand heavy wraps and furs and boots in some states. The roses and other flowers are blooming sweetly and innocently here.

Just back from the restaurant. Gee, it's hard to get into a restaurant or café in this part of the city at this hour of the morning. Working-men, taxi drivers, expressmen, policemen, and various kinds of clerks swarm into the restaurants at this hour and line up along the walls waiting for a chance to get to the counters or tables. Most every other door along some of these streets are restaurants and everyone is the same. One wonders if all these urbanites take their meals at the restaurant. How we must envy you people who have homes and good cooks who give you good food that is seasoned and good to eat!

About the only way one is able to tell when it is the fall of the year here is by the fog. When the fog begins to obscure the big clock on the Times Building then you know autumn is here. I can look down from my window upon Pershing's Square, a beautiful downtown park.[12] Its clumps of bamboo,

11. KKK is in reference to the Ku Klux Klan, a white supremacist hate group which, while it originated in the post-Civil War South, had members nationwide by the 1920s. See, for example, Nancy K. MacLean, *Behind the Mask of Chivalry: The Making of the Second Ku Klux Klan* (New York: Oxford University Press, 1995); and William Rawlings, *The Second Coming of the Invisible Empire: The Ku Klux Klan of the 1920s* (Macon: Mercer University Press, 2017).

12. Pershing Square is a small public park in downtown Los Angeles. "Welcome to Pershing Square Outdoor Concert and Event Center," https://www.laparks.org/pershingsquare/ (Accessed April 2, 2020).

its palms and pepper trees are so green and pretty and especially is it beautiful in the early morning.

It looks like a picture of perpetual springtime or whatever it is that artists call such pictures. There is always a bunch of free speech advocates—even at this hour—to let out some of their gas. They argue on the deity, royalty, drunkenness, religion, prohibition, communism, strikes, birth control, tips, astrology, evolution, vegetarianism, the third international, women's rights, men's wrongs, occultism, atheism, spiritualism, agnosticism, deism, and all the other isms to which mortal man has fallen heir. In this little assemblage, one will find politicians, professors, ministers, educators, and retired bankers who have come West for their health's sake.

Hundreds of train whistles rip the morning air as the transcontinental trains pull in at the giant Southern Pacific passenger station. Some of the tourists are looking on California's beauty for the first time and marveling. However, they will find other things to look upon—some of them less beautiful—when they have spent their savings and start looking for jobs. When one reads of California's wonderful brains, wealth, prosperity, and amazingly wonderful opportunities and climate, such as published in her stereotyped literature and shipped out by the car loads by her chambers of commerce, it is only natural that one should become the victim of the impression that California is a veritable hotbed of genius, the pot of gold that reposes at the end of the rainbow, the only place in existence where the plutocrats associate with the working stiffs. All who believe that stand on your head while I finish this.

Anyway, be that as it may, winter is coming on, and in the East it will be very severe, as usual, we of California are kicking one another's shins and fighting to get in line at the 'slave markets' (employment bureaus) where one can buy for ten dollars a dish washing job that pays eighteen dollars per week! But, then, we of California, have the climate, you see.

Wm. Nabors Writes from Arizona
October 18, 1925

After twenty strenuous hours we have arrived at Phoenix, Arizona, covering a distance of some five hundred miles and averaging twenty miles per hour. There were many notes taken en route, but 'twould take columns to narrate them, so we'll just pass them as uninteresting. But I would like to say a few worlds about the "Great White Waste." Of the three hundred miles of desert we crossed there were seven miles of road over what is known as the moving sand dunes. This is the only road the writer has ever heard of and most certainly the only one he has ever seen whose bed is continually shifting with moving sands. This piece of road is called the "boardwalk" and is only wide enough for one-way traffic. But of course, there are places every few hundred yards where one can pull out to the side and let any passing vehicles run by. If one should become careless and drive off the walk into the sand, as we saw no less than twenty that had, well, then it's just too bad. You are there and that's all. The sand all along there is from ten to a hundred feet deep, and its forty miles into Yuma, the nearest town. After we'd negotiated this dangerous seven miles successfully, we encountered no trouble until we hit Yuma, at which place we were held up by the custom officers who went through all our baggage, took our license numbers, asked numerous questions and finally okayed and permitted us to pass into Arizona. The day was just dawning as we pulled into Yuma. We stopped at the All-American Café for breakfast, and hardly had we left the machine when we were surrounded by a bunch of Indians, who were anxious to sell us funny looking souvenirs of everything from beads to baskets. Finally, after disposing of the Indians, some of whom could speak English, we breakfasted and again hit the trail.

Some of the road from Yuma to Phoenix is through lava bed, and impassably rough. The scenery is most beautiful. The variegated colored mountains loom up in the distance and stretch off towards the hazy boundary of old Mexico. For miles and miles, we saw nothing but rocks, about the size of half-bushel measure and perfectly round. They are called "Satan's Marbles." I've never read of any scientific explanation or theory of them. They've been burned or scorched by some terrific heat at some time or the other. Phoenix is a thriving little city of some forty thousand inhabitants. Its locale is in the very fertile Salt River Valley, and at the end of the old Santa Fe Trail. It is one of the most picturesque of the Western cities. Its architecture is a combination of Spanish Hacienda, Mexican architecture and modern structures. The agriculture and horticulture of this immediate part are to be envied. We see fruits and flowers that we've never seen before, not even in the Spanish markets at Los Angeles. Dates, pineapples, and loquats are the chief fruits grown here. These lines are being penned within a stone's throw of the state capitol. The law-makers here are a good-natured lot, who are an extraction of those of whom they come here to represent-cowboys, farmers, business men, and common people. They're addressed simply as John or Jim, by those with whom they are more familiar. There isn't the hustle and bustle here that one finds in the larger cities, and we're wont to remark that it is a sleepy town; but we're reminded that it is everything else but.

My companion en route is Dr. Moffet, noted Psychology lecturer and man of letters.[13] Although he usually speaks to full houses, he never attempts to bore me with his sub-conscious stuff when we're alone. While I sometimes 'cover' his lectures for the newspapers, I don't believe half he utters. Neither does he, I'm thinking. But "Doc," as I call him, is a pretty good buddy, at that. It is really amusing to note how some of those society dowagers clamor for "Doc's" attention. No, I'm not his press agent.

The New York of the South
June 8, 1926

Having left the southern boundary of the Lone Star State, where cotton is in bloom and where watermelons, cantaloupes, tomatoes, cherries, peaches, etc. are being shipped to the northern and eastern markets, some two days ago, we've come to the somewhat fondly termed "New York of the South"—Dallas.[14]

While our own magic city (Birmingham), has gone forward with amazingly rapid strides during the seven years that this humble writer was away, I must confess that Dallas, Tex., certainly deserved the honor—if there be any—of being called the New York of the south.[15] There have been more really large buildings erected in Dallas during the past three years than any other southern city through which he has traveled (and, not boasting, he has traveled through a good many of our larger cities). The Magnolia building here is the tallest structure in the south to-date (although there's one being rushed to completion in Houston that is thirty-four stories high). The Santa Fe building is a gigantic edifice, covering a part of three blocks, and there are numerous others here that are above the million-dollar class. Electric trains come roaring into Dallas from other smaller cities a hundred miles or so away. There are hundreds of communities working both in Dallas or Ft. Worth who ride the electric train from one

---

13. The editor was unable to discern the identity of Dr. Moffet.

14. On Dallas, Texas, during this time, see, for example, Robert B. Fairbanks, *For the City as a Whole: Planning, Politics and the Public Interest in Dallas, Texas, 1900–1965* (Columbus: Ohio State University Press, 1998); and Patricia Evridge Hill, *Dallas: The Making of a Modern City* (Austin: University of Texas Press, 1996).

15. Birmingham, Alabama, with its varied industries, had developed the nickname of "Magic City." It was not far from Nabors's hometown of Guntersville. See, James R. Bennett and Karen R. Utz, *Iron and Steel: A Guide to the Birmingham Area Industrial Heritage* (Tuscaloosa: University of Alabama Press, 2010).

city to the other every day. (The cities are less than forty miles apart). One finds the hustle and bustle and the slam-bang rush more so in Dallas than any other southern city. It has the atmosphere of some of our larger northern metropolises. Yet Dallas is pleasantly—if not extremely—southern. The Sunday blue laws that are so rigidly enforced in Birmingham are noticeably lax here. There is a general air of individual freedom in Dallas that makes one feel more or less at home. Of course, about the street corners one may see the usual clustering array of gaudily attired young drug store cowboys, who chat nonchalantly of everything but literature. If I were given two guesses in which to select from the current literature those publications that conform more nearly to their respective tastes, I should say either the so-called True Story and the confessional type of publication or the well-known movie magazine. That, however, is not reflecting upon the youth of Dallas. They merely portray those common American characteristics of blatant baubling, surface rippling and camaraderie. Dallas, to use the well-known Chamber of Commerce phrase, is an "up and at 'em" city.

Wm Nabors

Dallas to St. Louis, May 30, 1926

Denver
August 24, 1926

A blue Sunday in Denver is not unlike a blue Sunday in Birmingham or Los Angeles or even New York.[16] But a few people are on the streets today. The weather is cool (almost cold) and cloudy. Straw hats and overcoats are not an unusual combination here.

Was up to Pikes Peak yesterday. Pikes Peak is only eight miles up (up is right) from Colorado Springs, the millionaire's resort. In negotiating the eight miles, one is elevated to an altitude of more than 14,000 feet. Snow had begun to fall on Pikes Peak before we were up there an hour.[17]

Thousands of tourists lined the roads throughout Colorado at this season. Excellent roads are to be found all over the state. California is the only state in the West that surpasses Colorado for good roads.

---

16. On Denver, Colorado, in the 1920s, see, for example, Denver Post, *Denver Memories* (Pediment Publishing, 2017); and Denver Post, *Denver Memories II: The Early Years and the 1940s* (Pediment Publishing, 2018); and Amy Zimmer, *Lost Denver* (Pavilion, 2016).

17. Today, using US-24 W and the Pikes Peak Toll Road, it is a 29.8-mile drive from Colorado Springs to Pikes Peak.

Denver is a beautiful city, and considered the best lighted city in the United States. But even here one finds streets that are dimly lighted and uninviting. Denver has a notorious underworld element. The cops patrol the tenderloin district three and four abreast. Denver, like San Francisco, has its Chinatown, though not as imposing. Also, like San Francisco, it has a mint, but one sees little of the money. Since the daring mint robbery here a couple or more years ago, visitors are not admitted into the mint except with passes from the proper authorities. Of the twelve state capitals I have seen in the West, the Colorado State Capitol is the most beautiful. The city water is snow water and very beautiful or so they say. One sees missions and places of worship next door to shooting galleries and cheap lodging houses where painted women sulk in the doorways and puff cigarettes.

The West still has its "bad actors." A mail train was held up a few miles north of here in Wyoming.

Those of you whose appetites are poor, I would advise you to come to Denver. The air here gives one an appetite like that of the sea. But, should you decide to come, be sure to have plenty of money, or good security, for it takes lots of money to go but little way in these parts.

Wm. Nabors Writes from New York
February 1, 1927

The first gray streaks of dawn found this lonely wanderer writer descending the gang-plank from the *S.S. Montana*, of Antwerp and Hamburg, which docked here at five this morning after having been tossed and buffeted about by an eighty-mile-an hour gale that lashed our starboard from the northward, angering the turbulent waters that whipped o'er the deck like cannon shots, freezing in huge sheets as the mad waves receded.[18] Such is the North Atlantic in winter. As we ploughed slowly through the ice caked waters of New York harbor, we could discern the out-line of the Statue of Liberty, visibly cloaked with snow, looming up in all her resplendent, austere beauty through the misty freezing fog that hung about New York's sky-line like an impenetrable pall. America's most beloved statue was standing guard over the harbor waters of America's greatest city, as the ice encrusted waters lashed relentlessly against her imposing, impregnable base.

---

18. On the SS *Wheatland Montana*, see Chapter 1, Footnote 15.

New York City, to the Southerner, seems so impossibly polyglot. All the hustle, bustle, rush, clangor, slam and bang are New York's. The interminable canyons of staggering skyscrapers seem to echo the deafening din and noise that reverberate up from her streets of soothing organisms, more familiarly known as human beings. Business men, factory workers, shoppers, dock workers, deck hands, sailors with rolling gait, buxom ladies and ones sedate mill up and down in a hopelessly conglomerate inextricable endless stream. Such is the kaleidoscopic panorama that one beholds on Broadway in New York, the world's busiest thoroughfare. Far better writers than this humble wanderer have attempted to describe New York; so why should I seek to put in black and white an impression that can only be gained through the optic nerve? Broadway butterflies, coquettishly and elaborately gowned, flit up and down through the theatrical districts of Gotham. How quickly time rolls by! Some of them, nay, many of them, may someday be glad of the chance to peddle newspapers, like the ragged, wizened faced old lady you see standing over there on the corner of Times Square! Fur clad money changers, the international bankers who hang out in Wall St., descend marble steps from gorgeously appointed dens and offices to enter waiting limousines and be whisked away to the club or links; while in contrast to this enviable, comfortable picture are hungry Americans parading the streets with signs: "employment wanted," dangling from their backs. 'Fate' plays some queer pranks? Elevated trains, of from five to ten cars each, rush by o'er head with their cargoes of human freight; so do the surface cars and taxies, while underground in the subways hundreds of thousands of beings are being rushed at break-neck speed to their respective destinations. The immensity of this colossal metropolis is beyond the grasp of mere human minds. The door of the Italian consulate here was blown out yesterday by a powerful bomb, an infernal machine, placed there by New York's black-hand.[19] Gang warfare and murder are ever rampant in New York, and crime is extant, most every third door is a speakeasy or saloon, wherein convivial imbibers may appease the thirst and tipple to the heart's content. Fog horns on incoming and out-bound steamers rent the air. A bunch of youthful criminals, all hand cuffed together, some of whom looked pitifully adolescent, is being led from the city bastille, preparatory to entraining for commitment to the "big house up the river," Sing Sing.

---

19. The Italian consulate, located at 20 East 22nd Street, was bombed on January 17, 1927. In the aftermath, two Russian immigrants, Meyer Schumyatzsky and Reuben Taer, were arrested. Jack O'Brien, "Police Arrest Two as Bomb Plotters after Italian Consulate Blast Here," *Daily News* [New York], January 18, 1927.

Twilight again descends o'er New York, and as the lights flicker on a freezing vaporous fog enshrouds the world's money center.

The Melting Pot
March 1, 1927

I trust that the gentle readers who compose the *Advertiser*'s clientele will forgive my temerity in submitting with such maddening regularity these boreful [*sic*] epistles. But I shall have the audacity to boast that this is the second one contributed to the columns of our paper since the one submitted from Denver Colo., several months ago. Had not my wits been taking a siesta I should not have assumed to tax your patience; but to those of you who may never come to New York (you won't miss much if you don't), I shall try to describe in my humble way the ever changing scenes that one beholds when out for a stroll, without thought or design, through the quaint streets of lower New York late of a winter's evening.

Lengthening shadows and many angled, grotesque reflects of weather-stained, sooty tenements, sprawl out over the cobblestone in fading caricature as twilight drapes her misty veil about the spires and steeples of New York's lower East-side. A stroll at twilight through the slums of the Bowery, the squalid abode of the lowly and poverty-stricken, long rows of ugly, six story houses loom up in unbroken monotony block after block. Clotheslines suspended high over the alleyways dangle in variegated colors and fibers the family "wash."[20] Ragged and dirty little urchins play about the uninviting steps that lead up from the sidewalks to tiers of dingy "homes." The Bowery is indeed a picturesque thoroughfare, and one known to sailors in every port where men go "down to sea in ships." From dark cellar-ways exhale damp, sickening odors to become dissolved in the pervading dreary atmosphere. One is obsessed with a sort of depressed and lonesome feeling at beholding so many unpleasant scenes. All the beauty seems to have vanished from the drowsy street, long since defiled by time, and in its stead is but a miserable, decadent perspective.

Bewhiskered Hebrews attired in ancient costumes, peddling fruits and vegetables hundreds of little carts parked along the sidewalks Jewish women, jabbering in Yiddish and rolling baby buggies—the future merchants of America! A burley policeman who talks in the dialect of the underworld: "Dis," "dat,"

---

20. On the Bowery, see, for example, Stephen Paul DeVillo, *The Bowery: The Strange History of New York's Oldest Street* (New York: Skyhorse Publishing, 2017); and Eric Ferrara, *The Bowery: A History of Grit, Graft, and Grandeur* (Charleston, SC: The History Press, 2011).

"youse," "wot," etc. A forlorn and wrinkled little woman, whose stringy tufts of course, gray hair protrude through the holes in a worn and torn kerchief which is tied about her head, lies asleep on the concrete steps of a deserted cathedral. A gush of cold wind riffles the hem of her hard-used dress, but the reclining form does not stir from her trance-like slumber. Just another "has been" caught in the swiftly receding tide of life. Impatiently waiting, imploringly praying, to be whirled into the Great Unknown. Contemptuous flappers in conspicuous frippery, animals of her own specie, pass her by without even a shuddering glance. One observes with bitter disgust the cold, cruel, heartless indifference of the bustling bipeds who pride themselves upon being humans. But such is life amid this writhing, seething human sea of seven million surging souls.

The usual array of phony salesmen who hang out around Brooklyn Bridge. Hundreds of hungry looking men of all ages and nationalities standing in the bread-line for half a block, waiting to receive their dole of bread and tin cup of pale coffee. An old man with gray mustache and huge of frame, whose pockets bulge with useless trinkets, goes down the street muttering to himself. Another aesthetic looking individual sits drooped in a doorway, trying to force a pencil into the neck of a small bottle; breaking both the phial and a certain law of physics. Evidently a victim of some form of insanity. Verily, the most lonely and hermetic lives are lived in the largest cities.

Smartly clad theatre goers jammed in the foyer of a Jewish theatre. Furs, silks, satins, beads and tinsel sparkle and glisten under the soft white lights like flakes of mica. Some two or three thousand Communists gathered about the office of a radical newspaper, gesticulating excitedly and talking in English, Russian and Hebraic. Lonesome looking, dreamy-eyed seamen, wandering subjects of many flags, who know no home but the salty waves, sit around the piers on huge boxes that are labeled with strange names to far away and Levantine ports. Late in the evening to Forty-second and Broadway, and there to browse amongst the musty shelves of favorite old books in the great library.

------·•·------

Thoughts and Scenes While Strolling in New York
April 19, 1927

In the apartment across the air-shaft some lonesome mortal (perhaps another stray Southerner) is playing "Swanee River" on a piano. He (or she) perhaps isn't aware that the reminiscent peals of that old southern song are falling appreciably on the ear of a lonely Dixie wanderer.

Today has been another one of those wretchedly blue and miserably gloomy Sundays. A light rain fell in the morning and few people other than those who have to work rain or shine, day or night, week-day or Sunday, ventured into the streets. I spent most of the long, drab day within the nerve frazzling confines of my pseudo-hospitable room, reading newspapers and nursing an aggravating cold and sore throat. Perhaps I deviate from the conventional in mentioning any physical infirmities; but this detestable la grippe has kept me penned up in this prison-like room until I've become as dull as the color of the wall paper above my head.

As night dragged on a damp, heavy fog enveloped the city, obscuring the tops of the mammoth buildings that tower skyward like jagged peaks. The imposing structures seemed to take on a dismal aspect, their grey walls looming up through the clouds of mist like menacing ghosts.

The solitary loneliness of my room became so unbearable that I sallied forth for a stroll through the dimly lighted streets on the West Side, which is quite an adventure for a stranger in New York.

You can never tell when you turn a corner in the big city whether you're going to jab your parasol in your best friend's eye, be held up by a bandit or bawled out by a cop for dropping your flock!

Ventured down one of those dimly-lit streets of the jumbled brick houses with the iron steps and broken sidewalks. Danger seemed to lurk in every darkened door-way. It was one of those thoroughfares of five story, dingy tenements and aerial clothes lines, where buxom women of diversified personalities sit with their eyes glued to the window. Like fatted hens with their bobbling heads protruding from ensconcing chicken coops, they keep a vigilant eye on the urbanized little Huckleberry Finns who play about the sidewalk, blending coveted morsels by Webster, the Bible and etiquette in the form of epitaphs to their more fortunate little neighbors across the street. These strange women seem to be entranced by the humming of passing vehicles, the intermittent roaring of the elevated, the haggling of street peddlers and the gloating of cab drivers. Their conceptions of geography are embodied in the red and blue lines of a subway map, and their knowledge of history consists of the unpleasant memories of more crowded ghettoes on the other side of the pond. They have—

Pardon my digression. I meant to describe my stroll, not to elaborate upon these strange and foreign creatures who are a part of this great city's personality.

Freakish looking gents in flashy silk shirts and 'loud' neck-ties, and with antiquated derbies cocked at a rakish angle, loiter about the darkened doorways that leap up to God only knows what. They eye you with a look that makes you quicken your step, lest a blow from a "billie" or a black-jack should lay you low. They are the conscienceless denizens of the underworld. No one is eligible to their fraternity who isn't capable of doing murder, if the case demands. They are the blokes and iron-jaws who are known to the police departments of a dozen cities. "Political protection" probably explains their freedom. Wine glasses tinkle like falling icicles in one of those exclusive night clubs in the "Roaring Forties," where sleek haired, nimble footed waiters in tuxedos maneuver gracefully from table to table, serving those elite squanderers who sip at rare wines and sparkling champagne, and mince at filet mignon and smoke and babble and prattle till the early hours of morning, when the toilers of the city are rising to go to work.

Strains of music, alternately low and rhythmic and loud and intelligent, float out on the foggy air from an Italian dance hall. Yes, they dance in New York on Sunday.

No one seems to give a hoot what the other fellow does, so long as he minds his own business. That is easily understood when you stop to consider that about seventy per cent of New York is foreign; people whose habits, tastes, customs, temperaments, etc., differ from our own. A night patrolman standing by a lamppost twirling his inexorable night stick. The sight of a cop in one of these dark streets makes one feel more safe. What strange and unbelievable stories these cops can tell!

Paused for a moment in front of the church of the Transfiguration, which has been immortalized in novel and play as the "little church around the corner." Many celebrities have consummated connubial contracts within the walls of this well-known old edifice.

Dropped in for a cup of tea at the Bohemian Inn in Greenwich Village, where the motley little group of writers and artists gather nightly to chat with contemporaries and to patronize the blind old violinist, whose little place is a haven of atmosphere and inspiration to the struggling artists.[21]

Arrived back in the room without mishap, though much fatigued from the stroll. Fell to reviewing a story by a young Russian writer, one that has been translated into English by a very good friend of mine. I detest these young

---

21. On Greenwich Village, see, for example, Caroline F. Ware, *Greenwich Village, 1920–1930* (Berkeley: University of California Press, 1994).

authors who are forever trying to ape H.L. Mencken.[22] If only there could come another Maxim Gorky, with his "Creatures that Once Were Men!"[23]

Montreal, Canada
May 10, 1927

As these boreful [*sic*] lines are being penned, I am sitting by my window (mine for a period), gazing out upon the endless lines of restless humanity that file past in the streets below. As the curtains of night are being drawn about this quaint metropolis, and the city assumes the proportions of some strange Arabian dream, thousands of wearied mortals are repairing to their respective habiliments after another long day's toil; while to others more fortunately endowed with the luxuries of life, the night is participated in one hilarious unrelenting lark.

There are saloons on every corner; and I haven't as yet seen a "drunk." Compared with little old New York, Montreal is a Sunday school town! For five cents one may get a glass of good, old-fashioned beer that would cost you thirty cents in any New York speakeasy! It is almost out of the question to get a half decent room in Montreal for less than fifteen dollars per week. All of which goes to show how many Americans, or, rather, "Yanks" come to Canada to spend their money and vacations.

Spring has arrived in this latitude somewhat behind schedule. Being delayed, perhaps, by the ice flows in the North Atlantic. But spring is now in evidence in every street and square. Even the visages of these urban citizens seem to radiate that carefree cheerfulness that comes with the bursting of buds and the blooming of lilacs. The parks and squares are being transformed from desolate winter scenes to delectable pictures of spring, and about the emerald carpets of vibrant new grass sit hundreds of the Reign's loyal but lonely subjects. Nine persons out of every ten speak the French language.

As I sit within the lonely confines of this unpretentious little room, on whose dingy walls hang the usual cheap paintings and faded pictures that

---

22. Henry Louis "H.L." Mencken (1880–1956) was a prominent journalist and cultural critic. During the time this letter was written, Mencken's most controversial work was *A Book of Prefaces* (1917). See, for example, Terry Teachout, *The Skeptic: A Life of H.L. Mencken* (New York: HarperCollins Publishers, 2002).

23. Born Alexei Maksimovich Peshkov, Maxim Gorky (1868–1936) was a renowned Russian author who wrote novels, short stories, and plays. See, for example, Richard Hare, *Maxim Gorky: Romantic Realist and Conservative Revolutionary* (New York: Oxford University Press, 1962).

eternally pursue the homeless transient, I seem to be living in a world long since passed with the centuries. Perhaps these feelings can be attributed to that agony of loneliness that comes over the lonesome wanderer who is hopelessly buried in the forgotten depths of a strange and foreign city. Were it not for my cheerful friend, the young artist with whom I am journeying to the Thousand Islands, I should surely go mad.[24]

Chicago, Ill.
June 21, 1927

These lines are being written aboard Northwestern train no. 3 between Milwaukee, Wis., and Chicago, and will in all probability be posted in Chicago, or at some point between Chicago and Detroit; thus, the heading.

Since this lowly writer wrote last from Montreal, Canada, he has traveled some four thousand miles. Of all the places included in my hurriedly scheduled itinerary, Quebec was the most interesting by far. Its quaint, serpentine streets and historic parks are reminiscent of our own New Orleans.

During my brief sojourn in Nova Scotia I saw and learned many interesting things. Perhaps the most interesting phenomena witnessed were the Northern Lights, which are visible a few hundred miles north of Montreal. Every city of any consequence was "covered" in our tour of the Dominion. Ottawa, Toronto, Winnipeg, and Hamilton were some of the principal cities in Canada. It would require a book to do justice to my study of Canada and her people. So, I will not try to "hog" too much of the good editor's valuable space. Suffice it to say, however, that whiskey is one big subject in Canada today. And no wonder! She is reaping a gigantic revenue from the thirsty citizens of the U.S., who are flocking up there by the tens of thousands to pour out their millions. At that rate, Canada will soon have paid off her war debt at our expense!

Spent a few hours at Niagara Falls, en route back to the states. The great cataract is well worth seeing, especially at night when the powerful colored lights are focused upon the misty vapor that ascends up from the rocks below the mighty falls. The lights (of every color) produce an awe-inspiring effect when blended with the roaring, tumbling, powerful falls. They (the lights) are located on the Canadian side of the river, and are appropriated for by the U.S. in order to charm the hundreds of thousands who visit them annually. We

---

24. The Thousand Islands are almost 2,000 islands in the St. Lawrence River.

stopped over a few days in Detroit, the home of a certain well-known car that is spelled with four letters. Can you guess it? Quite right; Ford's the name, and the Fords "wield" the "big stick" around Detroit.

For some reason which I can't very well explain, I never liked Chicago. You've seen cities like that. Some you can't like and some you can. Chicago, as you of course know, is the American headquarters of bootleggers and gangsters. One never knows when a machine gun will start barking in the streets of "Chi," as the city is called in this neck of the woods. There are a "million bums" hanging out in West Madison Street in Chicago. The windy city is noted for its freedom of speech; and soap-box orators, radicals and others seeking publicity hold their little meetings all along Madison and Monroe Streets in the evening. The largest buildings in the entire world are in Chicago. My "buddy," the artist with whom I am traveling from New York, used to go to school here at the Art Institute; and tells me the city has changed surprisingly since he left here for the East four years ago. But I prefer little ole New York to Chicago any old time. We shall leave Chicago for the East, and may stop off again in Detroit. Hoping the patient one who happens to try to read this will consider that it was written aboard a train!

— • —

London to New York
September 13, 1927

It is in the dead of night and we are far out in the mid-Atlantic. I am trying desperately to get these lines typed on an ancient typewriter whose stubborn mechanism is long since obsolete.

The boat is rocking and rolling and the waves are slapping and flapping against the sturdy sides of this old sea-going tub as if some angry god were chastising an unruly child, or mocking at the infinitesimal mite of steel and wood that dares to brave the waves of his coveted finger-bowl. One never feels so small and unimportant than when in the middle of the ocean in the care of a still and starry night. One can smell the profusion of indiscernible odors that go with ships; you can hear the wheezing and feel the vibration of the belligerent engines as they battle with the waves in plowing their ways slowly, steadily through the valleys and mountains of water.

This is the fourth time that the writer has crossed the Atlantic this year. The last letter I submitted to the home paper was written in Chicago; and now, two months later, I am returning from jolly old London. But we wanderers know no distance; at least we don't measure it in miles. This time last year I was down in the Southwest, in the heart of the oil industry; and this time two years ago I was on the Pacific Ocean, somewhere between the Bering Strait and Port Pedro. These lines will be mailed in New York and I'm only sorry that I haven't time to describe some of the long-to-be remembered scenes and places I chanced upon while strolling through Limehouse and other picturesque thoroughfares in mighty London—London of the dense, misty fogs and the thousands of homeless, hungry human beings. I found that Americans are looked down upon as idle spendthrifts and squandering snobs by the average European. And no wonder those poor, underfed people have formed such exaggerated opinion of the Americans! Our aristocratic snobs who go to Europe to squander their wealth and wallow around in pampered luxury have branded us a bunch of intolerable parasites who have more money than conscience or brains.

You must remember that in Europe—and especially is it true of England—there are two distinct classes in society—the extremely rich and the extremely poor. The middle or bourgeois class have had to suffer the brunt of the recent war and consequently have been reduced to a state of penury that is really more pathetic than the plight of the working class, who have always been use to such conditions. In short, the common people or the masses of Europe are becoming "class conscience" and radicalism is flourishing everywhere and with threatening momentum. One shudders to think what would happen if the least little spark ignites the revengeful fury of these millions of discontented and exploited people. Everywhere in England one hears talk of an impending conflict with Soviet Russia. England and Russia have severed diplomatic relations long since, and things are getting in a bad way generally on the other side of the pond. Taken altogether their prospective is indeed a gloomy one to contemplate. So much for that. More later.

Somewhere on the high seas

In Paradise Valley
October 4, 1927

Another beautiful day has burst forth into a cosmic blossom, flooding this blissful Virginia valley with an ocean of sunlight. The golden rim of the big red sun is just peeping over the serrated skyline of the Blue Ridge mountains

47

as these lines are being written. The embryo day had hardly broken through its inky shell when I awoke this morning. Outside my window, on the rusty iron fence that encircles my cottage (mine for a time!) was a myriad of beautiful, dew-bathed blossoms—golden, purple, crimson and white—on riotous display and vying, one with the other in fragrance, luster, and tender loveliness. A delicate vine of emerald shade—perhaps a purged and subdued species of the Virginia Creeper? Entwined the spear-pointed pickets, and to its fragile fronds clung crystal spheres of scented dew, as if they had been so placed that the infinite seer might read in them the fate of the races.

On a dead twig just a few feet above the vibrant veil of wined tracery and the aesthetic panorama of blossoms and half secluded by the fading foliage of an apple tree, a russet-colored bird twittered softly, shook itself, picked at a fussy feather and then issued forth a series of shrieking, disconcerting notes, notes that were incoherent, embarrassing and potently out of harmony with the dew and the dying apple leaves. The feathered little orchestra must have seen my disapproval, for his countenance assumed that of a guilty schoolboy, and he flitted away on the flimsy pretext of finding his breakfast. I glanced at the dead twig from which the little radical had flown. It swayed ever so lightly in the grey dawn, as if it, too, were nodding its approval of its little guest's hasty departure.

Now birds waking from their sleep, dew-kissed blossoms and delicate vines whose tiny, tender leaves are lined with crystal dewdrops, may not be interesting things to write about but they certainly are soothing to a city-tired optic in the cool dawn of a late Indian summer. And besides, I venture the thought that these beautiful little creatures of nature more nearly personify the Great Creator than anything else man can look upon.

A few miles down this historic old Shenandoah Valley from where I sit writing is the spot where George Washington, after Braddock's defeat, built old Fort Loudoun and established his headquarters during the French and Indian War. The house which he occupied is still standing, though now a pathetic relic that is being slowly defaced by a species of fungi. This valley was a veritable trampling ground for both the Southern and Northern forces during the Civil War, and it is said that some of these little towns changed hands as many as seventy-two times during that never-to-be-forgotten struggle.

I should like to elaborate upon some of the wonders of this tragic valley, but I will not tax the good Editor's patience by taking up so much of his valuable space. More another day.

—•◦•—

Where Bigotry Begins
October 18, 1927

One notes with astonishment and no little sadness the pharisaism and narrowmindedness that are extant in parts of the Old South. I won't attempt here to define these phenomena further or to attribute them to any particular source, for their origin probably could be traced back beyond the Puritan witch burners of the early days in our New England states.

Naturally one wouldn't expect to find as many liberal-minded persons in the more backward parts of the South as one encounters in the West, or even in the larger and more cosmopolitan cities of the Northeast, for that matter.

An incident which the writer experienced recently while hiking from the National Capitol to the remote and sparsely settled regions of the Blue Ridge country in Virginia, illustrates very clearly what he is driving at.

Upon my arrival in New York from London, I found that the days and nights I had devoted to the perusal of musty but cherished manuscripts while abroad, had impaired my health to the extent that I deemed it wise to desert the city for a period.

Realizing that the mountain air and the climate of the south were conducive to health, I straightway purchased a hiking outfit and a railroad ticket to Washington, D.C., from which point I was to become a jack-of-all-trades, work along at odd jobs and, incidentally, take notes on the characteristics of the people with whom I came in contact.

I was now two days out of Washington and about seventy-five miles southwest of that city. My brow was grimy with an admixture of dust and sweat, and I was footsore and much fatigued as I straggled into a little cross-roads hamlet just as the sun was setting. This second leg of my hike had been an enervating one, and I sought food and a place of rest for the night.

I stopped in front of a greasy dingy, sooty-looking place that might be called a combination of blacksmith shop, general repair and garage.

I disengaged the pack from my tired shoulders and inquired of the bespectacled patriarch who was tinkering away at a nearby workbench, if there was any place in the village where one might obtain food and lodging.

Instead of answering my questions as a civilized individual would be expected to do, he assumed, I thought, an attitude that was altogether too personal. "Where ye from?" he blurted out, in a manner that denoted surprise more than inquisitiveness.

Realizing the suspicion and enmity with which these ignorant mountain-eers look upon strangers, I informed him that I was merely hiking for my health and looking for work.

"Blarst me if I ever hyeard of a feller hiking fer his health afore," he admit-ted. And I doubt if he had, for he didn't seem to know that the Civil War was over!

I reminded him again of my mission to his shop, which seemed to rouse him momentarily from the wonderment into which he had been plunged by my unheralded presence. "Why-er-lemme see," he stammered scratching his head and trying to remember which of the dozen or so inhabitants of the town had ever taken in a traveler.

"Why ye might go across over thar to the Widder Yancey's; I allow as how she might take ye in for the night," he suggested.

I thanked him for the information, bade him goodnight and took my departure.

When I stepped upon the screaky boards of "Widder" Yancey's hospitable porch, I could see my old friend the blacksmith still gazing at me.

Now I have dined at the Ritz Carlton and some of the most exclusive places in New York; I have mixed and mingled with the elite passengers on such ships as the *Leviathan*; I have gone to theatres where royalty was present and have sat in libraries with some of the great and intelligent thinkers of our day, but never have I felt more despised or uncomfortable than the time at this little mountain village in Virginia![25]

The Widow Yancey was an embodiment of all the unpleasant and distaste-ful qualities that a woman can assume.

She was a tall, skinny, fidgety creature whose face somehow reminded one of an eagle or some other carnivorous fowl of prey—a perfect specimen of busy-body. One of those nicety-nice individuals who seem to delight in bulging the fact that his house is The House of Respectability.

The fussy little minister of the town's church boarded there and also the professor of the local high school, a person whom I afterwards discovered to be

---

25. The *Leviathan* began as the *Vaterland*, a German ship. In 1917, the U.S. confiscated the ship and renamed it. The ship operated as a troop ship during World War I. After the war, the ship was part of the U.S. Lines. "The Ocean Liner Leviathan," National Museum of American History, https://americanhistory.si.edu/collections/object-groups/the-ocean-liner-leviathan (Accessed April 10, 2020).

unusually dull and disgustingly dumb, but one who nevertheless held the future of the community's development—in his fanatic palm.

Mrs. Yancey, after having satisfied her curiosity as to my mode of living, personal habits, sobriety, etc., agreed to understand that so long as I enjoyed the luxuries of her domesticity, I could associate with the best families of the town, but that I could not lower my dignity and status as a gentleman by having discourse with the pretty young maid or any of the other "servants" who slaved thereabouts!

It seems that she had come of an aristocratic old Southern family who had lost everything in the Civil War except these impoverished ideas.

I deduced that perhaps she had an uncle or some male relative who had been fortunate enough to get kicked by one of Lee's or Jackson's mules during the war, thus giving her a certain sense of prestige and accounting for her intolerable haughtiness.

I secured a position as book keeper with a big plantation owner who, incidentally, was a widower and occasional consort of Mrs. Yancey's.

One fine morning the sanctified creature who officiates in all the affairs of the cleric, actually caught me, mind you, in conversation with an old darkey! Naturally he had to open up his big holy generous heart and divulge everything to my nosy landlady who informed me very indignantly that my welcome had come to an abrupt termination. She also emphasized the fact that she doubted very much if I could secure a place with any other "respectable family" in town if they knew or had the remotest idea that I had been talking with "niggers."

I came away with this conclusion: Intelligent social reform, liberalism and advancement have as much chance where such bigotry is in saddle as a scholar would have of being heard at Dayton, Tenn.[26]

All of which is by the way of saying that the South will remain for several years etc.—unless some unforeseen miracle of education should emancipate it—a land of superstition and ignorance and until these two forms of blight and deterioration have been wiped from the sunny breadth of our Dixie, bigotry will continue the cantankerous monster that it is.

---

26. Dayton, Tennessee, is where the Scopes Trial took place in 1925. See, for example, Edward J. Larson, *Summer for the Gods: The Scopes Trial and America's Continuing Debate over Science and Religion* (New York: Basic Books, 2020).

The Meditations of a Wanderer
November 1, 1927

This humble writer attributes what encouragement he got in his early efforts at writing to the kind Editor of the *Advertiser*, who has always been very considerate and generous in granting space (which perhaps he could have put to more profitable use!) in his paper to my feeble literary efforts.

Thus, it is with pleasure and due retrospection that I send him a copy of one of my poems which was recently awarded the prize in a poetry contest that attracted some of the foremost contemporary poets of Virginia.

Today has been a beautiful, though lonely, Sunday. Though, as to be expected, many lonely Sundays must pass over the heads of the confirmed wanderers! How many otherwise lovely Sundays in the past—especially of late years—have been marred by the pangs of loneliness!

How often is the question asked of cosmopolites—the wandering, sophisticated men of the world, "Do you ever get homesick?"

The answer, if an honest one, must be in the affirmative. As one unfortunately catalogued with that class, I can truly say that in the brief, fleeting hours of my glory, or in the agony of my loneliness, the unpleasant symptoms of nostalgia—the crave to be with loved ones and the longing for the old fireside—are ever present.

Just so many barnacles are we, clinging, we know not why, in futile desperation to the dull, inanimate hull of that wandering raft, that goal-less craft that is christened Fate!

How often have I left my writing in the dead of night to wander through interminable streets in the great city of New York, for no other reason than loneliness!

Not so long ago, as I stood upon that magnificent structure that is known as London Bridge—that masterpiece of steel and stone that spans the Thames River—I actually fancied, as I stood gazing down at the flickering lights of mighty London, that I was home again, and that the panorama of fog-dimmed lights were greeting me from humble, friendly farm-houses in the far-away valleys of Alabama! That is a brand of loneliness that few home-loving provincials ever know; and 'tis best they don't.

How many artists, poets and composers who choose no particular spot, but the world, as their homes, have written of this maddening depression in the misty vacuum of the past!

One gleams a thread of such melancholy running in unbroken continuity all through the works of Edgar Allan Poe. Wm. Blake, the great English poet and artist, as he was dying in poverty, sent a little child out with his last shilling to buy a pencil with which to write on the subject that I have this day chosen as my theme.[27]

To borrow one of O. Henry's well-known phrases, we are homeless, though we have a thousand homes; and friendless, yet the races of the earth are our friends.[28]

A Grave Is Made
November 8, 1927

This is a beautiful morning. The sun is shining down upon us in all its golden splendor and there isn't the tiniest speck of cloud to mar the unbroken blue in all the sky about this drowsy little southern village.

A few birds are twittering softly among the golden foliage of the apple trees outside my window. They seem to know that winter is lingering but for a day; and that where the blossoms now grow the snow will soon blow, and the skies will be murky and grey.

From my window I can see the simple folk of the village passing along the sidewalks. They are all in their "Sunday clothes," and many of them are carrying wreathes and great bunches of beautiful flowers.

My kind and motherly land lady tells me that there's to be a funeral in the village today. She has given me a brief biography of the deceased, a sort of story thumbnail sketch that I have converted into story form. Of course, I have rearranged the facts and placed them in order of sequence, so as to give the story its proper continuity and perspective.

Perhaps there are many little boys and girls reading the *Advertiser* who would have liked to know the little hero of this post mortem story—a little boy who overcame, one might say, insurmountable obstacles in attaining his goal.

---

27. Edgar Allan Poe (1809–1849) was an American author and poet, famous for poems like "The Raven" and short stories like the "Tell-Tale Heart." William Blake (1757–1827) was an English poet and painter. On Poe, see, Jerome McGann, *The Poet Edgar Allan Poe: Alien Angel* (Cambridge: Harvard University Press, 1994). On Blake, see, Peter Ackroyd, *Blake: A Biography* (New York: Alfred A. Knopf, 1996).

28. William Sydney Porter, better known as O. Henry, attained fame for writing short stories like "The Gift of the Magi" and "The Ransom of Red Chief." See, for example, David Stuart, *O. Henry: A Biography of William Sydney Porter* (New York: Stein & Day, 1990); and Gerald Langford, *Alias O. Henry: A Biography of William Sidney Porter* (New York: Macmillan, 1957).

Peter Gregory had the great misfortune of being born a cripple.[29] And to add further misfortune to his embarrassing physical deformity (he was a hunchback), the gods of Fate deemed it wise to orphan him in the infantile stage of his life.

Little Peter was taken to raise by a paternal uncle, than whom no one would have been more cruel or beastly inhuman. The ignorant old uncle despised little Peter for his physical deformity, and was too ashamed of the little fellow to send him to school. Consequently, the bright-eyed little cripple was never allowed to go to town with his uncle like most other little boys do on Saturdays in the South.

Little Peter had to content himself with wearing the discarded shoes and clothes of his larger cousins, which were many sizes too big for his dwarfed little frame. No one cared enough for him to mend his stockings and clothes, or to even sew buttons on the ragged little shirts he had to wear.

The little hunchback had to stay at home and water the horses, look after the cows, feed the pigs and do all the many chores about the farmhouse while his larger and more fortunate cousins were away at school.

When "company" came to the home of old Ed Gregory, little Peter was ushered out and locked in a clothes closet some place until the company had gone. And oftentimes he had to sleep on a pallet in the barn when the neighbors would come to spend the night.

But Peter had a clear, beautiful able mind that more than offset the ugly features of his twisted little body.

He knew that he was despised by his uncle, that his cousins poked fun at him and even called him a camel, and that the other children in the neighborhood would stand and gaze at his deformed little person in silly wonderment. But all these things Peter didn't mind, for he would smile in his humble, pathetic little way and go humping off to play with his little dog, the only friend he had.

When Peter was nine years old, he learned to read and write. He had bargained with his cousins to do all their chores if they in turn would teach him to read in the books like they did.

Old Ed Gregory died of an "alcoholic heart," and at the age of ten little Peter was thrown out to shift for himself and from then until he was fifteen Peter was nothing more than a little slave to the many different families that had kept him. He couldn't go to school, for no one would assume the responsibility of boarding the little fellow, buying his clothes and giving him the care and

---

29. The editor could not find any information on Peter Gregory. There were multiple men by that name in Virginia during that time period.

attention that other children get. But now that he had learned to read and write, he became very fond of reading, and so spent what few pennies he could get together for books.

When other little boys of his age had begun to have "sweethearts" and were invited to all the little parties and communal affairs, little Peter was over-looked, and often had to stay at his place of adoption alone, for all the girls were ashamed to be seen talking to him. The boys, too, shunned him as if he were some contagious disease. All this Peter realized, and he must have been very sad, for no little boy would like to live in such lonely isolation.

From each family Peter learned a few things that he never forgot. And as he was kicked and cuffed from place to place his knowledge of human nature and his wisdom of books increased. He found time to devote a few hours each night to the perusal of his studies, and by the time he was fifteen and had his few scant belongings bundled up to hit the road for Richmond, there was no smarter or better educated boy in the valley.

We don't know what Peter did or how he got along in the big, strange city of Richmond. But he must have converted all of his hard knocks into stepping-stones, for today a great doctor—a hunchback little man who has done much towards eliminating disease—is being interred in the local cemetery, and many prominent people from the cities and the high places of learning have come to pay honor to Peter Gregory.

Whither are We Drifting
November 15, 1927

"Uncle Tobie" Grimes and old Henry Higgins are no different from the hundreds of other confirmed provincial "kickers" who assemble every evening on the store porches of our cross-roads hamlets to exchange "chaws" of their favorite brand of the weed and incidentally to bemoan the rapid-fire changes that an unprecedented age of progress is bringing about.

I offer the following in substantiation.

I'le be darned if I c'n figger out what the world's comin' to if sich as this keeps up," lamented uncle Tobie as he transferred a life-sized cud of tobacco from one side of his bewhiskered face to the other and pointed an indicating finger at two smartly, but scantily, dressed little flappers who were out, it seemed to Uncle Tobie, for no other purpose than to exhibit two pairs of pretty garters that circumferenced two pairs of shapely nether limbs.

"Yes, be derned if 'taint ridiculus," echoed old Henry Higgins as he flapped his galluses in puzzled contemplation and spat an amber colored stream of tobacco juice abjectly, though with no mean accuracy, at the upturned end of a nearby salmon can.

"Them dresses oughter be at least a foot longer," alibied Uncle Tobie as he craned his wrinkled old neck to get a farewell peep at the disappearing garters.

"Well," sighed old Henry regretfully as the garters turned a corner and were lost to sight, "'taint worthwhile talkin' to 'em, I reckon."

"And another thing I don't like," grieved Uncle Tobie, is the way women air goin' about nowadays with their hair bobbed. Why some of 'em air plumb grey-headed; and they look worse'n sheared sheep."

"Aw, it's awful, Tobie—plumb awful the way the world's a-goin'," agreed old Henry.

Uncle Tobie was scratching around in the matted locks of his tousled hair and trying vainly to dig up further damaging evidence that he might cite in sustaining his contention that the world is rapidly going to the proverbial dogs, when suddenly a young upstart came dashing down the street at a break-neck speed in a late model of Mr. Ford's cradle robbers.

After much screaking of brakes and sliding of wheels, the mortgaged vehicle came to a stop in front of where the two savants were discussing the disgusting age of transition.

Old Henry was just on the verge of rebuking the brainless pilot in scathing terms, when Uncle Tobie, knitting his brows together and with strained optics focused intently upon the occupants of the presto-driven cabaret, interrogated, "Ain't that your boy in there, Henry?"

"Huh, believe it is Ezra," answered old Henry, in a tone that unmistakably denoted parental pride.

"Ma's down at the barber shop gittin' her hair cut, Pa; said to tell ye to come on down there, fer she lacked a quarter havin' enough to pay fer it," yelled Ezra from the car as he and the two pairs of garters went rattling off down the street again at break-neck speed.

"Well, looks like we might have a little rain, Tobie," remarked old Henry as he went stumbling off towards the barber shop.

The New Year
January 10, 1928

Now that the old year is being counted out to the tune of hilarious celebrations, riotous demonstrations and such nonsensical monkey-shines as the hoodlums can conjure up to increase the din and noise of our already maddening pandemonium, let us pause long enough between the explosions of the morons' fireworks to take a sort of spiritual inventory of the little-known things we call ourselves.

The New Year promises much in the way of nothing really constructive. Of course, we shall have newer and later-modeled Fords to increase the number of mortgages and furnish a topic of conversation as well as conveyance to many millions of people in months to come.

We are to have a new President appointed (it amounts to just about that when all the delegations file in the processions to the various convention halls to carry out cut-and-dried instructions and exhibit such gnashing of teeth and symptoms of delirium as are appropriate to the occasion) to grace the head of the White House table and incidentally tell us how surprisingly prosperous we are for the next four years. "And a leader shall come among ye—." But that doesn't mean that he will not be another Lincoln or that he won't use the same old hackneyed phrases in dodging the issues! One thing is almost certain: Our taxes will remain about as high in the next administration (whether it be Rep. or Dem.) as they are in the present one, and the service will be about as bad.

Luckily for our national lawmakers, they still have Muscle Shoals and the Boulder Canyon dam to hurl epitaphs at one another over when it's too wet to golf or too cold to go motoring.

The Knights of the Hooded order will try to have us believe that the Pope of Rome and a legion of Mussolini's Fascist soldiers will swarm over and take possession of this great materialistic commonwealth like the Germans were going to do during the World War if Al Smith of New York is elected President.[30] Likewise, the Republicans will tell us that unless we elect a Republican to fill that honored office, we shall suffer much privations, know the pangs of want

---

30. Alfred Smith (1873–1944) served four terms as the governor of New York and ran for president as the Democratic candidate in 1928. See, Robert A. Slayton, *Empire Statesman: The Rise and Redemption of Al Smith* (New York: Simon and Schuster, 2007).

and eventually land in that unpleasant place to which Dante designated the rich men!

So, while the politicians ransack the country let us ransack the closets in search of our last-year's raincoats, for we shall need them when the great national mud-slinging contest gets underway.

We seem to have worse and more booze in the country than at any time since the eighteenth amendment went into effect. In fact, the eighteenth amendment is being ignored in the northern part of the country pretty nearly as much as the fourteenth and fifteenth amendments are in the South.

The press is exploiting more sensational murders than at any time in history, and our legal procedure signifies a sign of judicial decay that is sickening, even to a Congressman.

The rich are getting richer and the poor are eating with more relish, even if with less regularity. There have been more Christmas baskets and other forms of charity distributed this year than ever before in the history of the country. Wonder why the "starving Armenians" and those "near East" sufferers whom we fed with our gigantic "drives" and "humane campaigns" a few years back aren't returning the compliments!

Look back over the year that has spiraled itself into the eternal coil, and you can discern many wobbles in the furrow that I've plowed. I've traveled some, absorbed a little knowledge—how infinitesimally little!—and made a few enemies as well as friends. I've done nothing to be proud of and many things to be ashamed of. Taken altogether, I can't see the world has been better by my having been in it. But that I'm still a part of it and the time has rolled around again to renew those noble resolutions that were forgotten last year long before the sap had begun its annual pilgrimage up the trunk of the early maple tree, I shall try again where I left off then. Our New Year's resolutions, though all very good and idealistic, just somehow don't seem to withstand the attrition of time and the agitation of a purely human heart!

As those puerile lines are being written in this phlegmatic South Carolina village, I entertain no delusions regarding the "bright and prosperous" year that is now before me. Indeed, I should be happy to know that the gains that this year may hold for me would be great enough to compensate for the losses sustained last year!

On Whom Are You Betting
January 31, 1928

When the political dice have been thoroughly loaded for the quadrennial game and each of the major parties "set in" at the table in one grand scramble to be the first in putting over the fancy shenanigan that will decide the winner and cinch the coveted presidential stake, few of us small-fry spectators will realize what is happening, and many more of us will refuse to give a hoot.

To indulge in idle speculation here would only be a waste of printers' ink and a burden on the type-setter, not to mention the boredom such puerile "copy" would heap upon the editor. One should remember (but in this I am the most flagrant disregarder) that there is a limit to all things even to an editor's patience. But if you will bear with me, and bear no ill feelings toward me for revealing my political trend, I shall include in a brief list the names of a few out-standing men of our time (as viewed from my periscope), any one of whom I should vote for were the chance given:

Borah of Idaho (whoa I've gone! And conveyed the impression that I'm a Socialist, honest I?) Reed of Missouri (I'm not altogether "wet"), Ritchie of Maryland (again I'm not wet), Hunt of Arizona (governor and a great man, but comparatively unknown), Brookhart of Iowa (an Independent Rep.) and the well-known Senator Norris.[31] There are a few others but I promised to abbreviate the list. Yes; we've agreed: none of the above listed is within the realm of probability. Now speaking of the "possibles"—

Hoover is a great man and very potently a capable one. At least he demonstrated his greatness to the satisfaction of our Southern flood sufferers and his capability was proved during that agonizing martial period some ten years ago,

---

31. Republican William Borah (1865–1940) served in the U.S. Senate from 1907–1940. See, Robert James Maddox, *William E. Borah and American Foreign Policy* (Baton Rouge: Louisiana State University Press, 1970). Democrat James A. Reed (1861–1944) served in the U.S. Senate from 1911–1929. See, "James Alexander Reed," Biographical Directory of the United States Congress, 1774–Present, https://bioguideretro.congress.gov/Home/MemberDetails?memIndex=r000118 (Accessed April 6, 2020). Democrat Albert Ritchie (1876–1936) served as governor of Maryland from 1920–1935. See, Michael T. Walsh, *Baltimore Prohibition: Wet and Dry in the Free State* (Mount Pleasant, SC: The History Press, 2017). On Hunt, see Chapter 1, Footnote 1. Republican Smith W. Brookhart (1869–1944) served in the U.S. Senate from 1922–1926. See, George William McDaniel, *Smith Wildman Brookhart: Iowa's Renegade Republican* (Iowa City: Iowa State Press, 1995). George W. Norris (1861–1944) served in the U.S. Senate from 1913–1943; for most of his career he ran as a Republican. See, Richard Lowitt, *George W. Norris: The Triumph of a Progressive, 1933–1944* (Chicago: University of Illinois Press, 1978).

when he came very nearly to Hooverizing us to death in his efforts at patriotism. But Hoover's greatness, if nothing else, will prevent his being nominated.

Vice President Dawes, the great international banker and multimillionaire and "Al" Smith, the Tammany Hall progeny, are two "possibilities" pretty well in the spot-light.[32] Smith is by far the greater of the two. Dawes, like Mellon, is too enamored of money to care a whit about the common people's interest.[33] We even see "Big Bill" Thompson, who is boss of Chicago's saloons, gambling houses and machine gun nests, mentioned as a presidential possibility.[34] Holy shade of President Grant!

Personally, I think it would be a better, and by far a more economical scheme to appoint, say, Charles M. Schwab of the steel trust and J.P. Morgan of Wall Street for that matter, to flip coins in deciding this presidential question, winner take all![35] Now how does that strike you for a novel idea, eh? Didn't think it of me, did you? So's your old man! But I persist in digressing. Since the anti-evolutionists and KKKs have found no gifted teacher to take the place of Bryan, unless they should decide to come to a common understanding and confer that honor upon the Hon. J. Thomas Heflin, things will be getting in admittedly a bad way in the "Solid South."[36] But these leading elements, it seems to me, are a bit dubious of this man Heflin and you can't blame them; for nobody knows whose back yard he'll be ramping around in. The records show that our Tom has used some mighty fine judgement, as well as courage, in framing his vote on certain important issues of the past and he's just liable to start out like that again. Hence the fanatics are gun shy of him.

Regardless of the velocity of the political winds, some of the craft will weather the gale, and when the stage is set in Washington for the new production

---

32. Charles G. Dawes (1865–1951) served as Vice President during the Calvin Coolidge administration. See, Annette B. Dunlap, *Charles Gates Dawes: A Life* (Evanston, IL: Northwestern University Press, 2016). On Smith, see Chapter 2, Footnote 30.

33. Andrew Mellon (1855–1937) served as Secretary of the Treasury from 1921–1932. See, David Cannadine, *Mellon: An American Life* (New York: Vintage, 2008).

34. William Hale Thompson (1869–1944) served two terms as mayor of Chicago and had connections with mobster Al Capone. See, Lloyd Wendt and Herman Kogan, *Big Bill of Chicago* (Evanston, IL: Northwestern University Press, 2005).

35. Charles M. Schwab (1862–1939) was a famous U.S. steel magnate. See, Robert Hessen, *Steel Titan: The Life of Charles M. Schwab* (Pittsburgh: University of Pittsburgh Press, 1990). John Pierpont Morgan (1837–1913) was a financier known for railroads, U.S. Steel, and General Electric. Jean Strouse, *Morgan: American Financier* (New York: Random House, 1999).

36. Bryan is in reference to Populist and Scopes Trial prosecutor William Jennings Bryan. Democrat James Thomas Heflin (1869–1951), also known as "Cotton Tom," represented Alabama in the U.S. Senate from 1920–1931. Elbert L. Watson, "J. Thomas Heflin, *Encyclopedia of Alabama*, http://www.encyclopedi aofalabama.org/article/h-2952 (Accessed April 7, 2020).

it is very likely that we'll have a change of scenery. At least there will be new voices to utter the repartee of slapstick. American cupidity a la Washington and its state department in Nicaragua, as demonstrated by a series of magnanimous blunders in effecting the administration's desired coup d'état in that helpless little Republic, is now in a fair way to prevail. Mr. Marion Alexander, who for five months during the Sacasa revolution in Nicaragua was the Associated Press correspondent in that country, and incidentally the only correspondent down there who was not working in the interest of President Coolidge or big business, says it is ridiculous what the administration is getting away with down there under the brazen subterfuge of "protection."

Of course, that isn't news to the writer; he has met liberal speakers and leaders by the dozens in New York who were evicted from their native Nicaragua on the flimsy pretext of upholding the mandates and dignity of the Monroe Doctrine.

Just mention the farce our American bankers are staging in Nicaragua under the sacred name of Democratic government to any citizen who is threatened with intelligence, and you have given him food for monstrous gigglement!

If you doubt the truth of this allegation, let me suggest that you read Bertram Wolfe's history of the Nicaragua revolution. Or better still, try to explain, if you can, why the administration refused to allow Sen. Borah and a committee of investigators to go to Nicaragua and investigate conditions down there!

Notwithstanding all of this, President Coolidge will arise to address the big Pan-American peace blow-out next week in Havana, Cuba. And I dare predict, that if you'll just keep tabs on the papers that publish that speech—they all will—you will very probably discover that our president has maintained his sphinxlike silence in regards to Nicaragua and the man-treatment she's receiving!

Would be a prototype of Signor Mussolini of wopdum!

Yours for a complete dissolution!

Nabors Collides with Luck
May 1, 1928

Design to see in these few lines an expression of his most respectful gratitude who herein dissipates your generous patience with this inconsequential narrative. So, without further indulgence in superfluous apologies, he now obliterates all thoughts of you and a possible perusal, and so bends his resourceful genius to spinning a thread on which to string this odious yarn.

When the good ship *Moon Dance* glided into dock at pier eight-forty in this enigma of cities (New York) a fortnight or so ago from the palm clad isle of zephyr-caressed Cuba, this enterprising weaver of hackneyed fabrications was amongst the august parcels of advanced organisms that disgorged themselves from the jaded deck.

All our hero had in his pockets (now this is confidential and not to be whispered about) were his hands and a cablegram from a certain friendly book-man imploring him (our hero) to return to New York immediately. Not being encumbered with any bulky or weighty pieces of unnecessary luggage—such as the petty bourgeois display for purposes conspicuous—our entertaining narrator very democratically dismantled himself from a cumbersome overcoat and contemptuously ignored all the humble solicitations of conveyance vendors; preferring to hoof it up Eighth Avenue rather than associate with such low order of intelligence. (But just between you and me it's quite possible there were other very obvious reasons why he didn't employ a cab.)

On the eventful day of which we write our intellectual hero had forgotten to eat, which fact gave birth to a thought (admittedly a disconcerting one) that remained uppermost in his lofty mind; and that was to locate a certain familiar book establishment on Twenty-third Street, where thrived a congenial acquaintance by the name of Ralph Adimari.[37] Now try and imagine, if you are so able to distort your mind, the delectable predicament our friend was in when he discovered with much discomfort and not a little blasphemy that the purveyor of knowledge, book establishment and all had suffered a change of address! Of course, such things change with maddening regularity in this great and uncertain city of New York. And it's probably a good thing at that, for if the citizenry didn't have a change of address at least twice per annum they'd get to knowing more about their fellow hypocrite's business than is compatible even with friendship. So, you see if everybody stayed in one place very long things would soon come to a showdown; and in that case the whole mob would demand a shuffle of addresses. But in saying all this the writer is merely leading his innocent but mistreated readers on a digressing chase; so, off the tangent and back to the substance of the discussion, as the philosophers say.

Where were we? Oh, yes; we had left our stranded hero standing near a deserted bookery, inhaling the odiferous fumes of a nearby cafeteria and exhaling a life-size stream of choice invectives. The odium of such predicament (thus

---

37. On Adimari, see Chapter 1, Footnote 18.

we are told in the eulogium of business magazines) has spurred men of probably less initiative to the acquisition of great wealth and social prestige. But no. No such luck for our hero. It seemed as if he were doomed to grovel his lowly way among the accursed of the earth. It was expedient that something be done instantly, if not sooner.

His resourcefulness had been challenged. To smile in the unpleasant face of old Mother Adversity only seemed to accentuate her wrath. So, he discarded that theory as utterly ludicrous. The gravity of the occasion necessitated something more consistent with practicality; and so, he set about devising means of detaching himself from his worldly possessions, which were encased in a fourteen by twenty-six, leather-bound. Having thus reflected, he proceeded to emulate the reactions of other wretches of whom he had read in similar predicament, and immediately started off in quest of the nearest pawnshop. Dame Fortune had so arranged it that the closest such emporium in proximity was a couple of blocks away, otherwise our thrilling story might not have ended so happily. Suffice to say that at a busy intersection on Sixth Avenue our dejected, dispirited, and disfranchised hero was unexpectedly jostled; not by a speeding vehicle that left grim death in its wake, but by Ralph Adimari, bookman and one-time acquaintance, but now benefactor, godfather, lifesaver or what have you?

Art a la Greenwich Village
May 22, 1928

There are, within my limited scope of acquaintances, some half a dozen artists of genuine talent and accomplishment. So, it is not of these chaps I write.

It is Wm. Forrest, whose paintings are recognized abroad as well as in this country, and S.H. Pickering, the well-known Westerner, with whom I have been more or less in constant association for the past twelve months, to whom I am indebted for the knowledge that enables me here to pass opinions on the Greenwich Village artist, or rather, imitator.[38]

Though my schooling in the fine arts has been a sort of haphazard one, I have, in fact (and I say this without vestige of shame) spent more time and energy in the pursuit of that ecstatic stimuli derived from the muses than I have in catering to my own welfare. Yea, I have, tenanted both Pickering's and

---

38. On Pickering, see Chapter 1, Footnote 16.

Forrest's studios more nights than there are years in my age.[39] But then I mustn't let you know too much about our "private parties!"

In order to appreciate or, should I say, evaluate, the arty Villager it is necessary for one to spend at least six months in the atmosphere that emanates from that part of New York City. Though I dare venture that thirty days would be ample time in which to drive any rationally-minded person insane! Now I must confess here that I have been more or less indifferent and antipathetic toward most things (which perhaps [unclear] to a crazy, poetic constitutional fault of mine, and cannot well be obviated) considered "proper" and "correct" in society. But then I have the consolation of knowing that Shakespeare and Beethoven, and even Christ, were in revolt against the tastes of their time!

First, let us assume that we are on a sort of inspection tour of the Art colony of Greenwich Village, and we are now about to enter our first real studio. You perhaps observed as you came through the street door and paused in the vestibule to clink the big brass knocker that officiates as doorbell, that all the letter-boxes bore the legends of "Dr.," "Artist," etc. Well, that is merely to impress you with the little fact that you're no longer among mortals of ordinary clay, such as the rest of us prefer to be.

Your very being immediately responds to the pulsating Bohemian atmosphere of the gilded hall into which we have now come. You are momentarily stunned upon entering the aesthetic sanctum of, let us say, our friend, Mr. Dauber, by the gay and multicolored Indian prints, tapestries, fancy strappings, etc., that greets you from the walls of his exquisitely cozy domicile. You of course are pleased with the soft glow of blended lights that mitigate the curious and odd-looking jugs, jars, vases, antique pieces of Elizabethan furniture, the silken-pillowed lounge, the portable ash-tray and the easel, not to mention all the mysterious-looking canvases of cubist painting that stare at you from every corner, angle, and crevice.

You also observe the conspicuous display of uncut literature in his paneled and highly-decorated bookcase, not to refer to the aggregation of large 12 mo., gold-embossed Persian inlaid, Florentine Ooze leather bound volumes of expensive reading matter piled lavishly upon his mantelpiece.

It strikes you as being singularly strange that among all those handsome-looking, heavily-gilt books there isn't a single volume by an American author! But we forget to inform you that everything American is considered extremely,

---

39. There was a well-known Scottish painter/engraver named William Forrest (1805–1889) but he died almost 40 years before this article was penned. The editor had no luck finding a William Forrest who fit Nabors's timeline.

nay, impossibly, vulgar, and that to praise anything by an American author, except possibly Poe and Whitman, or, if you would be more modern, Mencken, simply isn't done.

As we enter the studio our gifted painter is habited in his smock, and standing near the easel, with brush poised as if he were about to commit the final stroke de perfecto to some great masterpiece. But upon seeing us intrude like so many hero worshippers, a sort of Mephistophelian smile transfigures his paint-besmudged face, and he bows most gracefully and greets each of us very cordially as we are introduced. He begs leave to remove his smock, and accordingly dons a smoking-jacket that is more appropriate to the occasion. We are all comfortably seated and he at once (as is the way of such gifted creatures) starts to unreel the silken ribbon of conversation.

Our host very gracefully fetches each of us, without once consulting our temperance, a cup of blazing potcheen (it isn't to be drunk until the little blaze has burned out), and frames an apology (they all do it in New York) to the effect that he has just run out of scotch, and that his favorite bootlegger is down to Atlantic City for the weekend. We mumble a word or two in admiration of his extremely ugly paintings and pretend to be deeply interested in an outrageous thing that's still wet on the easel. He very impressively dismisses the thing with a sweep of his hand, explaining that some old Park Avenue dowager, who has more money than knowledge of art, has contracted for the thing in order to impress an unsuspecting Count, who promises much in the way of matrimony.

Thus having spent an evening in such environs and having so thoroughly enjoyed (though we should be arrested for profaning the language were we to honestly express our minds) the rare brilliance of such profound personality as Mr. Dauber, we come away fully convinced that about nine-tenths of the Village artists are fakers, pure and simple, and that the other tenth are so enwrapped with vanity and hypocrisy as to be utterly impossible. We have that feeling that one has who had paid five dollars to see on Broadway a slapstick comedy that could be seen over on Eighth Avenue for twenty-five cents.

These Sundays
June 19, 1928

Edgar Allan Poe once wrote a short humorous story in which he showed how three Sundays could come in a week. Now we don't attempt here to conjure up any such calculus in mentioning the "day of rest." However, Sundays do seem to roll 'round with maddening regularity—the New York variety of Sundays, we mean.

We have no particular grudge against Sunday itself, and we should be the very last one to sign a petition to have it erased from the calendar; but the trouble with us cliff dwellers here in New York—pity us—is that there are no fine watermelon patches near where one might slip into and enjoy—oh, how can we think of it!—the evening at his neighbor's expense. Nor are there any nice, cool, shady streams near—at least not in fifty miles—where one might sit on old Mother Nature's perfumed carpet and lure Sir Trout from the azure depths of his favorite pool.

About the only thing one can do in New York on Sunday is to loll about in the parks and look at the pictures in the rotogravure section of the Sunday "supplements" until it is time to go the theatre or to the speak-easy. There hasn't been a new joke cracked on the stage in ten years; and if one goes into a speakeasy, the chances are about ten to one that the evidence will be found next morning on a marble slab somewhere in the morgue. So, what is one to do?—stay in one's room or apartment until the very walls become contemptuous of him.

With you who read these tearful lines it is difficult—oh, so different. You have those dear friends whom you can bore with a visit; or, better, you can tie yourselves to those pleasant communal affairs—the "all-day singings," etc., where it doesn't cost you a young fortune to be pleasantly entertained.

The advantages you have over us urban sardines are many, and are more conducive to health, wealth, happiness and even to personality than are the few advantages afforded by the big city. You just ought to see how they kick, shove, jostle and pack us about here in this hopelessly over-crowded metropolis! Why, no self-respecting cowpuncher would even think of inflicting such punishment on a herd of Texas steers!

And speaking of friends—if we, by chance, should meet while strolling about in the interminable streets of this great city merely a couple of speaking acquaintances, we seek consolation in our loneliness by flattering ourselves with the illusion that we, too, have friends; but those "friends" are usually the type that are bereft of any noble qualities the word may imply. The fault, however, is not theirs; it comes naturally with the other artificialities that such environs inevitably produce. Like so many moths, we spiral around in a swift, fickle and uncertain cycle.

CHAPTER 3

Passionate Philosopher, 1931-1934

"All that we see or seem is but a dream within a dream."
—Edgar Allan Poe

On Thoughts of Home
February 18, 1931

It has been so long since we submitted any "copy" to the *Advertiser* that we rather fear we've forgotten the requirements governing outside correspondence. However, as our good editor has on various occasions in the past extended to us a certain latitude of expression bordering one might almost say, on the patronizing—since he has so generously and graciously left those things to our own discretion, we shall try and respect this indulgence by keeping our paragraphs within reasonable spatial bounds.

It is not without regret and commiseration that we observe in the press of the country the multitudinous complaints, the sad information regarding the hardships and miseries which tens of thousands of our indigent Southern brothers are having to endure consequent of the present world-wide economic depression. But let's hope that the present hard times, though perhaps unprecedented in scope, are epidemic in nature rather than endemic, and that we shall soon again enjoy the fruits of the Cornucopia—that fabled "horn of plenty."

Though bad as times are in the South, they are doubtless much worse in the big metropolitan centers of the North and East, where countless hundreds of thousands are dependent altogether upon charity for subsistence. In a recent contribution to the *Birmingham News*, apropos an editorial in that paper on unemployment and its attendant miseries, we stated that in our opinion, judging from the data that have recently been adduced on the subject, there are approximately eight hundred thousand unemployed in New York City alone.

One sees bread-lines most everywhere one turns here in New York; men, women, and children stand shivering in the snow in the long queues, awaiting their mites of bread and soup, distributed as charity by the various social and welfare organizations in order to keep body and soul together. But perhaps on the obverse side of the picture may be soon discovered the proverbial "silver lining" of the cloud that now darkens so many little homes in our land.

A very dear little friend of ours, through whose kindness we are enabled to keep in touch with the news and happenings there at home (as the impermanency of residence unfortunately won't allow us to subscribe by the month or year to the home paper), has enlightened us regarding the many physical changes that have occurred in the vicinity of Guntersville since last it was our pleasure to be in the old home-town. For instance, we are informed that a big, new bridge now spans the Tennessee where once we had to depend upon the antiquated methods of the ferryman to facilitate and expedite matters of transportation. We are also told that the wheels of industry are humming their modern utilitarian lays in a new cotton mill contiguous to the once drowsy streets we trod in school days.[1] To him who is estranged from home and friends this news comes as good tidings, as a reassuring harbinger of progress.

There are other bits of intelligence which we're pleased to glean from the interesting and enlightening pages of the *Advertiser*. For instance, as we peruse, eagerly, avidly, voraciously the lines of this dear old indispensable medium of local news and information we're pleased to learn that he was once our professor at the old M.C.H.S. and is now, thanks to the justness of Providence, a judge of Marshall County. And we learn with equal gratification that another of our school-day heroes—him who used to thrill us with his oratorical power, his inspiring eloquence, has been given magistracy—we refer to Mr. Chas. Kennamer of Guntersville, whom President Hoover has sagaciously appointed to a U.S. judgeship.[2]

We rejoice also to note that the *Advertiser* has absorbed the *Democrat*, its ancient neighborly rival. If you'll permit us a moment's retrospection—our

1. The Saratoga Victory Mills opened in 1928. Whitney A. Snow and Barbara J. Snow, *Lake Guntersville* (Mount Pleasant, SC: The History Press, 2018), 103.
2. Charles B. Kennamer (1874–1955) practiced law in Guntersville and was appointed a federal judge in 1931. Smith, 73, 76.

vanity prompts us to turn back the pages of time, and recall the remarks which a little poem of ours elicited some fifteen or sixteen years ago. It was one of our first efforts at poesy, and was entitled, lest our memory betray us, "The Blue and the Gray."[3] Our first childish efforts at self-expression are perhaps our dearest ones; and the awful seriousness with which sensitive young persons take themselves naturally renders them liable to a variety of injuries, both real and imaginary, to which the less precocious of juvenilia are fortunately immune. Being unhappily in the former class, we shall never forget the deprecatory remarks with which the then editor of the *Democrat* damned, and perhaps not altogether unjustly, our little poem. And likewise, we shall always love the editor of the *Advertiser* for publishing and defending it.[4]

It has been many, many months since a letter of ours has appeared in these columns; and so, we dare not risk incurring the editor's "blue pencil" by exhausting his patience further with this trivia. However, we might be pardoned for explaining here that subsequent to our last effusion we have visited the snow-bound shores of Alaska and basked (sweltered?) in the tropical sun of Panama; we have revisited the Hollywood movie colony in balmy California, and at present we are one of the "sardines" that inhabit these snow-swept man-made canyons of New York City: ensconced securely, if perhaps not too comfortably and vegetating, as it were, quite contentedly for the time being with the poets, artists, sculptors and others of the intelligentsia that comprise the Bohemia that is known as Greenwich Village.

As an interesting sidelight on prohibition enforcement in the North and East, it may not be inappropriate to note that within a radius of five or six blocks from our apartment, go whatever direction one will, there are dozens of little basement-restaurants—known locally as wine-cellars—where colorful crowds of learned and brilliant people gather every evening to wine and dine and indulge in sophisticated discourse. There is a sort of freemasonry, a

---

3. On December 23, 1915, the *Guntersville Democrat* published the following: "We submit herewith, for charitable criticism, Willie Nabors's first encounter with the Muses. We publish it to encourage Willie who is only 15 years old, to other efforts, but warn him that Pegasus is a dangerous steed and he will find Parnassus a giddy height." The poem "War Times" read as follows: "It was those brave old soldiers who fought to save our land, with dark, cold nights and snowy days, and death on ev'ry hand! Those rough blue coated Yankees, who took the children's home, and burn'd their shelter o'er them, and left them wide to roam. The widows and the orphans, all pray'd for war to cease, and God in Heaven heard them, and bless'd our land with peace!" "Willie's Effort," *Guntersville Democrat*, December 23, 1915.

4. Nabors mixed up the *Guntersville Advertiser* and the *Guntersville Democrat*. It was the latter that actually published his poem "War Times." In 1915, the editors of the *Guntersville Advertiser* were T. Burke and H.H. Williams while Caius G. Fennell edited the *Guntersville Democrat*.

spirit of comradery prevailing in these intellectual circles. Everyone seems to gravitate to his own intellectual level; and all newcomers, especially if they be witty and brilliant and apt at repartee, are accepted without question. But one must know something of literature, must have traveled some and be familiar with the Fine Arts in order to break into these little social circles or cliques. In these places the poor starving poet rubs elbows with the statesmen; over there a bejeweled dowager entertains an exaggerating globe-trotter; over here a young society "deb" is chatting in a young scholar in a threadbare suit and mean, soleless shoes. These little places are very reasonable in price which accounts for their great popularity with intellectuals. One may have a spaghetti dinner and a bottle of wine for the modest sum of one dollar. Or, if you only go in to quaff the merry juice of the grape and talk, as most of them seem to do, then you can have your glass of wine for fifteen cents! And strangely enough, should you perchance imbibe too freely and become confused in your sense of direction, then the obliging young cop on the corner will very politely and very correctly instruct you in the "show me the way to go home."

The Face Upon the Snow
March 11, 1931

As I sit here at my writing table looking out upon a little court that is merengued with snow, my capricious fancy seems to conjure up a host of fantastic images—extraordinary little phantoms, as transient and evanescent as the frozen crystals upon which they dance, who somehow seem to glide imperceptibly about in the drab shadows which twilight spreads across the mass of whiteness beneath my window. And as I gaze thus vacantly out upon this quiet, cold scene, I find myself unconsciously tracing the likeness of a sad, young face upon the pallid canvas below me.

One of my neighbors in the building here, a talented young sculptor who occupies the apartment adjoining my own, invited me over last evening to tea, and incidentally to appraise me of a piece of work upon which he is now engaged. The subject that prompted his present undertaking is certainly an inspiring one; but one which, owing to the sublimity of its very nature, belongs properly to the medium of poetry rather than sculpture. The subject in question is the sad young face which I keep seeing before me in the snow.

There is an average of one suicide a day in this great city of millions of struggling human beings; this city of hopes and fears, of ambitions and disappointments, of abject poverty and incalculable wealth, of flattering successes and hopeless failures. One of these recent suicides—her of whom I write in this rather morbid mood—was a beautiful young woman in her early twenties. Her body was recovered from the icy depths of the East River by a young patrolman who heard her scream and saw her leap into the river from a deserted pier. All efforts at resuscitation resulted in failure; and the young lady, whoever she was, succeeded in the awful design that spurred her to seek out that dark and lonely point along New York's terrible waterfront in the dead hours of midnight.

The young woman was very careful to have nothing in her purse by which she might be identified; nor was there any card or scrap of paper or any description found upon her person. But her beauty was so striking, her features so remarkably accentuated, that the police concluded that they would have little difficulty in establishing her identity once the newspapers published the story. However, the story was printed and reprinted, and featured in most every one of the twenty-some daily papers published in New York; but no one ever came forward to identify her or to claim the body.

The young woman was obviously a person of some culture and refinement; for the delicacy and correctness of taste, as revealed by the harmonious color-scheme of the brown ensemble in which she was so exquisitely and charmingly got up, are not so easily effected by just every shop girl one meets in the space of a day. Everything about her, from the arrangement of her luxurious tresses to the design of her little shoes, implied taste and refinement.

Before consigning the unclaimed body to an unmarked grave in potters' field, a death-mask or cast of the dead woman's face was made of plaster-of-Paris. And this cast is one of the most interesting studies of a human face that I have ever seen. The sorrows, the dismal failures, the tragic defeats of ten generations of womanhood are recorded here—stamped ineradicably upon every beautiful lineament of this young face. How many disappointments, how much discouragement, how much suffering are written in the little furrows that mar the beauty of the forehead that lies this snowy evening in that gloomy repository where sleep the city's poor.

Who and what was she? Perhaps this question will never be answered. She might have been my sister—or yours. Certainly, it is that she was somebody's daughter. But the troubled little soul shall be vexed no more: she finds surcease tonight in the embrace of that great mother who will also enfold you and me when we too have left the land of the living.

Whom Shall We Elect?
March 2, 1932

Much water has flowed under the bridge since your humble correspondent took it upon himself to pester our good editor with these little nothings. In fact, it has been "nigh onto" a year now since you saw a piece in the dear old *Advertiser* with my illustrious name signed to it.

We hear the question on every hand-or-lip-today, "who is going to be our next President?"

Perhaps you do not greatly care. Well, there may be something to say on that attitude; but then if we all felt that way, I fear our government would go—or finish going?—to pot. After all, though we may not feel like saying with the impassioned Decatur "My Country, right or wrong," yet it is our country—yours and mine—and we should be pretty proud and jealous of our heritage; and strive to keep it the great thing that he whose birthday we celebrate on the 22nd envisioned it—the land of the free and the home of the brave, a government by the people for the people and of the people. A real, honest-to-goodness (not-oh, heavens no! the kind we have today) Democracy, wherein everyone has equal rights to share in its good fruits as well as perils and misfortunes. But oh, where is this Democracy? Whither has it flown? What have we in its stead? God pity us!

But then I did not mean to give you a lecture on advanced political economy; and so, let's return to our presidential guessing business.

Not having been in the South in several years now, I do not pretend to know whom popular sentiment favors for the highest executive office within our bestowal. But here in New York there are about as many opinions as there are possible candidates. Perhaps Governor Franklin D. Roosevelt, of New York, has a slight edge on the Democratic field just now, although Al Smith's straightforward, outspoken stand against prohibition seems to be bringing him new prestige and strength among the millions of sincere voters [who] have a just grievance against prohibition; as it breeds gangster rule, and all the other hellish and un-American things which we of the South have been fortunate in escaping.

Right here in New York City (I blush to say it!) conditions are utterly unbelievable, and all because of prohibition and the consequent train of crimes it has engendered. In the Greenwich Village section of New York City—a section long famous for its artists, poets, sculptors, writers and intellectuals in general—in this section today a lady is not safe to walk the streets unescorted. Bands of foreign-born hoodlums and young thugs, who detest quite openly everything American, prowl the streets at night, inflicting injuries and insults on whomsoever they please. They will insult your lady friend in a most shockingly base and vulgar manner, and beat you into insensibility or actually murder you if you stop to remonstrate! I do not exaggerate in the least. I have traveled pretty well over the earth in the role of a seaman, visiting all the well-known hell-holes of which you have heard—Barbary Coast in San Francisco, the French section of old New Orleans, the tough sections of Montreal and Chicago, of Los Angeles, Seattle, Houston, Vancouver, British Columbia, or down in the coastal cities of the tropics—yet never have I seen anything, ever in my days as an oil worker in the wild boom towns of the great Southwest, to compare with the total depravity which one encounters right here in New York City today! But I did not mean to write a story on New York's wickedness. (Perhaps I will deal at length with it in a later letter.)

Where were we? Oh, yes! We were probably discussing our presidential probabilities. So, Prohibition being an urgent and burning issue in the North and East, Al Smith may just possibly keep Franklin Roosevelt from getting the nomination in Chicago in June. In which case, both Roosevelt and himself (Smith) being eliminated, most anyone is liable to be nominated to head the Democratic ticket—Garner of Texas, the present speaker of the House, and "Alfalfa Bill" Murray, the fighting governor of Oklahoma, are mentioned as possibilities here. Newton D. Baker, of Ohio, and Governor Ritchie, of Maryland, are also mentioned as "dark horses," should the convention find itself in deadlock over Roosevelt and Smith.[5] However, much may happen between now and June. For one thing, we seem to be facing another big war in the Far East. I shouldn't be surprised were the U.S. and England involved in the mess before it is over. In which event the whole world would undergo a complete political and economic change as the inevitable outcome. Communism, of which one hears so much in New York, may possibly spread over the entire earth if we go into

5. John N. Garner (1868–1967) served as U.S. Vice President from 1933–1941. See, O.C. Fisher, *Cactus Jack: A Biography of John Nance Garner* (Texian Press, 1978). Democrat William H. Murray (1869–1956) represented Oklahoma in the U.S. House of Representatives from 1913–1917 and as governor from 1931–1935. See, "Murray, William Henry David," Oklahoma Historical Society, https://www.okhistory.org/publications/enc/entry.php?entry=MU014 (Accessed April 7, 2020). Newton D. Baker (1871–1937) served as Secretary of War from 1916–1921. See, Douglas B. Craig, *Progressives at War: William G. McAdoo and Newton D. Baker, 1863–1941* (Baltimore: Johns Hopkins University Press, 2013). On Ritchie, see Chapter 2, Footnote 31.

another great war. Our rulers should ponder this seriously ere they leap; or Karl Marx's politico-economic philosophy is already spreading like wild-fire right here in the United States—as witness the recent hunger march on Washington, D.C. Woe be unto the present system of society if our great warlords rush us headlong into another great conflagration! Remember this little prophecy! The next five years may show you much of which you haven't even dreamed.

In the next letter I may describe the change that has suddenly come over New York City as a result of the great panic, of prohibition and other things.

Meeting a Great Poet
April 13, 1932

Several years ago, at a goldmining camp in Skull Valley, Arizona, I heard a picturesque old wanderer recite for the first time the great poem, "The Man with the Hoe," by Edwin Markham.[6] I was only an adventurous youth then, in the impressionistic or formative period of life and I was so influenced by the poem, and by the dramatic way in which it was delivered, that I resolved to read all the poetry of Edwin Markham as soon as I should find a place where one could procure his books. And so, accordingly, a few months later I found myself in San Francisco, waiting for a ship to Alaska, and in the meanwhile spending all my spare time in the public library, reading, as I had vowed I would, all I could find of the great poet's poems.

The years passed by, one by one, and I rolled on, like the proverbial stone, and though I may not have "gathered any moss," yet I feel that I am today indebted to some of that "rolling" for a goodly portion of whatever polish I may have acquired in the intervening years.

I have read many, many poets and sojourned in many strange and out-of-the-way places since the night I heard that wonderful poem recited to half hundred rough and rugged miners amid the wild, desolate wastes of western Arizona. But it was only on Tuesday night of this week that I met Edwin Markham in person for the first time. I was returning to my humble lodgings about three o'clock in the morning, and as I turned a corner in the street, I ran pell-mell, into an artist, a fine old friend of mine, whom I had not seen in quite some time—and himself a man of some renown.

The street at this point was rather dimly lighted; but I observed that my artist friend was accompanied by a very unusual and striking personality, a

6. On Markham, see Chapter 1, Footnote 20.

stranger to me. I was very simply introduced as "a young Southern poet," and in the exchange of salutations I didn't quite get Markham's name; so, I asked if he'd kindly spell it for me, as the mispronunciation of proper names is often the cause of embarrassment. The great man very obligingly complied by spelling his name for me, at which juncture the artist mentioned "The Man with the Hoe."

Of course, I was surprised, and quite overjoyed at meeting in so unexpected a manner him whom I had so long admired. So, I suggested, quite naturally, that we three repair to some little coffee house for a chat and breakfast. The great bard didn't happen to be familiar with the immediate neighborhood where we were; but he intimated in no uncertain terms that he'd rather go someplace where we could get a glass of good wine. The artist cut in by reminding us that the hour was then long past three in the morning, and that all the little wine-cellars had to close up by order of law at three a.m. so, despairing of the inspiriting product of the vineyard, we compromised by going for breakfast.

As we started walking away, I happened to notice coincidentally enough, that diagonally across the street and opposite to where we had met, stood the famous old house in which Washington Irving once lived. I did not mention this fact to my companions, and I don't think either of them observed it. However, we walked down a quiet side-street and into an unpretentious little coffee house, such as one will see most anywhere in New York. We were seated at a plain little wooden table under a miserable light, and while waiting on the orders, I seized the opportunity to scrutinize my bewhiskered hero in the old slouch hat.

He is now quite well along in years—perhaps eighty or thereabouts—but still very robust and active, both mentally and physically. His hair is now snow-white, and falls in an undulating mass down about his venerable shoulders, giving him a somewhat patriarchal look. But his eyes—oh! Those are the characteristic features of the poet, deep, dark and thoughtful pools, which, upon evincing interest or sympathy in the object they survey sparkle with the old divine fire, and seem to actually grow darker and deeper as he becomes more engrossed in his subject, whether it be poetry or the outrageous injustices of a sick society.

His skin is unblemished and almost baby-pink, betokening a life spent largely in the open. He is of medium height, and inclined a little to stoutness. His clothes were expensive and well-tailored, but worn with that habitual carelessness which bespeaks the poet, the artist or the literary man—a sort of studied dishevelment.

As to his credo—well, like most poets, he finds much looking in the present system of things. He is convinced that capitalism is doomed. But he is somewhat inclined towards religion, and believes in a personal God. In other words, he is a fine American of the old school—a good man, a friend to the poor, and a great poet.

Learning to Write
May 11, 1932

The vernal equinox again swings us into the notice of that awful star (the sun) which is the author, the genesis, the source, the alpha and omega of all our petty careers here upon this diminutive spheroid, and as the Bird of Time comes fluttering down from the void of eternity, she again comes bringing tender green leaves, to cheer us on in our appointed ways—inspiring and reassuring tokens of another promise fulfilled. And thus, again we thrill at the thought of swinging in the cosmic swing!

And now that that violent fluorescent outburst is off my chest, I feel somewhat as I imagine a deflated windbag must feel after hitting a snag! So, let me try to make amends by saying (or does it sound more like barking?) that, spring is here; the leaves are out. Is that better? Thank you. Water please!

Now of your industrious, studious, ambitious girls and boys who are at present concerning yourselves seriously with the subtleties, the trick, the gymnastics, the chemistry—in other words, the technique of good writing—then never, never begin an article in the high keys which I employed in starting this one! That is, never begin one in that pitch if you would have it printed. The good editor would merely shrug his weary tolerant shoulder and say," Well, it's spring, I guess, that makes them write that way. Poor things! They all go nutty in the spring." And your fine poetical outburst would presently find its flowering leaves reposing serenely in the nearby wastebasket. Take warning, O ye embryo scribes!

It was recently my unbounded delight to plague to tears an otherwise intelligent audience that had come to pay good money to hear me luxuriate at some length in a worthless lecture on poetry. I remembered my dear adjective-scarred old editor-friends, and so accordingly advised all the future poets who might be among my patient but disgusted auditors to always strive for brevity, and to never say that in five words which could be conveniently crammed into two. (And here I see you rising to say that, like many another preacher, I find it somehow inconvenient to practice what I preach!) Very, very (one of those "verys," for instance, could very, very well be dispensed with?) well. But don't you try it. I might be pardoned for paraphrasing old Walt Whitman in saying that, it has taken many, many barrels of ink and much disappointment and heartache to bring me where I am today. But (to be further egotistical) I know HOW to say that which I would express, and this makes a world of difference to the editor. If the editor perceives that you know HOW to write whatever it is you wish to convey, then he, out of deference to his craft if nothing else, will allow you a certain latitude of expression which he would not extend to the neophyte, the tyro who might ramble all over a whole page and say nothing—and say it very awfully indeed. Trial and error were the two instructors whom I am most indebted to for whatever I may know of writing. But it is my sincerest wish that you who are bent upon becoming devotees of the pen will be fortunate in going as far as you can go in school-college-university, and in your choice of the great masters of literature who you would have influence you in shaping or forming your style.

Personally, of our great American authors, I have been most influenced, perhaps, by Poe, Irving, Hawthorne and probably Stephen Crane, and of the English writers, by De Quincey, Thackeray, Dickens, Oliver Goldsmith (who most influenced Irving), and perhaps Fielding of the *Tom Jones* fame. To the French I owe much to Victor Hugo, to de Balzac, to Gautier, and, of course, to Dumas. To the Russians I'm perhaps most indebted to Dostoyevsky, Tolstoy, and Gorky. So, study the great masters if you would become expressive writers—and spare the editors much!

Old Familiar Tunes
May 10, 1933

Although the gladdening month of May now comes hounding in like a playful whitecap atop the blue-green wave of summer, I have not as yet seen a single full-blown leaf as to reassure me and to allay the fears which a severe winter has engendered in a constitution apparently too delicate to cope with the climatic rigors of this latitude.

One is still sensible of a tinge of frost in the air, but the sun is shining brightly this last day of April; and the streets and sidewalks of New York are literally packed and jammed with human beings, and those creatures who look and act like apes, or, more properly gorillas!

This winter has been the worst one in every aspect, that has ever passed over my head. I have gone from one cold right into another, and am just now getting up from a prolonged siege of the "flu."

It is so good to be out in the sunshine and able to walk around again after one has been laid up in some old dark poet's attic for weeks on end. The buds everywhere are swelling and in process of complying with the inexorable laws of the equinoxes. One's nostrils dilate in hungry welcome to the delicious perfumes of spring, and a tremor of ecstasy thrills one upon approaching the little parks where the silver willows are dressing in their tenderest green, and the young blades of grass are slashing and stabbing away at the whispering breeze like little rascally pirates.

All day long I have been humming under my breath that beautiful old "homesick" song, "Swanee River," and it reminds me of a rather humorous little sketch which Mark Twain once wrote about an old tune which he had begun to hum in the morning, and kept it up all day and night, and simply could not get rid of the thing until he had got somebody else to humming it!

Sitting by my little garret window, looking out upon the courtyard below, I sometimes fall to imagining that I'm back in the old south again—oh, how long it's been, and how lonesome one gets!—and that it is spring and I am again behind the plow, turning up the warm, friendly soil which I have not seen in all these years; and gazing at the hazy, smokey summits of the distant hills, and listening to the plaintive calls of the whippoorwill as "quittin' time" rolls round. Yes, in those moments I am back home again, a carefree happy, barefoot boy, that knows all the little secrets so dear to the hearts of the juvenile naturalists; such as, for instance, where the earliest and prettiest violets grow, and where this and that bird has its nest; where the best fish are to be caught and where the deepest swimmin' holes are. As Eugene Field so beautifully expressed it in one of his fine little poems:

"I was very learned then,
But that was long ago."[7]

And then one recalls others pleasant events and scenes. The old fashioned "breakdown" country dances, which everyone so thoroughly and heartily enjoyed, and which are not duplicated anywhere else in the world. The so-called "barn dances" which we used to attend in Hollywood a few years ago

---

7. Eugene Field (1850–1895) was an American poet who wrote mainly for children. See, Robert Conrow, *Field Days: The Life, Times, & Reputation of Eugene Field* (New York: Charles Scribner's Sons, 1974).

were very artificial and commercial—as everything that Hollywood does is apt to be—in comparison to our real old Southern "breakdowns."

Yes, spring has come again to this latitude; but it is late, very late, and not at all like the springs that I'm thinking of as I sit here dreaming of the hills and mountains far to the south—the very hills and mountains that you may be looking upon at this moment!

On Human Weaknesses
May 24, 1933

There is nothing to me quite so mortifying and upsetting as the knowledge that I may have brought pain or injury on some true and tried old friend on those lamentable occasions when one is somehow drawn into a stupid argument or a quarrel.

I can think of no pangs comparable to those that bloom in contrition.

On a recent unhappy occasion, I was so foolish as to quarrel with a dear old friend, over some silly trifle that did not amount to a row of pins. (The most serious quarrels it seems, are those that arise over inconsequential things.)

I was so thoroughly miserable about it all that I simply could not sleep a wink until I had gone over to his apartment and apologized for what I considered my utter selfishness.

I found my old friend in quite as agitated and unhappy frame of mind as myself. He had an old smoking jacket thrown over his shoulders and his sad, intelligent face looked more drawn and weary than I had ever noticed before. He had been pacing up and down in his study (he's a novelist) for more than an hour, he said.

We sat down, and had a long heart-to-heart talk, which kept us there until the ghostly face of dawn came peeping in at the windows and his handclasp was never firmer nor warmer than when he bade me goodnight at the street-door, with that understanding smile which can mean so much and which is so much more eloquent than ever the tongue can hope to be!

Walking back to my own poor lodgings, I fell to musing upon the vicissitudes of life, and upon the pathetic figures which we mortals cut here with our petty ambitions, our ridiculous vanities ("vanity, all is vanity," said the great Solomon), and our absurd egos. The gentle Shakespeare expressed it quite fully in his famous observation by Puck: "What fools these mortals be!"

I was aroused from these ungratifying meditations by hearing someone call, or rather shout my name from the entrance of a pretentious hotel which I was then passing. A deep bass voice boomed out: "Is that you, Nabors?" It was Captain Allen, the famous English globetrotter, an adventurer whom I had met and drunk with on many and diverse points of the globe in days past. (I might piously remark here, however, that I do not drink, no nor even smoke today—a regular goody-goody, you know!)

Well, old Cap'n Allen (For he's getting well on in years now) is the same becoming, good natured cosmopolite that he was a decade ago, when we first met in Alaska.

Like most Englishmen of an adventurous turn, he has a repertory of really original and remarkable stories. He once met O. Henry in Central America, while that lovable American was a fugitive from justice (he had robbed a bank in Texas during his wild-oats days, before he had begun to write the stories which have made his name world famous and immortal).

Captain Allen also knew Mark Twain, Jack London, Bret Harte, and Stephen Crane personally, and he was a friend of the brilliant Ambrose Bierce, who disappeared in the desolate mountains of Mexico, after having written his famous "Devil's Dictionary," and he has never been heard of since.

The jolly old Cap'n soldiered with Kipling out India way, and has seen service in darkest Africa. He is a profound student of human nature as well as of the affairs of the world. A natural psychologist, he is not to be taken in easily by the shams and pretensions which he encounters on every side of him wherever he may be. Still his Irish-English heart is as big as his old beer-tank, which is quite ample enough, yet despite his great weakness for drink he is nevertheless in many ways a really admirable and charming old fellow. Lively and full of deviltry, but the gentlemen always, and the very soul of civility. Yes, the genial amiable old wanderer was full to the brim of New York's "happy-days-are-here-again" beer; and he was spreading sunshine and good cheer wherever he went, and I almost regretted that my total abstention prevented me from again going up to the bar with him and renewing the pleasant times of *auld lang syne*!

Loneliness
June 14, 1933

Full many a night have I wandered alone through the interminable streets of this great city, my heart overcast with heaviness and my mind burdened with the struggles of existence and thoughts of happier days at home.

Why is it I choose to write on the subject of loneliness? I do not know. Perhaps it's because in the vernal season a young man's fancy turns to love.

The Good Book tells us that it is not good for man to be alone. And oh, how terribly true it is! That was the reason the Creator of all that we are and behold had for making a woman. Man needs woman, his complement, to nurse, to soothe and to solace, to inspire and encourage him in those hours when the battles of life seem to go against him.

But alas! I fear that it is to be my unhappy fate never to know the magic and healing touch, the soft and tender caresses of a loving woman. And this thought leaves in its train a sadness that is most crushing to the spirit.

Why should I not have the company and companionship of charming and adorable women, of the gentle and beautiful creatures whom I have always worshipped from a distance? Why am I doomed to be always and eternally alone, as though I were but a detached spectator of the intensely vital drama of life, a sort of weedy reed upon which the winds of chance (or my chance) may blow their sad and melancholic notes?

Why? Why? I ask myself, but the echo does not return to answer me.

At the theatres (when I go—which is seldom of late) I am always alone; at the beaches—alone. I dine alone, live alone. If you meet me in the streets you will nearly always find me alone. I make my living, such as it is, by my pen; and consequently, I always work alone. A more solitary person it would be difficult to meet. Yet I am not averse to meeting people; and I like to hear people talk, to listen to their opinions. But very few I care to know personally or to meet socially. And this is not because I am "high-hat" or snobbish. The worst types of fools, to me, are the snobs and snooty highbrows. I think President Roosevelt had that type of creature in mind the other day when he spoke to the graduating cadets at the U.S. Naval Academy, and advised them, the future admirals of the navy, never to become clannish and "stuck-up," but to always keep in touch with the common people of the country. Good advice, and from a great president. Too bad that more of our rulers, governors, mayors, etc.—were not endowed with some of the President's liberality and good old common (a misnomer!) sense. But this is neither the place nor the time to pen the eulogy which his great acts demand, and besides, actions such as his are their own best eulogies—they're mightier than the pen.

But I started out to write on loneliness; and maybe, if I can't adhere to my theme, I can at least have the goodness to spare you any further digressions by here taking my timely leave of you. And so, adieu!

———•·•———

Luxury
July 5, 1933

To the oriental department of the great public library here in New York I repaired recently in quest of some enlightening data concerning Lafcadio Hearn, the great American writer who migrated to Japan and became, to all intents and purposes, an oriental.[8] And while engaged in this pleasant research I had the pleasure (for it is ever a pleasure to me to meet a person of gentle nature and endowments) and good fortune to make the acquaintance of a cultured and aristocratic Japanese gentleman, who happened to be in the diplomatic service of his country.

He had been educated in England (Oxford), and of course spoke English as well as or better than myself. Naturally our conversation turned to the object of my quest; and I discovered, to my great delight, that he himself was not only an admirer of Hearn, but a student and collector of Hearn items; that he had in his possession several books, documents, articles, etc., long since out of print, as well as one or two original manuscripts in longhand, for which he had paid a considerable sum at auctions.

It happened that he had been favorably impressed by an article of mine on Edwin Markham the poet, whom he had met socially and greatly admired; and so, he invited me up (uptown, that is) to spend the weekend with him.[9]

I found that he possessed a fine and really quite comprehensive library for a town apartment. But what I most marveled at and what struck me most of all was the graceful and delicate touches of refinement revealed in the arrangement

---

8. Author Lafcadio Hearn (1850–1904) was known for writing books on Japanese culture, myths, and folklore. While born in Greece, he was raised in Ireland and as a teen, moved to the U.S. See, Paul Murray, *A Fantastic Journey: The Life and Literature of Lafcadio Hearn* (Ann Arbor: University of Michigan Press, 1997).

9. On Markham, see Chapter 1, Footnote 20.

of his various establishments. The jewels and art objects imbued with centuries of traditional oriental culture which one discovered in the most unexpected and pleasing little nooks, corners and crannies; the little altar (for most Japanese are devoutly religious in their way), the various devotional pieces, the tapestries, the bronze, silver and gold Buddhas, and all kinds of little metal blossoms, and especially the sacred lotus flowers, all of solid gold or silver, and worth a king's ransom. The rare and exquisite antique plate, the expensive ceramics, lacquer objects and whatnot.

The gold, jade and ivory trinkets, all so charmingly arranged; the strings of old and precious beads, delicately wrought by great artists, the rare old prints, the exquisite and priceless vases, incrusted with gems and each with its historical or romantic story. The delicate etchings, the old paintings, the masterful carvings; the hand-made and beautifully bound old volumes of lore, poetry, etc., all went to make the home ideal for those who appreciate and can afford this form of luxury.

Personally, however, these trinkets, toys, baubles, etc., smack too much of the dilettante and the connoisseur for me. To one brought up to humbler surroundings they're too rich for my blood and somehow seem pagan and corrupting. I thought of the dear old prophet who lamented that his friend had fallen to worshipping idols and strange gods. I fear my conscience would not permit me to luxuriate amid such priceless and elegant trappings, while my less fortunate brothers and sisters were tramping the inhospitable streets with hungry mouths and bitter faces. But let's back to our subject.

The hospitality of my aristocratic friend was genuine and complete, if perhaps a bit sumptuous for my taste. I had hardly stirred from the soft, silken embrace of my bed in the morning when there came a light tapping at my door. I bade the tapper enter, and it turned out to be the valet de chambre, as the French say, with the morning paper and a glass of orange juice on a little silver tray. His master had inquired concerning my health, and had commissioned him, also an oriental, to convey to me the greetings of the day. Telling me that breakfast would be served in the library, and with much gracious bowing and smiling he backed out of the room.

My clothes were brought in, all freshly cleaned and pressed; my shoes were polished and set by the bed, and my warm perfumed bath was drawn and waiting!

If all these graceful gestures of civility and hospitality had not amused me, I fear they might have flattered me into conceit, or maybe inspired envy or avarice by way of emulation. But I came from the soil, where the tastes are simple and few, and go back to the soil one day I shall go; and all the luxuries of the world would not help me!

———•·•———

Prison Prayers
July 19, 1933

My heart was touched by the simple little petition for prayer which appeared in the *Advertiser* a few days ago, signed by four inmates of the county jail there on behalf of their fellow prisoner who was going away to commence his long toil.

I myself was a tenant for a night in those uninviting cells whence that little petition emanated, and I can truthfully say it was the most unpleasant and wretched experience of a rather colorful life.

I have long since forgotten who the jailer was at that time (for this was years and years ago); but I distinctly remember—ah, how could I ever forget it!—that he was a genial, kindly-disposed soul who was the father of two very charming young daughters and the burning of shame and humiliation which suffered my boyish face (I was in the eighth grade at school, and had been caught at a moonshine still) when I first discovered those girls looking at me through the bars in their sweet, sisterly little ways—how could I ever forget it! I could read the pity on their pretty faces as the tears in my eyes blurred their fair images from my vision, and my darling little mother—I can still see the wearied and anxious look on her sweet face as she came down from the hills bright and early in her best rustic dress, and little bonnet whose shadows but ill-concealed the broken heart beneath the cheering smile.

But for the consolation of those who languish in prisons, whithersoever they be; who are deprived, justly or unjustly, of their freedom, one might pardonably suggest the beautiful thought in the lines of Richard Lovelace's famous poem composed in prison: "Stone walls do not a prison make, nor iron bars a cage."

Some of the greatest personalities the world has ever produced have been cast into prisons and bound in chains. God Himself, we are told, once interceded on behalf of two of our fellow prisoners—Paul and Silas. And John Bunyan, the great author of "Pilgrim's Progress," was bound in a filthy dungeon for many, many long and weary years. Yet he did not abandon hope. He too prayed and petitioned for prayers. And his great work lives and is still being read today, long after his persecutors have been forgotten and consigned to oblivion.

The immortal Cervantes, creator of the loveable "Don Quixote," and the greatest writer the Spanish nation has ever produced, was many years in chains and forced to labor with one hand after having suffered the loss of the other one!

The purest, the sweetest and most divine souls this planet has seen have been sent to the cross, to the stake and to the wrack; have starved and rotted in dungeons and gibbets.

William Shakespeare, the greatest and most sublime figure in the world's literature, ran away from his hometown in order to escape prison! And the debtor's prison has claimed some of the most inspired geniuses of all time.

The world's most profound and wise philosopher—Socrates—was sentenced to death for some trifling offense; forced to drink a cup of poison. And the imagination could hardly conceive a more revolting and gruesome sight than that presented by the great French poet of the fifteenth century, when left dangling from the gibbet like some mocking specter while the fowls of the air pecked his eyes and consumed his flesh!

The record of the human role when viewed from the historical perspective, is indeed a sad, sorry thing to contemplate. As a significant commentary upon the mental and moral defects and aberrations seemingly inherent in our species, it might be interesting to note that not less than one-twentieth of the population of the earth have been residents of prisons. Both sage and saint, prince and pauper have known the gloomy confines of the bastille. And to those black abodes have gone great statesmen, and the generals who supported their opinions with arms.

Did not Oscar Wilde write his great "De Profundis" while starving in a filthy English prison? And in his incomparably beautiful "Ballad of Reading Jail" we find that he too had stood many a night contemplating the splendors of the firmaments from his little barred windows—dreaming and looking out upon.

"That little patch of blue
Men call the sky."

The Little Flower Girl
August 2, 1933

She stands at a corner of a downtown street, selling her little flowers to whosoever will buy them. Her eyes are big and soft and brown, and always look as if they were about to say, "Well, my goodness gracious!"

She is nine, and her name is Julia. She has been selling flowers for more than a year now, in order to support herself and a poor old aunt who is nearly blind from cataracts.

I met her one rainy evening months and months ago, as I was on my way down from the library. I was attracted by her alert and expressive eyes and the keen, searching glance they gave one.

When she told me her name, I called her Juliet, and she wanted to know what Juliet meant. I told her it meant "sweetheart," and she got a great kick out of that. So since then we have been very good friends. I always buy a flower (but I never take one) from her before I leave. I told her that the dime was merely for the privilege of smelling the flowers; and now she always holds them out to me when I walk up.

She is very dainty and cleanly about her person (she washes her dress and things herself, she says). When we first met her little shoes were out at the toes, and her dress was all faded and worn from much wear and washing. There are three or four multi-millionaires living in the neighborhood (where she sells her flowers) but not one of them has even so much as offered to buy her a pair of stockings! And she says the "swells" seldom ever buy a flower from her.

An old man passed along one evening and handed her an ugly metal ring, which looked like lead. When I came by later, she held it out for my approval; and when I told her it was cheap and ugly, she took it off and threw it into the gutter. And so, I somehow felt that I was responsible for Juliet's not having a pretty ring for her finger. What was one to do? I had been intending to get a new hat that very day, as I had been going about in a shabby, old fet, while all New York was blossoming out in straws. But here was Juliet without a ring; and besides, a ring is more becoming on a girl's finger than a straw hat is on a man's head. The question was settled. Juliet got the ring—and I don't like straw hats anyway!

Little Juliet is the only girlfriend I have in New York and the evenings I don't see her seem somehow strangely empty and dull. Once I didn't have even a dime for her flowers; and I walked uptown through another street rather than have her think I was becoming stingy with my dimes! And I know the very sight of her would have cheered me up wonderfully that evening, as I was just getting up from a long illness and felt lonely and in need of someone to talk with.

The other Sunday Juliet and her aunt were my guests at the beach. What an ill-assorted trip we were! Little Juliet, so pretty and winsome and gay; poor old feeble-witted auntie, who just sits and fumbles with her handkerchief, and says "yes" or "no," or nothing; and myself, perhaps a bit too thoughtful and sad-faced for a young man.

We made auntie comfortable on the sands of the beach under a big parasol, with food and drinks, while Juliet and I went on the merry-go-round, the airplanes, the speedboats, the Ferris wheel, the scenic railway, and whatnot. Juliet was thoroughly happy and tired when night came and both she and auntie fell asleep in the underground train on the way back to the city. One was tired and happy, and the other was only tired—very tired!

In Retrospect
August 16, 1933

It was not without pleasure that I noted the happy bit of news in the *Advertiser* the other day concerning the laudable accomplishment of Miss Pearl Hipp (of Tyronza, Ark.) in the field of sculpture.[10]

I had the pleasure of meeting Miss Hipp a few years since at the home of an uncle of mine in Arkansas, where we were both guests. We attended a big camp-meeting together, and spent many enjoyable hours in "pleasant converse." And all that I can say is if she is as talented as she is beautiful, then the world's sculptors had better watch out!

While adverting to this particularly romantic and happy period of my life, I might add that at the time of my visit in Arkansas I became infatuated with the little brown-eyed daughter of a wealthy planter there. And our pretty little romance remained in bud (though it never blossomed into the "master passion of life" called love) until I returned to Texas, and later wandered off down into Mexico, where I really did fall in love with a spirited little thoroughbred of a senorita, who could flash a smile that would just knock a man's legs right out from under him. And I realized then how very appropriate is the word "fell" in connection with love!

Her father was an old Castilian general who had one of those jaw-dislocating names and an inordinate hatred for the "Americanos" that was positively refreshing in its ferocity. But his pepperish little filly out-generaled the fire-eating old warrior so often and so beautifully that it made him look like Don Quixote fighting the windmills.

---

10. Pearl Hipp (1904–1975), daughter of James and Margaret Hipp, grew up in the Cranford and Grassy communities near Guntersville, Alabama. By 1920, she and her parents had moved to Tyronza, Arkansas. In 1938, she married Max E. Hyatt. U.S., Find a Grave, 1600s-Current; Alabama, County Marriages, 1805–1967; and 1910, 1920, 1930, 1940 U.S. Federal Census.

Many times, I risked my fool head in order to meet her on an evening within the protecting shadows of a big banana palm, which was our favorite rendezvous. And at our last meeting we were discovered by a malicious old woman, a servant who had been a part of the general's household for more years than Carmelita and I had been on earth. It seemed that avaricious old wretch had followed Carmelita in the moonlight from her room to our little tryst, for the sole purpose of collecting blackmail; for her young mistress immediately tore a bracelet from her pretty arm and flung it in the old woman's face, with the proper opinions of her in Spanish which I was glad for once that I couldn't understand!

This Carmelita was an irrepressible little bundle of the most amazing and delightful contradictions and inconsistencies I've ever encountered. She could always be relied upon to do the exact opposite of what one expected of her. Her adventurous little heart was as inconstant and impermanent in its affections as a message written on water. And having known her, one could the more fully appreciate Shakespeare's characterization of her sex: "Frailty, thy name is woman."

If you are familiar with Prosper Mérimée's immortal "Carmen," then you can appreciate something of the nature and disposition of my flaming little inamorata; for the protagonist in Mérimée's fascinating masterpiece is almost an exact prototype of the bewitching little flirt that took possession of my heart. She seemed to interpret everything in life as a sort of challenge to her ineffably daring spirit. Some remote egotistical tendency, perhaps inherited from her old warrior father (for "the life of the flesh," saith the old prophet, "is in the blood"), impelled her to conquer, to subdue and surmount all that she encountered here. And the impression she made on my whole organism, body and soul, was so profound that to this day when I hear her name my heart seems to leap up into my throat!

It not infrequently results in tragedy when a man of strong passions falls in love with a woman of this type. One remembers the agony that was De Quincy's when that great genius fell in love with a woman of the streets, and spent a fortune and a great part of his life trying to find her again after he had become famous as a writer. And one recalls off-hand many great Frenchmen who were victims of the same misfortune, and what an innumerable procession of poets have found joy, and fame, in beguiling their muse to rhapsodize the demi monde.

Hoboes and Royalty
December 6, 1933

The other evening I passed in front of the Fifth Avenue Play House, attracted by an advertisement on the boards to the effect that Dan O'Brien, the hobo (there is a decided distinction between a hobo and a tramp!) philosopher king of the hoboes, would appear in person, prologuing the "Beggars Opera."[11]

Seeing the name of the famous and jolly old Irishman on the program recalled to me the night of our first meeting, in a dingy little coffee house on Rue Saint Antoine in Montreal, Canada, a few years since; and of our "bumping into each other" again later in the quaint old French section of New Orleans. And as I stood thus immersed in retrospection, who should come out of the theater but old Dan himself, his white, silken hair falling down about his shoulders a la Walt Whitman. He wears a big, black slouch hat and overalls—always the overalls! With his hat off he looks something like the picture of old Patrick Henry we used to see in our "history books."

With this picturesque wit and poet-philosopher was a fashionably dressed woman; whose pleasant face, graceful carriage and charming manners suggested the aristocrat. Old Dan introduced us in his brief, easy-going way, but I didn't get the woman's name. He hailed a taxi, assisted the lady in, and then literally pushed me in behind her, despite my protestations of a previous engagement. He barked something at the driver, and we were whirled downtown through the maze of evening traffic to a little Italian restaurant somewhere in Greenwich Village.

Wine was set before us, and we quickly fell in with the convivial atmosphere of the place. The soft lights, and soften music of the orchestra; the glitter and sparkle of the urbane and well-dressed guests; the pleasant pastoral subjects of the murals on the stuccos, all conduced to the relaxed and expansive sort of cheerfulness which one so enjoys on such occasions.

I soon discovered that the aristocratic-looking woman in black was a most charming and interesting person, one who seemed to know everybody and everything worthwhile. I kept wondering just who she could be, this highly intellectual person who talked so easily, so charmingly, and with absolutely no affectation or pose whatever. For some vague, unknown reason I fancied that

---

11. On O'Brien, see Chapter 1, Footnote 1.

she was Fannie Hurst, the novelist of whose conversational powers I had heard so much over the dinner tables of Greenwich Village.

"Haven't you two met before?" queried old Dan, who must have observed the I-don't-seem-to-recall-who expression on my face.

We confessed that we hadn't.

"Why, this is Countess Andreyev, widow of the great Russian writer," announced Dan in a matter-of-face way, bowing toward the countess.[12]

I gasped.

"Not—you don't mean the great Leonid N. Andreyev—he of 'The Seven That Were Hanged,' do you?"

"That's right," assured the old poet-philosopher, with the composure and placidity of a sphinx.

"Why—er—this is a most pleasant and unexpected honor, Madame Andreyev," I spluttered, blushed and bowed.

And indeed, it was. She told us—me, mostly—as she and Dan had known each other for a long time—many marvelous little stories and anecdotes of the great dramatist's life and career in the old Russia of the last century.

Madame Andreyev now owns a "beauty salon" here in New York, and says she is making out rather nicely. Her son, now grown to manhood, is working in a big apartment house uptown. He is also following in the footsteps of his distinguished father by aspiring to be a writer. Luck to him!

A Cold World
January 3, 1934

The Christmas tree in Madison Square at Twenty-third Street and Broadway is a beautiful, dazzling thing to look upon with its hundreds of vari-colored lights sparkling through the mantle of snow which drapes its graceful boughs like some frosted veil from fairyland. Where is the artist with line so soft and sensitive, with colors so radiant and luminous as to express something of the magic of the lovely scene?

But there are other scenes less beautiful to look upon as the city lies blanketed in the heaviest snowfall in years, almost a foot!

The coming of the big snows in the cities of the North is contemplated by the very poor with something akin to horror. To them it means untold

---

12. On Countess Andreyev, see Chapter 1, Footnote 22.

sufferings, and hardships the like of which people who live in milder climates can have no conception.

As I was passing through a poor tenement district this evening, I saw a frail, thinly-clad woman and a little child of six or so huddled together to keep warm in a darkened doorway. The weather was twenty degrees below freezing, and the wind was biting cold. Out upon the sidewalk in the front of where they stood shivering lay their meager earthly belongings—some ancient furniture and an odd assortment of household effects. The things were thrown together in a heterogeneous heap, as though the evicting officers who had thus so cruelly dispossessed them were angry at them for being poor.

One sees so many of these wretched scenes nowadays that one can't very well stop to commiserate with all the unhappy poor souls who one sees on the sidewalks guarding their miserable "belongings" until they are taken away to the city's storage houses, where they very likely will never see them again.

There was something fine about the woman's face; the brave, sweet way in which she bore her calamity indicated a nobility of soul and a spirit made for better things.

I approached them in the doorway in a hesitant, confused sort of manner; I did not know exactly what to say or how best to say it, as I did not want to embarrass the poor lady more than I could help.

I asked her if there was anything that I could do for them.

"You're awfully kind," she smiled.

"My husband has gone to see if he can find a place that we can move into. We're all sick, and he especially hasn't been able to do anything for weeks. We get behind with our rent and . . ."

"I understand your unhappy situation," I broke in, "for I know well what it is to be out of a position in a big city."

"My little daughter here and I," she continued, in order to divert the conversation to a less painful subject, "have been amusing ourselves by counting the people who go into that liquor store over there." She pointed, indicating one of the new liquor stores where intoxicating beverages are "sold in bottles to take out." There were several well-dressed but extremely vulgar-looking men staggering around on the sidewalk, drinking from quart bottles of bonded whisky. There was something of the animal—perhaps the swine—about them. Not one of them paid the least attention to the terrible social tragedy which was being enacted across the street from them.

I went over to a nearby restaurant to get some coffee and sandwiches for my new friends. And when I returned the husband was there with a little push-cart, hired with his last dollar, ready to move their scant belongings into an old vacant store, which a man said they could have for a week or so.

The husband was an elderly man who looked and spoke like a scholar or perhaps a professional man. There was a warm, sympathetic expression about his kindly features that suggested the face of Lincoln. His voice was soft and gentle; and he couldn't keep his sad, terror-haunted eyes off his brave little wife. He turned her coat-collar up about her neck, and kept apologizing for having been gone so long. She assured him that he hadn't been gone long, and that he must be "tired out and all frozen."

The poor man had a hacking cough and was very thin and emaciated. His old coat was threadbare and worn through at the elbows.

I pitched in and gave them a hand in moving, and did what little I could towards making them happy and comfortable in their new abode.

The poor scholar is the only surviving son of a great evangelist whose sermons were widely read and discussed in this country a couple of generations ago—the famous Dr. Talmage![13]

Our British Superiors
January 24, 1934

Stephen Foster, the gifted young man who wrote the most popular and beloved of our old Southern melodies and folks songs, such as "Old Black Joe," "My Old Kentucky Home," "Swanee River," "Old Folks at Home" and "Oh, Susannah," was seldom if ever in the South.

He came from Pittsburgh, Pa., and his sad passing—friendless and alone in Bellevue, the famous city hospital in New York—is only too typical of the awful fate that seems to stalk the unhappy creatures of genius in the world.

I often wonder why it is that English men of letters nearly always assume a superior attitude when they come to America, where so many of them have waxed rich, to lecture to the "vulgar conceited Yanks," as one of them called us.

---

13. Dr. Talmage is in reference to Thomas De Witt Talmage (1832–1902), a popular preacher in both the Reformed Church in America and the Presbyterian Church. During the course of two of his three marriages, he fathered seven children, only two of which were sons, Thomas and Frank. Thomas died of pneumonia in 1881 while Frank died in 1912. Either the scholar misrepresented himself as a son of Dr. Talmage, Nabors misunderstood, or Nabors lied. See, Ferenc M. Szasz, "T. DeWitt Talmage: Spiritual Tycoon of the Gilded Age," *Journal of Presbyterian History* 59, no. 1 (Spring 1981): 18–32; T. De Witt Talmage, *T. De Witt Talmage: As I Knew Him* (New York: E.P. Dutton and Co., 1912); and Find a Grave.

I sat last year in a distinguished audience of learned men and women here in New York and heard the Quixotic G.B. Shaw, London's intellectual cutup, make a bit of an ass of himself with his superior witticisms at the expense of us unregenerate homo Americanos, not omitting a slighting reference to our beloved President.

When one reflects that the unappreciative vulgar Americans (we can never appreciate anything really fine, to hear the superior foreigners tell it) have poured literally millions of dollars into the coffers of Mr. Shaw and his yelping colleague, Mr. Kipling, one should not, perhaps, be too harsh with them for thinking us an aggregation of downright fools!

Rudyard Kipling has now become a conservative mossback who hobnobs with the royalty whom he made famous (or infamous) only a few short years ago by criticizing them so ruthlessly in his barracks ballads. He, too, came to the good old gullible U.S.A., went out west flunkeying [*sic*] around and lifted a few fertile ideas from a really brilliant and gifted American writer—Bret Harte— which he later had the audacity to dress up in tales as his own!

This same Kipling, whom we made rich and famous by our vulgar patronage, went back to dear old England and wrote the inevitable book of ridicule of us, which always follows one of their flying visits to our shores.

They all do it!

Even the great Dickens himself couldn't refrain from it. Indeed, he might, with Thackeray, be said to have begun it. And I regret to say that Oscar Wilde, one of the most charming Europeans to ever set foot on our soil, was also tainted with the virus superiorities. He had hardly got back to England before the printing presses were working overtime, flooding the world with labels giving our price, cost, origin and quality, if any!

Back in the days when America was producing real American writers, and great ones, too, the proverbial worm was not slow to turn. One recalls Poe's charming little critique attacking, in his brilliant, inimitable way, the asinities and imbecilities of the imposing English. And there was Lowell's incomparable five essays in which he dealt so masterfully and so wittily with "a certain condescension in foreigners."[14]

Washington Irving, Hawthorne, Emerson, Holmes, Whitman, Mark Twain and, in fact, most all our truly great Americans have from time to time taken up the cudgels for Americans in the form of inspired pens that could deliver

---

14. James Russell Lowell (1819–1891) was an American poet and critic. See, Martin B. Duberman, *James Russell Lowell: Poet, Critic, Editor, Teacher, Diplomat* (Boston: Houghton Mifflin, Co., 1966).

opinions in that vital, sparkling, timeless medium which men have agreed to consider immortal.[15]

I am cognizant of the fact that we Southerners have inherited a perhaps just grievance against the English or their base betrayal of us during the Civil War. But then they were only running true to form in that—that is, seeking the highest market for their goods. And consequently, that fact has nothing whatever to do with the writer's present tirade against the base ingratitude of their men of letters, whose noble altruism impels them to seek the enlightenment of their distant boorish cousins!

Whither Civilization?
March 7, 1934

Would you believe it, according to the U.S. Flag Association, an old and patriotic society which has recently made an extensive study of crime, we have had more victims of murder in the United States during the past ten years than we had men killed in all of the six major wars in which we have been engaged?

According to the society's report, we have had killed in action in the Revolutionary, Mexican, Civil, Spanish and World wars [unclear] men; and there have been 120,000 people murdered here in the United States during the last decade! And this does not include the deaths from manslaughter or other causes, but from murder alone!

If Sherman was right, and "war is hell," then the sort of peace we have been having here for the past decade is certainly a disgrace!

And speaking of statistics, it might interest you to know something about the greatest metropolitan center of your country, and the largest city in the western hemisphere—New York.

To begin with, let's take the taxi cabs (since we all like to take them occasionally). There are some 20,000 taxis ("taxi" is really the plural form of this word, but nobody uses it thus) in the streets of New York (But not lately, for they're on strike and New York is having to hoof it for a change.)

There are some 18,000 policemen in New York City. Quite a good-sized city they would make? And about 12,000 firemen; 10,000 street sweepers.

---

15. Ralph Waldo Emerson (1803–1882) was a transcendentalist, poet, and essayist. See, Maurice York, *Ralph Waldo Emerson: The Infinitude of the Private Man* (Chicago: Wrightwood Press, 1994). Oliver Wendell Holmes (1809–1894) was an American physician and poet. See, William C. Dowling, *Oliver Wendell Holmes in Paris: Medicine, Theology, and the Autocrat of the Breakfast Table* (Lebanon, NH: University of New Hampshire Press, 2006).

The assessed property valuation of New York City is approximately $20,000,000,000. There are a billion dollars' worth of subways under the old burg; and there are streets here where the streams of traffic are flowing on five different levels at the same time; two elevated railways, one above the other; the surface street with its trolleys, taxis and whatnot, and two subways under the street, one below the other! And with the Zeppelins and aircraft of various descriptions which are always seen overhead, there could be said to be even six levels of traffic on some of the streets.

New York is, of course, the world's "theatrical center." There are even more big movie studios here than there are in Hollywood and Los Angeles; and every schoolboy knows that New York (Wall Street—a very short thoroughfare with a cemetery at one end of it and the East river at the other) is the world's financial center. New York is the world's center of the garment manufacturing industry. And New York is likewise the world's publishing center. There are some 21 big daily papers published here besides some nineteen hundred other publications, not to mention all the big book publishers. And New York has now become the world's first shipping center. Every hour in the day there are ships coming in and going out, to all points of the globe where men are engaged in commerce. New York is the world's diamond center—diamonds and other precious stones. There are streets here with nothing but diamond stores on them. New York is the world's leader in restaurants, cafes, cafeterias and other eating houses. New York is the world's first city for hotels, from 25 cents per night to $25 per day.

There are several buildings here over sixty stories high; and there is one—the Empire State building—that towers approximately a quarter of a mile above the sidewalk—102 stories. On cloudy days you can only see about two-thirds of the way up the giant skyscraper, the top third being above the clouds. You can go up to the top of it for a dollar. One big elevator will take you up some fifty stories, and then you get out and go into another one, which takes you up to the eighty-seventh story, and from there on up you have to walk. When you are reaching the 1,000-foot level going up in the building your ears will suddenly pop and you will feel momentarily rather queer, but it seldom proves serious to those venturing it.

New York has a population of about 7,000,000, and their nationalities predominate about as follows: Jews, two and a half millions; Italians, one and a quarter million; Germans, one million; Russians, one million; and Harlem, the Negro section here, is the world's largest Negro center.

Where are the Americans? Don't ask me. I've only met two of them here, one from the South and the other from the West!

Old Literary Landmarks
April 11, 1934

Hidden away in an obscure corner of Trinity churchyard, uptown at 155th Street and Broadway, is the unmarked grave of Alfred Tennyson Dickens, the oldest son of the great English writer. Only a few severed branches torn from some evergreen and a withered wreath long since laid upon the grave by some unknown hand that revered the great name of Dickens, are all the marks of remembrance that one will find at the grave today.

Dickens died suddenly here in New York some 22 years ago, on his first visit to this country. And his pallbearers of that day included the great Andrew Carnegie, and many statesmen and famous authors of the time.

Alfred Tennyson Dickens was named after the great Lord Alfred Tennyson, poet laureate of England, who stood sponsor for the first offspring of perhaps the greatest novelist in the world of literature—Charles Dickens.

Not far away from where Dickens' firstborn lies resting, there sleeps another whose name deserves honorable mention in the list of literary greats of his country—Clement Moore, the beloved poet whom every boy and girl remembers as the author of "The Night Before Christmas."

The writer used to visit the tiny old house in West 23rd Street—where now stands a row of swanky twenty-story apartment houses—where the American poet lived and wrote his famous little masterpiece.

And speaking of the old houses of famous literary men, I was passing by Edgar Allan Poe's old house down in Bleecker Street, in Greenwich Village (it, too, was torn down a few years since, and the site is now occupied by a big garage) late one snowy night when, suddenly recollecting where I was, I glanced up at the shuttered old windows in the dilapidated old empty house, and was not a little startled to see a dim light behind the old shutters in the very room where the poor half-mad poet had written some of his most fearfully fascinating tales and some of his most beautiful poetry. A couple of blocks away I found a policeman, and went back to investigate. We found that some four or five homeless men of the streets were cooking up their evening meal in the old fireplace. The cop was going to chase them out forthwith, but I interceded for the poor wretches and he finally permitted them to stay.

Mark Twain's old house on Fifth Avenue at Ninth Street has lately been taken over by a bunch of young ladies who are unemployed, and are selling books from little stands in the various parks of the city.

I know old good-hearted Mark wouldn't have hesitated to let them have the big, rambling old house, even if he had to move out himself in order to make way for them! That was Mark Twain. He actually went around amongst his literary and professional friends—authors, editors, doctors, lawyers, etc.—and begged them for money to give to the great Maxim Gorky, the poor Russian writer who was here in exile at the time. (Gorky is today considered, along with Shaw and one or two others, to be one of the world's greatest living writers.)

And to recur to Mark Twain again for a moment, the writer spent a most delightful evening last year with his great friend and biographer, Mr. Paine, who is getting along in years now, and has practically retired from literary labors.[16]

Every time I pass Washington Irving's little old house down in Irving Place, I imagine that I can see the great humorist burning the midnight oil over his books at the little wooden table where he always wrote.

Likewise, every time I pass by the little old hotel on 28th Street where O. Henry lived and wrote so much, I am reminded of his marvelous little masterpiece of a story called "The Furnished Room"—one of the last and greatest that he wrote.

Marshall County Genius
May 9, 1934

I have been thinking for some time that when, and if ever, I have the leisure and the funds to do the requisite research, and the freedom from the necessity of having to day after day be shackled to some stupefying and distasteful form of drudgery for which I am wholly unfitted, in order to earn a bare existence, that I would write a book on the outstanding accomplishments of our Southern men of genius and what they have contributed to the enlightenment and welfare of the world. A sort of appreciation or anthology of achievements, many of which, in this day of noise and confusion and fury, signifying nothing, perhaps, but the emptiness of superficial vulgarians, have become obscured and are comparatively little known, even in the South.

---

16. Author Albert Bigelow Paine (1861–1937) wrote a four-volume biography of Mark Twain. "Albert B. Paine, 76, Biographer Dead," *New York Times*, April 10, 1937.

I was rereading lately some of the works of Dr. John Allan Wyeth, of Alabama and New York, who attended the public school there at Guntersville and who, like the great Oliver Wendell Holmes and Sir Arthur Conan Doyle, was a charming and masterful writer as well as a great physician and surgeon, and while reading this great scholar the thought occurred to me: how very few, even of our professors and teachers, in Alabama are likely to be familiar with the works of this man of genius.[17] I can think of no better exercise for those students in our high schools and colleges who would become proficient in the difficult art of expression; who aspire to be writers, journalists and men and women of letters, than to have them study the graceful, scholarly and charming style of Dr. Wyeth. And with the good editor's consent—for I'm sure he could not devote space to better purpose—I will quote you a brief descriptive passage that is characteristic of this great writer's beautiful style and originality of observation. It is taken from his "The Life of General Forrest":

> "Now and then there comes upon the stage of life, in the theater of the world, a
>   man who so differs from the rest of—
> " 'The innumerable caravan that moves
> To that mysterious realm where each shall take
> His chamber in the silent halls of death.'"

That he catches the eye and ear at once and, as long as he moves in the scene, holds the attention of his fellows. When the sable curtain falls, and his part in the drama is over, we who remain to fill the minor roles find time in moments of reflection to ask ourselves: what manner of man was this, and wherein did he differ from others of his kind? By what mysterious alchemy did the elements in him combine to lift him to the stars, while we who just as earnestly, with upturned eyes and patient longing, strive to reach the immortals, stumble and fall, perish and are forgotten?

On the 13th day of July in the year 1821, in a rude frontier cabin, amid surroundings which told of poverty, and in the obscurity of a remote backwoods

---

17. Dr. John Allan Wyeth (1845–1922) was a native of Guntersville who, after moving to New York City, formed the New York Polyclinic Graduate Medical School and Hospital in 1881. In 1902, he became president of the American Medical Association. He enjoyed writing books like *With Sabre and Scalpel: The Autobiography of a Soldier and Surgeon*; *That Devil Forrest: Life of General Nathan Bedford Forrest*; and *History of LaGrange Military Academy and the Cadet Corps, 1857–1862*. See, Roderick Davis, "John Allan Wyeth," *Encyclopedia of Alabama*, http://www.encyclopediaofalabama.org/article/h-3522 (Accessed April 7, 2020); and Whitney A. Snow and Barbara J. Snow, *Wyeth City: Alabama's Model Industrial Experiment* (Birmingham, AL: Banner Digital Printing and Publishing, 2019).

settlement of middle Tennessee, there was born one of these rare beings. The light which first greeted his infant vision came through the cracks in the chinking between the logs of hewn cedar, or sent its penetrating rays beneath the riven boards of the roof, which in overlapping rows were laid upon the rafters and held in place by heavy poles and blocks, in lieu of nails. This humble cabin, which was his mother's home, claimed no more than eighteen by twenty feet of earth to rest upon, with a single room below and a half room or loft overhead. One end of this building was almost entirely given up to the broad fireplace, while in the middle of each side swung, on wooden hinges, a door. There was no need of a window, for light and air found ready access through the doorway and the cracks, and down through the wide squatty chimney. A pane of glass was a luxury as yet unknown to this primitive life. Around and near the house was a cleared patch of land containing several acres enclosed with a straight stake fence of cedar rails, and by short cross-fences divided into a yard immediately about the cabin; rearways of this was a garden, and a young orchard of apple, peach, pear, and plum trees. The yard fence ran parallel with the public road, so newly but through the forest that stumps and roots of trees still showed above the level of the ground, waiting to be removed by the slow process of decay.

What a vivid, clear-cut, and withal a poetic description. A little gem that even James Fenimore Cooper, who excelled in this department of literature, has not surpassed in his happiest moments.

Dr. Wyeth has also written some touching and lovely poetry of a very high order. A many-sided genius was this illustrious son of old Marshall County, whom, alas, only too few of us know and appreciate.

Uncle Bim From Georgia
May 16, 1934

The wandering relic of the Old South around whom these sentimental lines are written stood the other night on a corner of the busiest street in all the world; stood contemplating mad Manhattan's seething scene with a sort of dreamy bewilderment.

I knew him as soon as I laid eyes upon him. And I could see that he was profoundly and hopelessly lost, in all that fateful word implies! True, I did not know his name, nor from what state he came; but need one know where a rose was grown in order to recognize it?

Sartorially speaking, Uncle Bim—for such was the name he bore—wouldn't exactly have been taken for a fashion ad, unless, indeed, it was to illustrate the mode of haberdashery that prevailed in the cotton fields of Dixie some sixty years ago! His hat, to begin at the top of the list and read down, was a size too small, frazzled out at the brim and without a band, and the holes in the crown of this ancient adornment seemed to have come in assorted shapes and sizes. His kinky hair, lest we overlook his natural embellishments, had not been shorn in months, and was as white as the massa's cotton fields. And the lower portion of this ebony old phiz had also rioted in the same fleecy luxury. An old pair of brass rimmed, square "specks," with one of the absurdly tiny windows missing, was saddled a bit uncertainly upon the end of his big, flat nose. What occult reason he had for wearing them, I never found out; but he certainly wasn't wearing them to see with!

In lieu of a coat he was wearing one of those old-fashioned clawhammer affairs that passed out with the civil war. Long exposure to the Southern sun had reduced the pristine somber of this splendid garment to a sort of dullish-brown; while in the middle of the back were two big cloth-covered buttons, that might have served as tail-lights. A white and blue-striped hickory shirt was held together at the neck by a shoestring, which, strangely enough, had been tied with commendable art in a neat little bow, the two ends of the big shoelace falling down upon his breast a la the poet. This was the only article in his wonderful getup that might have suggested the temperament of the dreamer. He was living, as it were, and expressing himself on a shoestring! A pair of added overalls that were easily a couple of sizes too big were wrapped in some mysterious manner that only these old darkies seem to understand, very tightly about his legs, and tied at the ankles with a species of white cord, such as little boys sometimes effect when riding bicycles. This ample garment, more than aught else about him, suggested the rustic cage from which the ungainly bird had flown.

All this remarkable sartorial leafage appeared to have grown naturally out of a pair of monstrously large old shoes, which gave the poor wretch the appearance of being a sort of strange forked plant that had stemmed from two pots, and reversed nature by fusing in some mysterious alchemy for community of purpose at the nether extremity of the torso. A combination at once ludicrous and pathetic. If you can fancy a giant beetle standing on his hind legs, in the act of unfurling his wings, then you could appreciate the general effect and symmetry of Uncle Bim's getup.

In one hand he held a tiny red bundle, and in the other an impossibly crooked old walking staff.

A crowd of New York wisecracking gawks had coagulated about the corner of this great artery, and were contemplating our Uncle Bim with the most irreverential and unbecoming mirth, with unfeeling derision and that black curiosity with which the more vacuous of them just stop and stare at whatever is different.

With a feeling of fellowship, inspired partly by the courageous treatment our old visitor was receiving, and partly by a genuine liking for his kind, your sentimental narrator approached the old timer with: "What part of the South are you from, uncle?"

"Is yo-al a police?"

The old darkey was visibly frightened. He had the pathetic and helpless look of a little scared rabbit that expected the worst to befall him. "No, I'm not a policeman," I hastened to reassure him; "but you're from the South, aren't you!"

"Yes-suh; I'm Uncle Bim Brown f'om Georgia," he confessed.

His candid confession inspired a like frankness on my part, and I whispered to him that I was from old Alabama. At this happy piece of news Uncle Bim danced a little jig right there on the sidewalk. His dim old eyes brightened perceptibly with the diminishing fire of life, and then were blurred with tears. The old darkey's toil-worn hands were trembling with the repressed emotion that permitted no word to issue forth as he held my hand in his for a full minute. By some impish twist of wit, I was reminded of that tragic, comic little cartoon called "When a Feller Needs a Friend."

The poor old fellow, broke, hungry and thoroughly exhausted from his long hike up from Georgia, was on his way to a little town in New England, where he hoped to arrive in time to see his brother, whom he had not seen in forty-five years, and who was thought to be dying.

I helped the old darkey what little I could, and after he had been refreshed with food and rest, I accompanied him to the edge of the great, bewildering city, and put him on the Boston road, with best wishes, good luck and what little cheer I could muster. After bidding him farewell, I returned to my lodgings, where I took up my violin and sawed away for an hour or more on that lovely old Southern melody, "Old Black Joe." Like Uncle Bim, I was homesick for Dixie, and the old song seemed so appropriate to the occasion. How aptly might the words of the beautiful melody be applied to the friendless old darkey

as he trudged his weary way, amongst unfeeling strangers, along the great high-
way towards Boston, the voice of his brother calling to him across the years back
to childhood, and the old darkey replying in the words of the old song;

"I'm coming, I'm coming,
For my head is bending low—"

From my window I could see the famous Bellevue Hospital a few blocks
away, in which Stephen Foster, the gifted young man who composed "Old
Black Joe," passed away penniless and alone. How strange is the road of destiny!

Editors
June 6, 1934

A few days ago, there came several score editors from the various cities
and municipalities of Texas, bent upon seeing the sights in the big town before
returning to their respective sanctums in the far-flung domain of the Lone Star
state. They had been on an extended tour of the United States and Canada,
and their delightful and informative trip was scheduled to end, as one of them
expressed it, "in one final big blowout, with desserts and everything," in New
York City, the mecca, the magnet and oasis of the western hemisphere.

The New York reporters (supposed to be the most alert, intelligent, and
well-informed in the world) who "covered" the feast and festivities of the provincial editors, presented a rather incongruous admixture of sophistication and
naiveté in their observation of the editing gentry from the great Southwest. It
seemed that the reporters had approached their assignments with the trepida-
tion born of the expectation of encountering a bunch of two-gun rowdies in
big sombreros and red flannel shirts. The kind, you know, who were editing the
little sheets in the West in Mark Twain's day. And one of them (the reporters)
lamented in his long writeup that there was not a single "ten-gallon hat" in
evidence amongst the whole contingent of editors! "Why," he mourned, "you
wouldn't distinguish them from so many Wall Street brokers, lawyers and business men."

The writer was appointed to an associate editorship of a New York publishing firm last year; and in that capacity had occasion to contact many of
the metropolitan editors, both famous and obscure. And he can state without
prejudice that the editors whom he has met in the South and in the West have

been usually as well dressed as, and a lot more intelligent than, the editors by and large of the North.

And speaking of editors, one of the greatest and most respected of the exalted fraternity (and I am not being facetious when I say "exalted fraternity") has just passed away in New England. His name is Willis J. Abbot. Mr. Abbot was a brilliant and prolific writer, and one of the remaining few who was looked upon as a sort of connecting-link between the old journalism and the new.[18] His warm, sympathetic understanding of humanity and his vivid imagination enabled him to touch to life the commonplace topics that in less gifted hands too often become only so much dull reading matter.

Mr. Abbot did his first reporting on the old *New Orleans Times-Democrat* in 1884. And one of his fellow workers there was the poor, half-blind Irish-Greek emigrant who was destined later to become one of the rare and glittering jewels in the diadem of world literature—Lafcadio Hearn. And if you'll pardon the slight digression, I should like to remark here that the life of Lafcadio Hearn was one of the most unfortunate, financially speaking, in the annals of literature. He almost starved to death in the great city of London when a young man strug-gling to become a writer, and was thrown into prison there for seeking alms in the streets. And during one of his tragic winters in this country (at Cincinnati) he actually slept in a big goodsbox down in the brush along the Ohio river, because he could not afford even the cheapest sort of room! He later tramped his way down to New Orleans, where he finally found a chance (at $2.25 a week!) to express the great talents that have since made him world-famous. Although the author of many brilliant works (the first editions of which you cannot buy today for a fortune), and the professor of English literature at the University of Tokyo in Japan, at the time of his death Lafcadio Hearn did not have enough money to pay for his burial! But let's return to our editors.

It was during Mr. Abbot's residence at New Orleans that the late Joseph Pulitzer of the *New York World* wired him to get an interview with Jefferson Davis, and to find out what the Confederate President thought of the character of General Grant. Mr. Abbot recorded years later that Mr. Davis impressed him more than any of the eight American Presidents he had known. But as to the question of General Grant's character, all the great Southerner replied was:

"My young friend, did you say that the old elm on Boston Common is still standing?"

18. Willis J. Abbot (1863–1934) was an American journalist who wrote numerous books relating to the military.

Mr. Abbot once held the position of editor-in-chief of one of Mr. Hearst's big New York dailies; which he characterized as "very remunerative employment in a lunatic asylum."[19] He later left Mr. Hearst and his sensational journalism for a more dignified if less remunerative position with another paper.

In the words of Mary Baker Eddy, founder of the *Christian Science Monitor*, for which paper he was writing at the time of his death, Willis John Abbot "injured no one, but blessed all mankind."[20]

The Fleet's Out
June 27, 1934

Those little boys who compose a not inconsiderable minority of the *Advertiser*'s readers must have begun to think by now that if your correspondent doesn't write an article on Uncle Sam's navy that's been visiting in New York lately, that he isn't worth his salt. And so, in order to keep in good standing with these boys, I'll have to tell you about the navy.

The Grand Fleet of the American navy—the combined Atlantic and Pacific fleets—has just weighted anchor and steamed out of New York harbor after an enjoyable stay—both for the sailors and for the city—of eighteen days.

Some forty thousand officers and men composed the personnel that manned this most impressive and formidable display of fighting craft ever seen in New York, and, for that matter, perhaps anywhere.

Nearly two million citizens, whose hard-earned money has made this gigantic armada possible, were interested visitors to the powerful man-o-war; while on the navy's side it's doubtful if many officers and men missed a chance to go ashore in the big town. However, be it said on behalf of the blue jackets, they were as peaceful and sober a navy as was ever turned loose in a big, wet, exciting metropolis, with the freedom to go and do whatever they pleased. Of course, for the officers there were the usual rounds of social affairs—balls, teas, dinners, theatre parties, and all the other swanky things that society folks like to do. The admirals were dressed out in enough gold braid to sink a man not accustomed to so precious a burden! However, even the admirals on this occasion were quite

---

19. William Randolph Hearst (1863–1951), the famous newspaper magnate, who later became the inspiration for the film *Citizen Kane* (1941). See, Ben Proctor, *William Randolph Hearst: The Later Years, 1911–1951* (New York: Oxford University Press, 2007).

20. Mary Baker Eddy (1821–1910) established the Church of Christ. In addition to authoring many books, she started the *Christian Science Sentinel*, *Christian Science Journal*, *Herald of Christian Science*, and *Christian Science Monitor*. See, Gillian Gill, *Mary Baker Eddy* (Boston: De Capo Press, 1998).

human. They were seen to take admiring little urchins (little girls, of course, for no manly little boys would stand for it!) in their arms and kiss them.

President Roosevelt—who, were I following the correct form of protocol, should have been mentioned first in this article—looked very fine and handsome as he boarded the reviewing cruiser bright and early. It was the first time that the writer had seen him since last fall. I can truthfully say that the President seemed to be the most happy and carefree person I saw in connection with Uncle Sam's great naval show here. For the most part the naval officers, and especially the high-ranking flag officers, seemed, to me at least, to be perhaps a little too austere and stern visage to ever be very popular with the rank and file of democracy. But maybe this was only because their rigid countenances were so in contrast to the cheerfulness of the President. And goodness knows, we are all aware that our President has more cares upon his fine manly shoulders in a moment than these admirals have in a lifetime! Still he (the President) knows how to smile. And what a smile! It's not merely one of those official (I almost said Hoover) grins that seem to become a sort of facial fixture with professional politicians. The President puts all the charm of a truly charming personality into his warm beaming smile.

Though we love our President ever so much, I am sure that those little boys who are reading these lines are wishing that I'd return to the navy with them. And so here goes.

There were two giant airplane-carriers here, and from the decks of these mighty ships—the biggest things afloat, except possibly icebergs—some two hundred airplanes took to the air, and performed all sorts of daring and thrilling stunts over New York for the benefit of the President and the people. I did not go aboard the big 'plane carriers, as I had already been on them in California waters some few years ago.

There were any number of great battleships, cruisers, destroyers, tenders and whatnot anchored in the Hudson River from the Battery at the lower end of Manhattan Island clear up to Yonkers, some twelve miles away!

I was on a couple of battleships and some three or four cruisers and destroyers. Needless to say, everything was as spick-and-span as was possible to be. Why, you could eat your dinner right off the decks, they were that clean! Everything was polished and shining like glass, and you could see yourself in the big guns almost like mirrors. (But I truly hope, boys, that you'll never, never have occasion to see yourselves in front of one of these big guns when she is going into action. God forbid that!)

About the only important war craft not represented with the fleet here were the submarines. These, I think, are the most romantic warships ever conceived by the ingenuity of man. Have you ever been on one, or more correctly, in one of them? Your correspondent went aboard one down in Panama once; and let him tell you, they're the most interesting and fearfully fascinating things you could ever imagine! Just fancy the great black ocean-waves closing in upon you as you slowly sink beneath the surface. But then I'd better stop here, or you will all be running away to join the navy!

—————

Home Sweet Home
July 4, 1934

How beautiful, how poignantly beautiful, and how dear to the hearts of us all is this immortal little masterpiece that was originally written on the back of an old envelope as the young poet-adventurer, John Howard Payne, sat one lonely evening in a strange land far, far from home.[21]

John Howard Payne, a gifted young New Yorker, roamed this wide world over, from the clay hills of Georgia to the scorching wastes of the great African desert where he became stranded, fell ill and died.

For more than twenty years the forgotten remains of the young poet lay beneath a slab in the shifting sands of the great desert; the very sands, perhaps, that had blown over Solomon's Temple, and that had seen great nations rise and fall, and hundreds of generations of men come and go in the ages that shifted them to and fro in that ancient cradle of civilization.

At a little village over on Long Island the other day your lonely correspondent stood with bowed head as the shades of evening closed around the humble old house that was once the home of the unfortunate poet, and the house that had inspired him to write his classic little ballad. And as I stood there in the deepening gloom of closing day, one poet-wanderer paying respect to another. I too was thinking of a home far, far away, and of the sweet, cheerful faces and pleasant voices so tender with love and sympathy—many of which I shall not see again. How well, and how often have I known that homesick feeling that came over the poor wandering poet as he sat alone in the great city of Paris, writing his little song on the back of the envelope, expressing the feelings of

———

21. American John Howard Payne (1791–1852) gained fame as an actor, poet, playwright, and songwriter. In 1841, he became American consul to Tunis. "From a Foreign Grave; John Howard Payne's Body Brought Home," *New York Times*, March 23, 1883.

the inarticulate millions of the world's sons and daughters who were destined to wander far afield!

"Be it ever so humble,
There's no place like home,"

After nearly half a century of neglect, the grave of John Howard Payne has become an international shrine, and people are coming from all over the globe to visit it. His remains were taken from the silent wastes of the great desert some fifty years ago and brought back to his homeland, to rest, as was only befitting, in the capital of his country—Washington, D.C.

In these uncertain times of newfangled philosophies, when the home as the most vital and central institution of life is being seriously challenged, and actually destroyed (as in Russia), one can turn to John Howard Payne with a fuller appreciation of the truth and lasting beauty of the sentiments so poignantly and so happily expressed in "Home, Sweet Home."

Thoughts on America
July 18, 1934

There seems to be a particularly active anti-Southern campaign being carried on in the East just now. And if anything were needed to convince the doubting Thomases of this very potent fact, then let them go to the big New York papers, consider their ways, and be wise!

The sensational manner in which the news of the Alabama Supreme Court's recent decision concerning the Scottsboro case was smeared in glaring headlines across the New York papers indicates, to me at least, something slightly more than the human (inhuman?) love of justice which is nurtured so assiduously in the breasts of our liberal Yankee cousins: It is indicative of the lamentable tendency to nationalism which is again spreading over the earth after a season of dormancy.[22]

One finds this unhappy spirit of sectionalism pervading and slowly envenoming even the pages of our dear old conservative magazines. And of course

---

22. In March 1931, two white women falsely accused nine black men of rape. The resulting trial rocked not just Scottsboro, Alabama, but the nation. On the Scottsboro Boys, see, for example, James Goodman, *Stories of Scottsboro* (New York: Vintage Books, 1994); and Dan T. Carter, *Scottsboro: A Tragedy of the American South* (Baton Rouge: Louisiana State University Press, 2007).

there are our (I'm now writing as a New Yorker) wise-cracking New York colum-
nists who are in fact but highly-paid subtle propagandists, and the unfortunate
part is, these widely publicized propaganda artists soon begin to wield a not
inconsiderable influence over our more American editors and educators; who
ought to know better, who should be able to perceive the colored gentleman in
the woodpile!

It is hardly necessary to include in our list of violent haters those loud,
vulgar, vicious little foreigners who style themselves communists. It is the
particular and sole business of these treacherous (at heart) little opportunists
to foment strife and discord in every possible and impossible way in order to
undermine our American institutions. I know many of them personally, having
lived amongst them here; but I don't know a one of them that I'd trust across the
street! They are prominently Jewish—Russian Jews, German Jews, Polish Jews,
etc., etc. Internationalists for the very good reason that they have no country!

Thanks to our great steel and coal barons and our big exploiting industrialists like the late old Judge Gary, and others of his ilk who worship only the
dollar, regardless of the sweat-stains and blood that might be upon it—thanks
to these "rugged individualists" our great country has been literally flooded with
the riff-raff and refuse of Europe.[23] The streets of our great cities today are full
of these little cowardly foreign-born gangsters, whose machine-gun bullets will
yet send many of us to our graves.

And I implore you to consider for a moment (you should have considered it long ago, and written your Congressman to that effect!) the disgusting
and outrageous spectacle of our movies. Why, there is not an American name
amongst our great movie producers! And behold these fine gentlemen teaching
our American boys and girls the delightful ways and manners of the brothel
and the underworld! But thank heavens, the churches at last have awakened to
the shocking and dangerous situation, and have begun an energetic campaign
against the disgusting filth hashed out by the lordly film magnates as entertainment! Ironically enough, we who were supposed to be (so we thought!) the
world's most enlightened and civilized people, have been the very last country
to discover the rottenness of our own movies; most of the big European countries having already banned the Hollywood garbage!

Things have come to such a pass in our country today that when an
American opens his mouth (and goodness knows few enough of us have had the

---

23. Elbert Henry Gary (1846–1927) was a lawyer and industrialist known primarily for his involvement
with U.S. Steel. See, Ida M. Tarbell, *The Life of Elbert H. Gary: The Story of Steel* (New York: D. Appleton
and Co., 1925).

courage to do it lately!) in defense of that which he has been taught to respect and revere, he is immediately bowled down by a chorus of yelping propagandists who shout "Ku-Kluxer" from their lofty pent-houses or from the head of their edifying columns.

To close my "Americanism" article on the note with which I began it, I will say here that I do not "believe" in capital punishment; that, even if I did, in my opinion the Negroes involved in the Scottsboro case have not received justice, whether it was in Alabama or in the Congo. And I am thoroughly ashamed of the fact that my home state—Alabama—led the list in lynching last year, with five. But if being an American and a believer in our American institutions as opposed to anything that Europe has to offer—if, I say, being a citizen makes one a "Ku-Kluxer," then for God's sake let me become a Kleagle at once!

In saying all this I am not unmindful that tomorrow is the Fourth of July. And, who knows? Maybe my purpose in writing this was to remind you that you are still (at least so I hope) Americans. And instead of the apathy and national indifference that have too often in the past encouraged us to "let John do it," let's make up our sluggish minds very definitely that in the future Sam shall do it—meaning, of course, none other than our beloved old Uncle Sam!

Now please do not conclude too hastily that your correspondent is being obviously inconsistent by advocating the very nationalism which he pretended above to deplore. It does not follow that because a man believes in peace and freedom that he will not gird his loins for battle when that peace is disturbed and that freedom is threatened. Quite the converse: the most peaceful and virtuous men are usually the best soldiers when summoned by the clarion call of duty!

Ghosts
August 1, 1934

No doubt there are few less pleasant and insubstantial creatures abroad in the world than the ectoplasmic (the stuff that ghosts are supposed to be made of as opposed to protoplasm, the material of life) visitants from another world who find it convenient occasionally to revisit their old stomping-grounds, usually in the role of fortune-teller or seer.

And in nervous and uncertain periods like the one we're witnessing over the earth today, these phenomena have a way of recurring to bedevil the visions and dreams of men, and to disturb their thoughts with all the dark, portentous signs usually prophetic, so we are told, of dire calamities and impending fearful evils.

Nearly every paper we pick up today has its lurid ghost-story, or its miracle-performing shadow of some patron saint or other traced in profile upon the usually inaccessible wall of some obscure church that nobody ever sees.

The belief in the existence of ghosts (haunts) is almost universal with the races of mankind, and extends back into the dark unhistoried eras of remote antiquity. Our oldest Bibles and legends are but little more than the chronicled doings of amazingly energetic and prolific ghosts. Indeed, the one thing that impresses the modern student of comparative religions perhaps more than anything else is the prevalence of the ghostly influence that would seem to be the very matrix, as it were, in which their truths and half-truths are embedded, like the pearls in the oyster. And naturally all the great temporal, secular and so-called profane (non-sacred) writers from time immemorial have had the wit to exploit this potent and fertile field in contriving their respective literary creations. Even the most superficial acquaintance with Shakespeare reveals that great master's prodigality of invention and exploitation of the ghostly elements in the drama. How well do we remember the ghost-scene in Hamlet, or the way in which Banquo's ghost returned to mock his slayers! Of course a great genius like Shakespeare would be too much of a psychologist not to appreciate the extent to which the latent fears, the heritage of a superstitious age, like smoldering, like the volcano in the mountain, in the dark recesses of the human mind, await the occasion to burst forth in blind destruction.

Now please do not conclude too quickly that you perceive in these hastily-scribbled lines the beginning of a long, tedious essay on ghosts, for such is not the case: your long-winded correspondent merely indulged in the above observations by way of excusing himself for that which follows!

Speaking of ghosts reminds me of a rather shameful little experience which I had once down on the lower East Side in this great melting-pot that is New York.

An artist friend of mine who had a garret studio down in that dark, mysterious Italian section around Brooklyn Bridge, was going away to his summer place in Maine, to "rest up a bit and do a little painting." And so, he kindly suggested that I save rent for the summer by occupying his studio. His suggestion was accepted, and I soon became the sole tenant of his unpretentious but artistically appointed studio; and thus, found myself in the midst of some half a million low-class Italians, the vast majority of whom could scarcely speak half-a-dozen words of English!

The district was a particularly tough one, and notorious for its underworld characters—the deadly black-hand gangs, the low white-slavers, the dope-smugglers, murderers, thieves, pick-pockets and the whole rogues-gallery of fiendish demons. What possessed the artist to ever move into such an impossible district I don't know, unless it was the love of romance, of adventure and "color," and the hatred of the conventional and commonplace that prompted his artist soul to seek such Jean Val Jean surroundings.

At first, I found his cool, pleasant studio quite to my liking. It contained all the modern conveniences: an electric refrigerator that made its own ice; an electric stove and cute little kitchenette equipped with every kind of electric appliance and gadget imaginable; everything so handy and comfy that about all there was left for one to do was to feel sorry for those less fortunately situated! The "living quarters" of this delightful atelier consisted of the usual lounges, book-cases, tables, piano, statues, paintings, and the bric-a-brac that one would expect to find in such a place. There was an "artist's dog-bed" with a wine-colored velvet covering and a nest of silken downy pillows piled about in confusion; and to offset this luxurious contraption there was a little Persian canopy overhead, with the delicate curtains held in place by heavy gold-colored cords. I almost blushed at the thought of sleeping in such a dainty, lady-like affair, even though no one could claim to have seen me getting into it! One side of the studio, of course, was given over to the artist's "north-light" (a big skylight set at an angle of perhaps thirty degrees, under which the artist usually works). As I say, the first few days there were really enjoyable ones; I could do my writing every evening with no one to disturb or distract me. Everything was as quiet as a tomb in the old four-story house. An old Italian inventor, who had a cunning, shifty look that I did not trust, lived on the floor immediately beneath me, and the other floors were occupied by what I took to be decent working people (all Italians), who came and went as silently as shadows, which in truth they suggested, being dressed as they were always in black. But let's get on with the breath-taking denouement of our little story!

Late one night as I sat writing by the light of a heavily-shaded lamp in my favorite little alcove, I became suddenly aware of someone standing behind my chair. I quickly looked around, but—only the old book-case was there! I was not a little startled at this, for I would have gambled my life that someone stood behind me. I got up, took a drink of cold water and then went and made myself a cup of coffee. While the coffee was percolating, I threw a window open and stepped out into a little balcony for a breath of fresh air. But in some vague, mysterious way I could still sense the presence of some strange force in that studio; something that did not so much alarm and terrify (the usual reactions to the fear of the unknown) me as it depressed me. I felt a sort of indescribably sad mood stealing over me, as though I'd just been apprised of some terrible tragedy. I tried lightly to shake the feeling off with the thought that perhaps overwork had put my nerves a little on the ragged edge, a fact which a visit to my friend the neurologist would no doubt confirm. I thus poured myself a cup of coffee and sat down preparatory to enjoying the delicious stimulant; but I never got to taste the coffee! The very air seemed suddenly to vibrate with a mysterious influence that I could not explain or comprehend, or that I had ever experienced before. I put on my hat and coat, extinguished the light and very quietly went out into the street. By the big clock in the Metropolitan tower I could see that it was then three in the morning. I took a long stroll (a dangerous and foolish thing to do in that section at that hour!) and did not return to the studio until dawn. The next night the same phenomenon occurred, but seemed somehow to be more pronounced in its effect. I simply had to leave the place!

I wired the artist that I could no longer be responsible for his studio, as I could not stay there.

"I understand," he answered; "that's why I'm here! Letter following."

In his letter he advised me that he was returning to dispose of his things; that he had experienced the same thing that I had; that he had been ashamed to mention it, as he feared, like myself, that it was merely a symptom of mental disorder.

I've often scrambled my meager brains in the fruitless endeavor to solve what will perhaps always remain a big question-mark: what was it? I've even wondered if perhaps it could have been that the subtle old Italian inventor was secretly trying out some strange new gas, or perhaps a powerful ray, on us!

———•———

Sunday Thoughts
August 8, 1934

Today being Sunday I lolled around the apartment most of the morning reading the Sunday paper and answering a few letters. Towards noon Homer Bevans, the sculptor, dropped in, and I prepared, in a bachelor's way, a light lunch for the two of us.[24] We had a most enjoyable talk about most everything

---

24. On Bevans, see Chapter 1, Footnote 23.

under the sun. Bevans comes of an old Chicago family, and in early life was a friend of Eugene Field, the poet. Of late years he has been living abroad, mostly in Paris, I believe.

Speaking of Europe, my friend thinks that the Austrian situation will eventually precipitate the world into another terrible holocaust. And by the way, while on the subject of wars and rumors of wars, did it perhaps ever occur to you that July, more than all the other months of the year put together, is apt to be the month having to do with wars? Do we not celebrate our Independence Day in July? So do the French and the Mexicans, and the Brazilians, and the Columbians, and the Italians, and in fact most of the independent countries of the world. Why is it?

I regret (if you'll pardon the kaleidoscope suddenness with which I change subjects!) to hear of Marie Dressler's passing.[25] She was a truly great actress, a talented interpreter of the author to the audience, and withal a woman of unusual personal charm. Your correspondent had the good fortune to meet her in Hollywood once, and I shall never forget her rare conversational charm, which was simplicity and sincerity itself, or rather themselves. She was not only a great stage and screen comedienne, but a benefactress as well to thousands of the poor down-and-outers, not merely of her own profession, but of all walks of life. She makes us laugh and forget troubles, and she could also weep with us in our tragedies. Her passing will be a terrible blow to the movie industry, which, on other accounts, is in a particularly unpleasant position at the moment.

This afternoon I accompanied my sculptor friend to his sip (he has a commission to do a bust of one of the ruling potentates of Europe, whither he was bound), and on my way back to my lodgings I strolled through the park, attracted thither by an Italian band, which consisted of some eight or ten pieces of brass and drum. The "music," though perhaps a bit pretentious for so limited a band, consisted of a few selections from the classics. However, whatever there might have been lacking in art was made up for by the great energy and gusto with which the pieces were rendered! But in truth I was more interested in a little baby bird, whom the early morning storm had prematurely and crudely dislodged from his nest, than I was in the "wop" music. The little fellow couldn't quite support himself on his fluttering little fuzzy wings, but he was very brave about it all, and tried again and again to follow the mother bird back up into the tree from whence he had been so unmercifully precipitated. The patient tenderness with which the little feathered mother tried to coax and

---

25. On Dressler, see Chapter 1, Footnote, 12.

help him back into the tree and out of the reach of the prowling cats was most touching to witness. I observed that she, though nervous to distraction, was nevertheless thoughtful enough in her frantic agitation to pick up tiny bits of grass, and other minute objects which I could not see and put them into the little fledgling's mouth, which was open and begging most of the time. She was trying desperately, and in the only way she knew, to get her baby back into his little swinging crib.

I picked the little fellow up and set him on a twig above my head. But somehow, I found it hard to walk away from him. Perhaps it was the music that made me a bit sentimental!

<hr />

Poverty and Riches
August 22, 1934

As summer slips past and autumn draws nigh the air becomes tinged with a pleasing, indefinable something that turns one's thoughts to the open road; that makes one want to get out of the crowded city and seek places that are more pastoral and pleasant.

Indian summer usually brings the loveliest weather of the year to the latitude around New York. The temperature is mild and balmy, and the sky is of a black transparency that is very tranquilizing to the spirit. But it can in nowise compare with the autumnal loveliness of our North Alabama, when the hills and mountains look as though they'd been touched to gold by the wand of some ubiquitous Midas; with here and there the flaming gumtree looming like a pillar of fire, and adding its magic touch to the landscape, as does the dogwood in the spring.

China-town, in my opinion, is about the most interesting and colorful part of New York City. There are some 25,000 Chinese in New York, and most of them live downtown in a circumscribed area of a few square blocks. It is one of the strangest and most picturesque sections of the lower East Side. And it is ever a pleasure to me to observe the pretty Chinese girls as they go about their shopping at the fruit and vegetable stalls and push-carts early in the morning. They are usually dressed in their quaint native costumes, which consist of black silk pajamas and a long slipover affair, such as the Russians go in for, with a plentiful splashing of big yellow flowers (in the cloth), which produce an exotic but not unpleasant butterfly effect. Some of these almond-eyed beauties are as slender and graceful as the poppy-stalk of their native land. They do not go in for cosmetics; but then they don't need them: their skin is very smooth and fine of texture, and the color of a pale autumn moon. There is a rare, translucent quality about the pigmentation of high-class Chinese that produces an almost unearthly pallor; which is perhaps why some writers refer to them as "celestials." Many of these young oriental women speak English quite fluently, having attended American schools and colleges; and some of them are immensely wealthy, being the daughters of big Chinese merchants and importers. (But it's no use, boys: these oriental lassies seldom ever marry an occidental!)

To turn from the bustling habitats of the living to the peaceful repositories of the dead: I like to browse, as it were, amongst the old graves in the ancient churchyards down town. Some of the inscriptions on the old headstones in Trinity church-yard are very quaint and interesting, and take one back to olden times. Some of them were put there as long ago as 1650. But many of them have long since become defaced, and their crude carvings obliterated by the ravage and blight of time. Indeed, some of the old stones themselves have crumbled away to dust, leaving, as Shakespeare would say, not a wrack-behind. Many notable personages connected with the early history of our country are buried here, and the old Trinity church property is now a very valuable one, being in the heart (if, indeed, such place could properly be said to have a heart!) of the great financial district, with towering skyscrapers puncturing the clouds on every side. A big traction company recently had to pay the trustees of the property a million dollars for the privilege of boring a subway tunnel deep down under the old church and graveyard!

And speaking of the financial district: I always feel very self-conscious when strolling through Wall Street and the contiguous strongholds of Mammon. The sidewalks and doorways are teeming with officers and detectives, scanning every face, on the lookout for trouble; especially since the great explosion down there a few years ago, in which some of the big buildings were wrecked. They never solved the crime! They found parts of the dray-wagon, which contained the explosives, and parts of the poor horse were found as far as three blocks away; but to this day it all remains a deep, dark mystery. Some think it was the work of radicals or anarchists; others believe it was some lunatic with a grievance against the institutions blown up. Be that as it may, they are so vigilant and cautious down there today that every vehicle that parks for five minutes is investigated!

The swanky restaurants and cafes that cater to the bankers and brokers in the financial district are now making a specialty (so one sees advertised on their windows) of mint juleps and other fancy cocktails; none of which is less than a dollar a "shot." One of the head waiters told me that the bills for some of these swell dinners (mostly for the drinks) sometimes run as high as seven hundred dollars! An ordinary steak that you could get in the average restaurant for 50 cents costs you $6.00 here!

It is quite a comedown from the ritzy cafes of the financial district to the cheap "hash foundries" and malodorous eating houses along the Bowery—that famous street of forgotten men. These latter gloomy refectories are always filled to capacity with the tattered battalions of the earth's disinherited, who have learnt to dine on a dime! The Bowery, for legions of these poor down-and-outers, is the last stop on the road to Potter's field. Tragedies more grim and dramatic than ever tragedian penned are being enacted each day and night in the dark, desperate haunts along that dismal thoroughfare. It is truly the street of forgotten men!

Food for Thought
September 12, 1934

Hour by hour the sun is receding southward; the evenings are growing cooler, the days shorter; another winter is drawing near. And with it comes the awful realization that, for many of us, there will not be another spring: Hunger and exposure will again decimate our unhappy numbers, as they did last year and the year before. With the temperature hovering at 15 degrees below zero, or 47 degrees below the freezing point (as was the case last year), and with thousands of us without overcoats, and with only a bowl of thin soup for the day—with these combinations facing us, many of us are likely to fall by the wayside ere the frigid blasts of winter shall have passed.

Approximately 22 per cent of the entire population of New York City, or nearly a million and a half people, are now on the relief rolls. And there are another million perilously near it; what with the pitiful sums they earn from the two or three days' work a week, which is all they are getting.

Let's turn our attention for a moment from this unpleasant prospect to one of a slightly different tone: There lives an eccentric old banker over on Park Avenue who is the sole occupant of a 24-room suite! For the palatial sty the old boy pays a hundred thousand dollars a year! He recently gave a quarter of a million dollars in lawyers' fees to keep another old banker from going to the penitentiary—where he probably belonged. All the life savings of a hundred thousand poor people were wiped away by the failure of the great banking institution which he and his fellow robbers successfully plundered! And yet we hear this type of creature putting up a great hue and cry about "our constitution," and the way the Roosevelt regime is taking "our liberties" away from us.

The "American Liberty League," which you no doubt have heard of or read about in the papers, is an organization composed of big bankers and their political henchmen who are out to try to undermine the present administration at Washington; the only administration we have had there in years that really has the interests of the country and the common people at heart.[26] This same "American Liberty League" (all enemies of the people usually parade as great patriots and constitution savers just as all hypocrites try to get into the churches to hide their dirty work!)—this same Liberty League outfit is headed by the great cigar-chewing windbag Al Smith, who is president of the Empire Trust Co., owners' of the largest building in the world![27] Next to Mr. Smith is a suave, diplomatic corporation lawyer named Davis (the same, who ran for president in 1924, and got the Democratic party the worst licking it ever had!), who is a tool for J.P. Morgan & Co., the greatest banking institution on earth![28] With Messrs. Smith and Davis in our great liberty-saving project is one Wadsworth, a reactionary Republican ex-senator who is interested only in making political capital out of the attendant publicity.[29] Mind you, these are the three distinguished gentlemen who are out to save our liberties for us and to try to prevent the Roosevelt administration from granting federal relief to some sixteen and a half million destitute Americans; honest people whom the diabolical machinations, the swinish activities of our big international bankers have reduced to a state of pauperage. We see the unfortunate victims of this vicious and selfish system of "the tooth and the claw," as president Roosevelt recently termed it, shivering in bread-lines and tramping the streets with hollow eyes and pinched faces—gaunt, poor things whom starvation is slowly putting an end to. Twenty thousand of them were buried in Potter's field last year!

---

26. Comprised of politicians who opposed Roosevelt's New Deal, the American Liberty League was formed in 1934. See, George Wolfskill, *The Revolt of the Conservatives: A History of the American Liberty League, 1934-1940* (Boston: Houghton Mifflin Co., 1962).

27. On Al Smith, see Chapter 2, Footnote 30.

28. Democrat John William Davis (1873–1955) lost badly to Calvin Coolidge in the 1924 presidential election. Prior to that, he had served as U.S. Solicitor General and as U.S. Ambassador to the United Kingdom. See, William Harbaugh, *Lawyers' Lawyer: The Life of John W. Davis* (New York: Oxford University Press, 1973).

29. Republican James Wolcott Wadsworth, Jr. (1877–1952) served New York as a Senator and later, as a Representative. See, Martin L. Fausold, *James W. Wadsworth, Jr.: The Gentleman from New York* (Syracuse: Syracuse University Press, 1975).

If you want to see something that will give you food for thought, come with me some morning at dawn to the ferry at East Twenty-third Street, in New York City. As the first faint rays of light begin to fall upon the fog that overhangs the East river, you will hear the rumble of heavy wagons being drawn by giant draught horses. Presently, the wagons will round a corner and make for the ferry. You will see a big Negro convict sitting on top of a load of plain pine coffins; and behind this wagon will come others, each with its convict driver and its load of coffins stacked five high. We will now step onto the ferry and follow them. Twenty minutes up the river we are landed at the ferry-ship at Hart's Island. Great gray buildings, heavily barred and gloomy to look upon, loom up in the distance. Although the sun is not yet risen, we see hundreds of convicts around us everywhere. A great yawning ditch now becomes the scene of much activity. The ditch is several feet deep and hundreds of feet long. We see the convicts dragging the pine boxes from the wagons (no careful handling here!) and passing them down into the great gaping ditch, where they are laid in long rows three deep. When the ditch is filled with its quota of men, women and children paupers, the guards bark out their orders and the shovels get busy. The light of day shall find them no more; nor shall the pangs of hunger have any terrors for them here—poor things!—who were they?

You come away feeling gloomy and sick at heart, and you shudder at the thought of being buried between two coffins, one above you and one beneath you, in a big common grave with strangers all around you!

The Great Sea Disaster
September 19, 1934

Your correspondent, accompanied by another journalist and a representative of the U.S. government, motored down the New Jersey coast Monday morning to see the burning hulk of the great sea-going queen, the *Morro Castle*, in which more than a hundred men, women, and children lost their lives between midnight and dawn Saturday morning.[30]

There she lay, a few yards from shore, her superstructure a smoldering mass of warped and twisted wreckage, and her lower decks all gutted and in frightful ruins—a great, black inferno of a coffin with the cindered remains of the poor creatures who were trapped like rats in her lower decks—who were deserted by the crew and left to perish!

---

30. On the SS *Morro Castle*, see Chapter 1, Footnote 2.

At 3:30 o'clock Saturday morning some two hundred persons were struggling for dear life in the cold, stormy sea (for a gale was raging at that hour) around this burning ship. About a hundred others, mostly members of the crew—be it said to their everlasting shame!—were in lifeboats and heading for the shore, some eight miles away. Old men who were too feeble and weak to swim for long, and elderly women who either could not swim or were too shocked and hysterical to try, were left behind, with the frightened and struggling little children, while our brave heroes of the crew (most all of whom were cheap foreigners, as the big shipping lines will not hire American seaman because they can get the foreigners for less wages!)—our brave heroes of the crew headed safely for the coast!

To add to the horrors of the ghastly scene the water was alive with great man-eating sharks, many of which were seen to grab children and women and disappear beneath the great black waves. A captain on one of the rescuing vessels testified that he turned his great flood-lights down upon the awful scene below him in the water, and counted no less than ten sharks splashing about in the midst of the poor helpless swimmers around the flaming ship!

Many couples, some of whom were on their honeymoon, kissed each other goodbye and leaped from the burning ship into the dark, raging ocean. Some made it to shore; some were never seen again. One young man, just married, was swimming with his young bride toward the shore when, suddenly hearing her scream, he turned in time to see her twisting as though in great agony, and then disappear beneath the waves! Another woman was swimming slowly but steadily toward land with her husband (they were middle-aged persons) when he called to her in a gasping, broken, pitiful voice: she could not see him as they were well away from the blazing ship, and it was dark as dark could be—"Go on, honey; keep it up—I can't—can't make it." With these heart-rending words, the poor fellow left his wife and this world behind him.

It was indeed a most sad and touching thing to see thousands of anxious relatives and friends coming with tear-stained and sorrowing faces to identify and to claim the bodies of their loved ones, who were laid out in a temporary morgue not far from where the great ship was still smoldering. The bodies that had been taken from the sea, or that had been washed in by the tide, were laid in long rows in the improvised morgue, with armed soldiers standing silently on guard. But the saddest thing of all to me was a pretty little curly-headed lad of some 5 of 6 summers. He looked more like a big doll than a boy of 5. Once so bright and handsome, the pride and joy of some proud father and mother, he was now cold and blue in death. Long, curling, beautiful lashes were closed over the little eyes that had looked upon a scene whose horrors would have petrified the stoutest heart. No one knows who he is, nor claims his little body. O sweet little casualty of the sea, would that we could touch you to life again and take you home with us! It is believed that his father and mother either perished in the flaming ship or were swallowed up by the raging sea.

This terrible tragedy of the sea should be a lesson to us easy-going Americans who permit our great ships, upon whose safety our very lives depend, to be manned by cheap, ignorant foreigners instead of by intelligent American sailors—thousands of whom are now starving around the waterfronts because they cannot get work!

The Little Lost Girl
September 26, 1934

Your correspondent was the honored recipient the other day of a most charming and friendly letter from a prominent and cultured lady in Marshall County. And from this pleasant communication he was not a little flattered to learn that some of his tedious articles which appear in the *Advertiser* are not only being read, but are being clipped out and saved! This lady—I shall not mention her name here—tells me that she has saved more than fifty specimens (though, of course, she didn't use exactly these words) from my rather erratic pen. Now I can think of no higher tribute to pay a writer than to tell him that his feeble effusions are being preserved for future reference. And, though I might dissent from her taste in writers—knowing as I do this particular one rather well—I shall nevertheless always be grateful to her for her thoughtful consideration. Nice, encouraging letters like hers are not often received by writers like me; and when they do come, it might be truly said to be a red-letter day! But I fear I'm tooting my little horn entirely too much!

While dining in one of the big automats the other evening I had a rather singular but pleasant experience.

In case you've never seen an "automat," I'll give you a brief description of one: a big self-service cafeteria that usually seats several hundred people at a time, many of them having mezzanine floors and little nooky alcoves for those who prefer to dine in retirement. The peculiarity of the automats as distinguished from the ordinary cafeterias is that everything is done by buttons, electrically. All the food—except of course the hot dishes, which are served by countermen at the steam tables—is in little glass compartments, everything very tastefully and sanitarily put up. You simply walk along with your tray, select the items of food you want and drop the specified number of nickels (cashiers will change your money into nickels) into the little slots, somewhat as you might play the slot machines which you may have seen in stores. The automats, by the way, are extremely popular in New York, where they've been operating for some twenty years. The food is both reasonable in price and good in quality, and there are no waiters to be tipped or to buzz around and bother one, as everything is mechanical, and one can eat without saying a word to anyone, if one so chooses. I've also been in automats in Philadelphia and in Chicago. I understand there are now more than a hundred of them in the country, some sixty of which are in New York City. The automats comprise one of the largest chains of restaurants in the world, and are rated at more than thirty million dollars. But to return to our little story.

As I sat in the automat sipping my coffee, with my face buried in the evening paper, I suddenly felt something tugging at my sleeve, somewhat as the big perch used to tug at my fishing line in the old Nabors millpond. Looking down, I was surprised to see a cute little golden-haired tot of perhaps three or four years. She surveyed me with a pair of big blue eyes that looked as though they were about to say, "Well, good-ness gracious! Why don't you notice a lady?"

"Hello, there, young lady!" I bowed, trying to comply with the demand in her eyes.

"Where's my mama?" she demanded, ignoring my salutation and pulling herself up to her full thirty inches with the imperious dignity of a queen.

"Your mama?" I asked, feeling rather humbled by the haughty manner of this high-toned young lady.

"Yes, my mama—you find her, you find her quick!" She issued these orders in rapid-fire succession, and with a tone of finality that precluded any argument or back talk whatever.

"Why-er—what does your mama look like?" I pleaded, hoping for a possible clue as to the good lady's identity.

"She looks like my mama!" she snapped, evincing her great disgust at my stupidity by casting a look of scorn upon my lowly person that made me feel just about as small as a penny. She next reached over and gave my nose a good stiff jerk, as if it wasn't long enough already!

"Oh, yes, your mama—I'll find her," I promised, getting up from the table and heading rapidly in the general direction of the steam-table, where I observe a dozen or so ladies waiting to be served. "Pardon me, ladies," I began, in a tone loud enough to be heard above the rattle and clatter of dishes, trays and silverware; "have any of you lost a little girl?" I had hardly delivered myself of these words before five or six women screamed and dashed for their tables. "It's quite all right, ladies: I've found her!" With this reassuring message I led the way very heroically to my table, where one of the ladies—presumably the long-lost mother pounced upon our little queen and proceeded to smother that young person with the most fervent, the most ardent kisses, as though they'd been separated for ten years instead of ten minutes! As the happy mama was leading her "previous possession" away the little imp, as if she hadn't punished me enough already turned and made a most frightful face at me! I quickly buried my nose in the paper again, lest she should decide to come back and give that prominent organ another stiff jerk for good measure.

On Brooklyn Bridge
October 3, 1934

As twilight drapes its misty veil about the spires and steeples and the towering walls across the way, it seems that I might be standing here looking out upon some wonder-scene in Fairyland instead of the great bustling, pulsating city of New York. As the day merges gradually, imperceptibly into night, and every object within the field of vision assumes a softer outline, the lights begin to twinkle faintly here and there over the great metropolis, and to blink and wink in all the colors of the rainbow on the tugs, scows, lighters, barges, tenders, ferryboats, freight-ships and the various other craft that compose the bewildering maze of traffic in New York harbor.

I often walk out upon Brooklyn Bridge in my solitary nocturnal strolls. And many a midnight have I stood here alone within the shadow of the great pedestal, looking down upon the river some three hundred feet below—lost in pleasant reverie, or maybe seeking forgetfulness of sorrow.

How many discouraged and defeated poor souls have turned their weary footsteps to this mighty work of steel and stone, hoping to find forgetfulness and rest in the bosom of the peaceful river far below! It would seem that the river is calling to them in a voice that we cannot hear: "Come unto me, ye that are weak and heavy laden, and I will give thee rest." I imagine that I can see them trouping past me here in the dead of night—the sad, silent haunted faces and the drooping shoulders that are weighted down with unspeakable cares.

We are apt to think, in our smugness, that only weaklings commit suicide. But this, however, is far from being true: there are circumstances in which it requires infinitely more courage and strength of will to die than to live and be, as weaklings usually are, a burden on society.

Perhaps the most tragic figure that ever sought oblivion from the railings of this bridge; that ever used these famous parapets as a gateway into Eternity, was an unknown young poetess, whose unhappy fate it was to be a woman of the streets, a Magdalene.

Late one winter's night many years ago a young policeman stood in a darkened doorway near Brooklyn Bridge, and wondered at the strange ritual which he beheld in the churchyard across the street. All New York lay blanketed under the heaviest snowfall in years, and out of the black night, soft, sparkling crystals still came swirling down with unrelenting persistence. A frail little slip of a girl some eighteen years was seen hurrying along the snowy street toward the darkened cathedral. She was thinly clad in an old worn coat, and as she glanced nervously about her it was observed that her face, though once beautiful, was now pitifully thin and emaciated. She entered the church-yard and fell on her knees in the snow, in an attitude of prayer. High overhead the snow had settled among the tracery of the Cathedral towers, and every niche was drifted full of the soft, fluffy flakes; and over the statue of the Saint in front of which the young woman knelt in prayer the snow was draped in soft, diaphanous folds, as if the sainted one was wearing a bridal veil—which beautiful symbol, alas, was not to be for the frail little creature in the old worn coat! The curling locks that peeped out from under her cheap little hat were all covered with snow while she bowed her troubled head in prayer. She struggled to her feet, dusted the snow from her hair and her clothes, and hurried away in the direction whence she came. The young policeman kept wondering at the strange behavior of the young woman in the old worn coat. And a couple of hours later, when the snowstorm had somewhat abated, his curiosity impelled him to follow the dim footprints in the snow, and see where they lead him to. He was not long in discovering the destination of the praying young woman in the old worn coat. A quarter of a mile out on Brooklyn Bridge he found the old worn coat laid carefully upon the railing, and pinned to the coat was a piece of paper. The young patrolman took the coat and the paper and repaired to the station-house with his information.

The body was recovered the next day; and the piece of paper contained one of the most beautiful poems that I've ever read. The poem and the policeman's story were published in one of the big New York papers; and a famous writer of that day was so impressed by the poem that he not only gave the young woman a decent burial but followed the hearse to the cemetery, where he spoke a few gentle words with bowed head, and placed a beautiful floral piece upon the new grave.

In the poem which the young poetess left behind her she contrasted the whiteness and the purity of the snow with the darkness and degradation of her unhappy career.

The first line, in each stanza of the poem was:

"The snow, the snow, the beautiful snow"

In closing these lines on Brooklyn Bridge, I might add that such is the irony of life that, when the kind-hearted author himself died a few years later in a foreign land, no one came to place a flower upon his grave, or to utter a few gentle words with bowed head!

Nabors Mill, 1898

Nabors Mill, 1921

Jud Nabors, circa 1915

William and Jud Nabors, 1925

Richard and Lucinda Nabors, circa 1950s

Donald and Riley Nabors, circa 1950s

Tempie Nabors Lumpkin; Dura Nabors Elrod; unidentified; Lula Nabors Vaughn;
unidentified; and Lucinda Nabors, circa 1930s.

Zola Nabors Vandenburg; Dura Nabors Elrod; Lucinda Nabors; Gladys Nabors Snow with daughter Annette; and Tempie Nabors Lumpkin, circa 1940.

William Nabors, circa 1920s.

William Nabors, Boxcar Betty (Hobo Queen); and Ben (Hobo) Benson at a party hosted by the *Bowery News* in 1957.[31]

31. "Bill Nabors, Boxcar Betty, Ben (Hobo) Benson and others at a *Bowery News* party," *Bowery News* 59 (Nov 1957), 5.

C H A P T E R   4

Tipsy Braggart, 1935-1937

"Other people are quite dreadful. The only possible society is oneself."
—Lord Goring from Oscar Wilde's *An Ideal Husband*

The Canal Project
January 2, 1935

The projected Tennessee-Guntersville-Warrior Canal is unquestionably one of the major developments of recent years, especially as concerns Marshall County and North Alabama.[1] And this great project should have not only the consideration and good wishes, but also the active support and co-operation of every citizen who is so fortunate to live in this progressive region.

The potentialities for progress, for social and economic advancement which a project of this nature and import contains is almost beyond calculation. Not only would it facilitate and expedite the exchange of commodities between intra-state points, but it would also have a decided effect in lowering the freight rates with which the shippers of this region have to contend. And needless to point out here that this in turn would benefit every farmer, and have a most salutary effect on business in general.

---

1. After years of construction, the TVA Guntersville Dam ultimately created Lake Guntersville in 1939. See, Whitney A. Snow and Barbara J. Snow, *Lake Guntersville* (Mount Pleasant, SC: The History Press, 2018). For more information on the TVA, see, for example, Erwin C. Hargrove, *Prisoners of Myth: The Leadership of the Tennessee Valley Authority, 1933–1990* (Princeton: Princeton University Press, 1994); and Matthew L. Downs, *Transforming the South: Federal Development in the Tennessee Valley, 1915–1960* (Baton Rouge: Louisiana State University Press, 2014).

One need not consult the histories of our various canals (by the way, there has just recently been a most interesting and informative book published on the history of the old Erie Canal)—to repeat, one need not go to the histories of the world's canals to appreciate the tremendous influence which they have exerted, in practically every instance from the days of Pharaoh down to modern times, in the material development of the regions which they have served. Indeed, the acceleration of activity has so exceeded expectations as to verge on the phenomenal. And if you think this smacks too much of the press-agent's fantastical exaggeration, I cordially invite you to study the histories of the various canals, not only in this country but in Europe.

If you allow me to inject a personal note (since it is germane to the subject) into this article, I will tell you about my own experience in canal construction.

In 1926, the first year that Alabama played in the Rose Bowl at Pasadena—(which your correspondent witnessed as a sport writer for young Cornelius Vanderbilt's *Los Angeles Daily News*)—in the autumn of 1925, I was sent over to Arizona, to represent the paper in that vast but rather arid commonwealth. My journalistic duties of course brought me into contact with the social, business and political leaders of the state. And I used to have the privilege (the only newspaper man to be granted this honor, I believe) of running in and out of old Gov. Geo. W. P. Hunt's office as often as I pleased—which was quite often, I assure you, as his was not only a genial and sunny nature, but he could retell a joke with as much zest and relish as the next one![2] I was in his office, by the way, at the time he received the formal notice of the death of the King of Siam; which sad intelligence was conveyed in a big state envelope with the royal insignia embossed thereupon, and edged in black. When the old governor had read the contents of the regal communication, he tossed the heavy missive over across the desk to me, with the explanation that he had been a personal friend of the old king during his term as U.S. Minister to Siam. I merely mention these little reminiscences by way of revealing what a truly democratic executive the old governor was. He is generally known out there as "The Father of Arizona," as he holds the singular record of having been seven times governor of his state! In the language of the Western cattlemen, he is "just as plain as an old shoe." And he would as soon stop in the street and talk with a laborer as to a banker! But let me not indulge in further anecdotal digression, for I set out to tell you something else!

When young Vanderbilt all but lost his shirt in his Los Angeles newspaper venture, and all of us young scribblers were left high and dry, with no more

2. On Hunt, see Chapter 1, Footnote 1.

job than the Wandering Jew, I went in to see the old governor and broke the sad news to him. "Humph!" he grunted, "that's nothing—I'll send you up to Northeastern Arizona as a commissary clerk on the big dam at Mesa Canyon." A couple of weeks later our exasperating young reporter bounced back into the old governor's office with a positive assurance that nobody but Blackfeet Indians (of whom there were plenty) could live in that God-forsaken frigid region. I can still see the dear old governor as he scratched his fine classical head as if puzzled as to just how to get rid of the young pest. "Well," he said, "I'll send you out on the Canal job as a concrete shooter, at nine dollars per day." And so, I went to the Gila Canal to run an electric concrete-gun for eight hours a day—that is, what time I wasn't gazing off over the date palms and hazy peaks towards Mexico!

My few weeks on the Gila Canal were among the happiest of my life. Hundreds of workers from all over the West, the Southwest, and the Northwest were working there together—all gay, adventurous, colorful young fellows who looked upon the earth as being their oyster!

The Gila Canal, at a cost of a few million, brought untold wealth to the Salt River Valley region around Phoenix. And the hundreds of employees brought thousands of dollars in business to the merchants and businessmen of the community. And the Tennessee-Guntersville-Warrior Canal would certainly do the same for North Alabama.

P.S. After having written the above article, I was pained to see in the *New York Times* that the dear old governor was dead (Christmas Day). I might add here that while doing newspaper work in Virginia in 1927, I received a fine and beautiful letter from Governor Hunt (which I still have), inviting me back to Phoenix to accept a good position.[3] Unfortunately, perhaps for me, I did not return to the West.

———•·•———

Our Poor Illiterates
January 23, 1935

In the last report issued from Montgomery on the subject of illiteracy, I was pained to note the appalling fact that approximately one out of every five persons (pity them!) between the ages of seven and twenty in Marshall County can neither read nor write. This is indeed a most shameful state of affairs, and

---

3. Actually, Hunt died on Christmas Eve. Berman.

one does not like to believe it of one's own country. But nevertheless, it's the stark truth, disgraceful though it be.

Of the some forty-eight states that comprise our great national common-wealth, Alabama (and I say it with shame) is right down near the bottom in edu-cational matters. Indeed, when compared with the great progressive states like Mass., N.Y., Wis., Calif., and others, it would seem that our beloved Alabama is rather more barbaric than civilized. Why even South Africa (and this is actually true) has a better record in this respect than does our Alabama! What with our racial heritage, our background and the good quality of our blood, the native intelligence of the (white) Alabamian is inferior to none in the world. And yet one among every five of us must remain steeped in the most abysmal ignorance for the mere lack of elemental instruction!

Whose is the fault? I do not pretend to know. But it would seem that some of the blame should be laid at the doors of our wealthier families, who own and exploit the resources of our state without, I fear, giving due consideration to the welfare and mental conditions of the disinherited. These wealthy individuals should know (but they are either too avaricious and greedy to care, or are too short-sighted and unimaginative to consider the future)—as I say, our ruling families—and, say what we will, wealth rules in Alabama as elsewhere—our ruling families ought to have the gumption to know that it is just such poor unlettered creatures as these that become the unwitting tools of dangerous and foolish demagogues and political spellbinders of the Huey Long stamp.[4] They (our wealthy citizens) should consider the fate of czaristic Russia. When the poor, harried, half-famished and illiterate peasantry, led on and incited by the inflaming oratory of a Lenin or a Trotsky—when finally, they turned in sheer desperation up on their ruthless exploiters, their wrath has no parallel in all history. Seventeen thousand of the ruling class were butchered in one day! And when the great lords and grand dames would cry out for mercy they were answered with bullets and bayonets. " 'Mine is the vengeance,' saith the Lord." And we are told He works in mysterious ways His wonders to perform.

"The Man with the Hoe," whose dark, brooding soul the great French painter, Millet, so masterfully pictured upon his famous canvas that it inspired my old friend Edwin Markham to express in a powerful poem of the same title something of the awful destiny of the race, when the man with the hoe and

---

4. Huey "Kingfish" Long (1893–1935) had a colorful history as governor of Louisiana and later U.S. Senator. He had presidential ambitions which were thwarted by an assassin's bullet. See, William Ivy Hair, *The Kingfish and His Realm: The Life and Times of Huey P. Long* (Baton Rouge: Louisiana State University Press, 1991).

his lowly toiling brothers shall have inherited the earth[5]. They who have the gift of interpreting the signs of the times might see in the great changes taking place throughout the world today the beginning of the fulfillment of that mighty prophecy in which it was foreseen that the lowly would one day inherit the earth.

Speaking of Edwin Markham, America's beloved and famous poet, who is now in his 83rd year, I had the pleasure recently of introducing him, by letter, to the Hon. John A. Lusk, of Guntersville, himself a distinguished and lovable personality.[6] Indeed, if we had more families like the Lusks, the Burkes, the Hortons, and my dear old schoolmaster J.O. ("Uncle Ollie") Johnston of Union Grove, who has devoted more than a quarter of a century of his honorable and useful life to the schoolroom—if we had more of these notable people who devote their time and energy without reserve in trying to extend a hand to our deserving fellows, then our record would not be quite so black.[7]

But let us return to our poor illiterates. (God knows, it's time we did!) I do not know what Marshall County is going to do about it, or for that matter just what can effectively be done to mitigate the awful pall of darkness that enshrouds too, too many of our fellow 'Bamians. To admit a few friendly rays of light into these unillumined souls is the noblest act that man can perform for man. They look upon us and our mysterious education as being their natural enemies in the fierce struggles for existence, the ceaseless and often cruel battles for life. Of course, I do not live in Marshall County, unhappily for me, as fate has decreed that I should wander far afield. I am only a poor poet who is struggling for an existence and a chance to write in a big, unfriendly city among strangers and in broken health. But I am doing the best I can (I do not mean to say this boastfully or egotistically) with my feeble light to make the path perhaps just a little lighter for those whose light is yet more feeble (pity the

---

5. Jean-François Millet (1814–1875) was a famous French artist. See, Julia Mary Cartwright Ady, *Jean François Millet, His Life and Letters* (London: Swan Sonnenschein & Co., 1902).

6. In 1895, John Alexander Lusk (1859–1939) constructed a brick building to house his law office. He gained a reputation as a solicitor and outstanding lawyer. Today, the family law firm still exists at Lusk & Lusk and is the oldest professional building in the city. Smith, 48.

7. J.O. "Ollie" Johnston (1871–1943) taught at Union Grove School, acted as a Justice of the Peace, and served as a Baptist minister. Janet Calhoun ed., *Trails & Traces, People & Places* (Albertville, AL: Creative Printers, 1994), 320; and Alabama, Deaths and Burials Index, 1881–1974. Attorney James Lindsay Burke (1850–1914) worked in publishing the *Marshall Tribune* and partnered in a steamboat business. Burke was elected 14 times as mayor of Guntersville. His son Yancey Burke became a long-time editor of a local newspaper. Smith, 46; and U.S., Find a Grave, 1600s-Current. In 1912, Oscar Horton (1886–1964) was appointed principal for the newly constructed Marshall County High School in Guntersville. In 1922, he was voted mayor but resigned to accept a position as county tax assessor; he was elected probate judge in 1928. Katherine Duncan and Larry Smith, *The History of Marshall County* (Albertville, AL: Thompson Printing Co., 1969), 147; Smith, 76, 70, 103–104; and U.S., Find a Grave Index, 1600s-Current.

thought!) than my own. If I had the money to spare, I would gladly take it out of my pocket and hire a teacher (and thereby give employment to at least one of the them) to go to as many of these poor illiterates as possible, and try to teach them the ancient art of conveying intelligence by the use of symbols—that is, to read and write. And furthermore, if I lived in Marshall County, I would do this personally, even if I had to labor in the fields all day for a livelihood, for those in my community who should need it. It should not be looked upon as merely performing a good deed for one of our fellow passengers on this great whirling globe; for it is in truth nothing more than our rightful duty to pass the sacred (yes, that is the word: sacred) torch of knowledge on to those who are laden and stumbling along the way. Tomorrow they may be our buddies in the trench somewhere. And how could we depend upon them to read or write the all-important message upon which our very lives might depend?

I shall recur to this timely and very important subject again in another article later on. Meanwhile what are you going to do—you who read these lines? What are you going to do for them who cannot read these lines?

———•—•——

Good Literature
January 30, 1935

While I did not write much this week—only about six thousand words on one of my books—I nevertheless more than made up for my lack of creative industry by doing what many people might consider a tremendous amount of reading.

I read again for the first time in a few years several chapters of the historical writings of Herodotus, the ancient Greek historian who, as you perhaps know, is known as "the father of history." And my latest impressions of him only tend to confirm those formed when first I read the chronicles of his Egyptian travels. His seems to be the genius of the raconteur rather than the historian. However, it is always worthwhile, from the writer's viewpoint at least, to study the ancient scholar for his fine classical style. He so palpably strains for effects in his childish exaggerations that his works have long since ceased to be considered reliable chronicles of an ancient world that flourished and faded long before Christ was born.

I also read, besides Herodotus, the "Annuals" of Tacitus, the old Roman historian of the first century A.D. While though Tacitus was obviously a sincere and scholarly historian, he is, to me at least, not nearly so interesting as the more colorful if less reliable old Greek. In fact, if it were not for the importance of his subject-matter, I fear he would be rather too tedious for the modern reader to go.

Next to Tacitus I read the "Satires" of Juvenal, the vitriolic old Roman poet-philosopher, who in my opinion was the greatest Roman of them all, including the courtly urban and erudite Horace (who always took care to be on the side of the emperors!) and that cringing, servile flatterer Martial. It will be recalled that this was the age that witnessed the massacre of the innocents (babies); which Maeterlinck has so powerfully dramatized for us in one of these great books; it was an age that saw emperor after emperor murdered in the most cold-blooded manners—poisoned for place, for profit or for power; it was a quite common practice for wives to poison their husbands, husbands to murder their wives; children to murder their parents, parents to destroy their offspring; crucifixions and diabolical plottings were the order of the day. In an age that was so totally and completely corrupt and profligate; that witnessed the most vile, loathsome and degenerate excesses of which we have any record, it is encouraging and reassuring to find the great satirist Juvenal speaking out with his fine manly independence against the monstrous enormities of the dissolute and debauched high places. What could be more high and noble than the following moral sentiments so powerfully expressed in one of the stinging indictments of the Roman world which the great pagan satirist has left us:

"Be brave, be just; and when your country's laws
Call you to witness in a dubious cause,
Though Phalaris plant his bull before your eye,
And, frowning, dictate to your lips the lie,
Think it a crime no tears can e'er efface
To purchase safety with compliance base;
At honor's cost a feverish span extend,
And sacrifice for life's only end.
Life! 'tis not life: who merits death is dead."

But the most delightful and enjoyable reading (I only read four books this week) was Gamaliel Bradford's "Journal," which is a literary man's diary that covers the years from 1883 to 1932, when that great and beautiful spirit passed on to his reward.[8] Bradford's "Journal" reminds me so much of the "Journal"

---

8. Gamaliel Bradford (1863–1932) was a famous poet and biographer. See, Van Wyck Brooks, ed., *The Journal of Gamaliel Bradford, 1883–1932* (Boston: Houghton Mifflin Co., 1933).

of Amiel, the great Swiss scholar of the last century; than whom none has written more beautifully, more tenderly, or with so profound an understanding of humanity. Amiel's was the most Christ-like of any personality I've encountered in the field of literature. And his "Journal" is one of the most beautiful records of a human soul ever penned by man.

But to return to Gamaliel Bradford. Mr. Bradford, though a New Englander, has written one of the finest, perhaps the finest, portraits of Gen. Robert E. Lee in existence. He has written many such full-length "portraits," as well as literally dozens of sketches of famous literary men and women, of statesmen, soldiers and people of action. Though not so prolific a writer as was Sainte-Beuve, the great French critic and master of portraiture of the nineteenth century, who wrote more than six hundred "portraits" of famous personages—while though not so voluminous as the indefatigable Frenchman, Bradford nevertheless managed to write more than twenty-five books! And when we consider the fact that he was a consummate and painstaking artist in all that he touched, and that he hardly ever knew a well day in his life—when we think of these things, then we feel ashamed of our feeble and futile efforts at literary production, of the meager and slender fruits of our intellectual labors!

Like the great Amiel, Gamaliel Bradford was a fine, noble, sympathetic man—a beautiful soul if ever there was one.

The Man from Alabama
July 17, 1935

The other evening, I went into the Cooper Union library, which is only some three or four blocks from my lodgings, to look up some data on a subject upon which I am doing some writing. Cooper Union, as you may know, is an old New York college which is famous for the noted men (and women) who have lectured there. It was at Cooper Union, by the way, that Abraham Lincoln made his great speech in '61, entitled "Right Makes Might." But to return to our subject.

While scanning through the index-cards for the information which I sought, a distinguished looking elderly gentleman with, among other things, grey hair, a monocle and a slight scholarly stoop, approached me, begged my pardon, and asked if I had not once given a lecture on Keats at a poetry club in Montreal. I admitted that I had. Whereupon he grasped my hand as if I had been a long-lost friend. I mention this inconsequential little incident only because it has a bearing upon our little story. In fact, it was this distinguished-looking person (who "turned out to be" a retired college professor) who introduced me to the man from Alabama.

When the old ex-professor learned that I was a Southerner, and from Alabama, he observed that it was rather co-incidental, his running into me there at that time, for, as he informed me, he had a neighbor, a "most extraordinary person," an artist, who occupied the flat across the hall from where he (the prof.) lived. I expressed a desire to know the man from Alabama; and, to make a long story longer, the professor took me along to his lodgings. He was a most gracious and civil host, and showed me about his unpretentious but comfortable quarters. We scanned, briefly, some of the titles of the few hundred volumes that comprised his library. And while I turned a few pages, at random, of one of his own books, written, I believe, as doctoral thesis—while I thus made a cursory inspection of his intellectual efforts, he busied himself with brewing tea and laying service for the library. I inferred, of course, three on a little reading table in that the extra set-up was for the man from Alabama; and in this my surmise was correct. When the tea and cakes were ready to serve, my host absented himself for a moment, and returned with a tall, dark-complexioned man of perhaps fifty or so, whose dark, luxurious hair, worn unusually long, had begun to assume a tinge of grey about the temples, forming a most striking and becoming frame for his pale, oval-shaped face. With the first glance at the man from Alabama one was struck by an indefinable something in his honest countenance that bespoke strength of character, firmness of purpose. Although his features were pronouncedly rugged, almost Lincolnesque, a closer study of his finely-chiseled face revealed certain very delicate, almost feminine lines, especially about the mouth; which attested the sensitivity and charm, and revealed the artist's soul of the man. And his manners and voice and general deportment were quite in keeping with his aristocratic appearance. His voice was soft and vibrant, and possessed a musical undertone or timbre that suggested rippling brooks and gay, light laughter. But there was a serious, almost sad look in the soft depths of his expressive brown eyes that told one that this man had known suffering, which, in fact was the case; for the bright, livid spots high on his cheeks hinted at the awful malady that shall one day carry him away—tuberculosis.

The man from Alabama—he had left Mobile when quite a young man, to study art abroad, and had like many another wandering 'Bamian, never gone back—he wore an old dark suit that, though much frayed and frazzled about the cuffs, was clean and neatly pressed. His linen was snowy white, though one suspected that the poor chap did his own laundry.

As an artist—and he most assuredly is a great painter, for it isn't just every dauber that is honored by the National Academy—as an artist, the man from Alabama (I shall not mention his name, for he might not forgive me for assuming that liberty, or license)—this great creative artist from Alabama, who is slowly dying in a cheap New York flat for the lack of recognition and the proper care and treatment, which he justly deserves and is certainly entitled to—this great Southern genius is absolutely devoid of the conceit and vanity which one usually associates with artists. Although a very learned, a very accomplished and gifted man, he is honest and candid in his opinions and expressions, and very considerate and respectful, almost to the point of humility, of the opinions and expressions of others. He was kind enough to show me some of his fine paintings—beautiful things conceived by a truly lofty imagination, and executed with masterly skill, consummate art. Looking up on his rare canvases, one was reminded of the famous line in Keats: "A thing of beauty is a joy forever." There was a nameless something, a noble striving, in every one of his paintings which I seemed to perceive in the man's personality. Swift's definition of culture (which was appropriated by Matthew Arnold!) might not be inapplicable in describing some of them—things of "sweetness and light." While I think I love beauty—that is, true beauty, beauty of the spirit—as much as Keats did, I nevertheless am so constituted that whenever I behold an object of surpassing beauty my first reaction is apt to be a pang of regret at the thought of how ephemeral, how transient is its tenure here, how soon to pass away. Nearly always I'm haunted, when contemplating a thing of beauty, by the words of the immortal Lincoln (who was quoting an ancient sage)—"This, too, shall pass away." But let us return to the man from Alabama.

Before you are long in this man's company you begin to feel that you are in the presence of a superior personality; his every gesture and observation suggests this fact; his very gentleness confirms it. He is not a person that clowns and fools nor one empty-pated wise-crackers would obtrude their inane buffooneries upon. Not that he would do or say ought to oppose it; it's just that there is some subtle, indefinable influence, more sensed than felt; some intangible force, a spiritual something about the man that commands respect and admiration. One would as soon think of joking with the Lord as to engage this poet in pointless small-talk and trite commonplaces. I imagine that his noble countenance conceals something of those fine, high qualities which Carlyle read in Tennyson's face—that nautical play of light and shade, of depth and warmth, of feeling and understanding sympathy which animate and beautify the countenance of those rare mortals possessed of that timeless thing we call the spirit.

But alas, the path of the poor creative artist is often beset with pitfalls, lined with thorns, and illuminated only by the unconquerable spirit. Such is the case of this great artist. If I had more money than were necessary to an existence here on this sentient plane, I should derive great pleasure from lending a helping hand to struggling poor geniuses like the man from Alabama.

Better Write than McIntyre
August 7, 1935

Since I have been receiving a few letters recently asking, among other things, if all the wonderful things which Mr. O.O. McIntyre writes in the papers about New York, are true, etc.., act., I trust I shall be forgiven for attempting to answer here collectively the queries propounded individually.[9]

For the benefit of those of you who have not had the advantage of a McIntyre correspondence course in New York-ese, I will tell you, briefly, who the gentleman is, whence he hails, and just what I think of his capacity, or incapacity as an observing journalist. Is that not enough?

O.O. (Oscar Odd) McIntyre comes, as he never tires of telling us in his edifying columns, from a small town in the Middle West—Ohio, I believe. He writes a syndicated column called "New York Day by Day," which is a sort of backstairs gossip, insipient small-talk and exaggerated tittle-tattle. And, incidentally, Mr. McIntyre has been having considerable difficulty of late trying to explain just how it happened that so many of his brilliant quips, sparkling bon mots, tart retorts, witty rejoinders and spicy observations were "lifted," bodily, from a book by another and more gifted, contemporary New York writer, without even so much as mentioning the offended author's name by way of compensation! Now, to the layman—that only tolerates but supports us "professionals"—to the laic, then, this thing of appropriating or annexing the other fellow's sage remarks and using them as one's own, may not seem to be much of a "breach of the amenities" to get hot and bothered about. But to a conscientious writer (and there still are such!) it is just plain thievery, as much, yea, more so than if the offender had made off with so much private or personal property. And especially is it inexcusable and unforgivable in a writer like McIntyre, who is published not only in most all of the big Hearst dailies in

---

9. Oscar Odd McIntyre (1883–1934) had a daily column, "New York Day by Day" which appeared in hundreds of newspapers throughout the country. See, Greg Daugherty, "Odd McIntyre: The Man Who Taught America about New York," *Smithsonian Magazine*, https://www.smithsonianmag.com/history/odd-mcintyre-the-man-who-taught-america-about-new-york-2317241/ (Accessed April 8, 2020).

this country, but in many other publications as well. Of course it is scarcely to be expected that a literary mountebank and stuffed shirt who seeks the applause and panders to the taste of the mob—it is hardly likely that such a purely ambitious hack would be sincere and big enough to acknowledge an indebtedness to a struggling, less fortunate fellow scribe.

I used to get a "kick" when I first came to New York several years ago, out of checking the great McIntyre up on some of the alleged New York wonders and marvels which it is his forte to retail (and wholesale!) with such gusto, albeit feigned naiveté, and always, of course, in the manner (the "inimitable McIntyre technique," don't 'cha know) of the folksy cracker-barrel raconteur. And there are actually times—pity him—when he seems to believe even his own stories!

McIntyre, like many another mediocre Hearst scribblers, was puffed into fame by the late Ray Long, when that enterprising go-getter was occupying the editorial sanctum of the *Cosmopolitan Magazine*, and other Hearst publications. (By the way, Long, once the highest-paid editor in the world, with a reputed salary of $180,000 per year, committed suicide in California the other day on account of financial worries!)[10] But back to our "great" McIntyre.

McIntyre has always impressed me as being a sort of literary imposter with a combination inferiority-exhibition complex. A sure indication that the fellow is a victim of an "inferiority complex" is the rather nauseating fact that he is eternally disporting himself in "reflected glory,"—that is, he always manages, if you will note, to have just been dining or hob-nobbing with some impossibly rich or some hopelessly famous, big-wig before sitting down to "do the daily stint," as he likes to call it. The height of his ambition, according to some of his fellow journalists, is to be the best-dressed man in the world! (exhibition complex?) When I say that he impresses me as being a sort of intellectual charlatan, or interloper, it should not be thought that I mean this as a personal attack upon McIntyre the man, which is most certainly not my intention; but rather as a candid analysis, or critique, of McIntyre the writer. In the words, or the approximate words, for I do not remember the exact quotation, of Shakespeare: "Who filches my purse takes nothing—it is trash; but he that takes my good name takes that which enriches him not, and leaves me poor indeed." And so back to our subject.

McIntyre is never so much himself as when he's being not himself—that is to say, when he's indulging his favorite imposture of make-believing that

---

10. Ray Long (1878–1935) was an American newspaper editor known for serving as editor of *Cosmopolitan* from 1919–1931. See, "Ray Long, Editor, Commits Suicide; Ill and Morose," *Brooklyn Times Union*, July 10, 1935.

he's the flat-footed oaf, the goggle-eyed yokel, the gaping rustic come to town to gawk, to shake the straw out of his hair and disport himself generally like the congenital cut-up that he isn't. In other words, he is simply not real: he is forever playing the stooge, the foil to the personality which he would be but cannot. His intellectual didoes and cavorting buffooneries are but the disgusting grimaces that conceal a literary tragedy. The empty barrel, saith an old proverb, makes the most noise . . .

It were a mere waste of time to discuss McIntyre as a writer were it not for the influence which he, with his astoundingly wide circulation, wields upon thousands of "embryo writers" throughout the land. The number of ambitious young would-be McIntyres who flock to New York annually in the fond hope of crashing the Hearst oligarchy or "journalese" would be truly laughable were it not tragic. He (McIntyre) builds up, with his pretty spider-web of words, a glamorous picture of "little 'ole New York" that is altogether false and misleading—a mere trap in which too, too many young people are ensnared and deluded, often to their ruin. His credo is typically Hearstian: a devout worshipper at the golden alter of success; success, meaning in this instance, of course, the financial variety. And like all intellectual bankrupts, he is bitterly jealous of serious writers of ability. I do not recall a single reference of his to a contemporary writer of genuine ability and talent that wasn't reeking of cheap envy. To paraphrase a current cigarette ad: There isn't a thought in a carload of MyIntyre's "canned" (syndicated) articles. Therefore, I repeat, it's better to write than merely to "McIntyre."

Sunday in Central Park
August 7, 1935

After a week of almost continuous rain and storms it is a genuine pleasure to see fresh and delicious weather again. Nothing is quite so depressing, to me, as dark, rainy weather in a great city. The very faces of the scurrying thousands on their way to and from work seem somehow haggard and grey. And then there are always the unfortunate poor beggars, ragged, bedraggled and miserable creatures, adding a somber tone to the wretched picture, especially in the squalid sections and among the dark, dingy, forbidding haunts of these forlorn and hopeless *lazzari*.

But ah, how different is the day, this lovely jewel of a Sunday here in Central Park! So bright and clear the sky, so serene and peaceful the day; the quietude of the woods broken only by the cheerful twittering of a squirrel, or the liquid sweetness of some airy songster, whose feathered little breast is light with the sheer joy, the thrill and the ecstasy of living. The light, musical laughter of three pretty little golden-haired tots under a big tree nearby is as pleasing as the delightful fragrance of the wild-flowers which is everywhere in the air today. I feel a boundless desire to take these pretty little children in my arms and caress them—loneliness, I guess. Yes: one can be lonely, very lonely, in a great city: Contemplating this happy scene in the lovely pastoral surroundings here in the very midst of a great city, carries me back in memory across the years to those precious childhood days in Alabama. Where, oh, where are those little playmates I knew and loved so well?—"But where are the snows of yesteryear?" Memory, like poetry, hath a bloom which time cannot blight. It is often the only refuge and solace of the lonely and the unhappy—thoughts of happier days gone by.

It was under this very tree that I sat one evening six years ago with my beloved companion and bosom friend, Jose Clemente, a charming young Spanish nobleman, who now, alas, lies in a hillside grave a few miles up the Hudson. Tuberculosis, developed as a consequence of the poison gas which he encountered while defending our flag during the World War, sent the gifted young scholar and poet to an early grave.[11] I often come here with a book of verse, which we used to read and enjoy together, and sit on this bench here under this fine old tree. And there are moments when I fancy that he is near me in spirit—perhaps the wish is father to the thought. But nevertheless, there is something reassuring in the thought. It would seem somehow so cold, so futile and so hopeless, so empty and unpurposeful if there were no existence beyond the grave. If this physical body, this frail and uncertain manifestation of natural law—if this were the only life vouchsafed us poor mortals, what a pitiful, mean, miserable span would be man's tenure among the phenomena of nature! Why, if this were all, we have precious little of which to boast: the parrots, the turtles, the elephants, and perhaps the whales outlive us many times; to say nothing of certain forms of inorganic life like, for instance, the trees; some of which live to be thousands of years old! No, I shall not believe that this sentient creature, man, this marvelous being who epitomizes all there is in organic development; this natural wonder at the apex of the evolution pyramid, who illustrates the very principles of his own existence here,"—I shall not believe that this being, man, who is, of all the forms of life on this planet, the only one endowed with

---

11. The editor was unable to discern the identity of this individual. Whoever this was, he is not to be confused with the famous painter and muralist Jose Clemente Orozco (1883–1949).

the faculty of reason and the concept of justice—I decline to believe that, when man lays down this fleshly body, he shall be no more. But let me not trespass further upon the precincts of the theologian!

As the sun declines behind the tops of the trees to the westward, and the pleasure-weary picnickers gather up their papers, books, baskets and babies preparatory to commencing the homeward trek, I am secretly elated at the thought of having this immediate part of the park all to myself. I like to sit here on the bench in the last minutes of the fading day, and imagine that I'm whatever I'd like to be, and with whomever I should love to be with at this hour. And especially do I like to fancy that I'm sitting here again with my talented young friend, the soldier-poet, lost in the spell of a beautiful poem, enchanted by the soft-cadenced recitations of a resonant, musical voice that has long since quitted these pleasant shades for the deeper shade of the grave. How fitting are the beautiful and moving lines which an ancient poet (Telemachus, the Greek) composed upon receipt of the news of the death of an old friend (Heraclitus, the philosopher):

"I weep as I remember
How often you and I
Have tired the sun with talking
And sent him down the sky."

From a Hospital Window[12]
September 4, 1935

As today is my 17th day in the hospital, and a beautiful Indian-summer Sunday at that, I will make-believe that you are my visitors, and so tell you just all about it.

I was run down by a speeding auto, and pretty badly smashed up: a bruised left side, some fractured ribs, a sprained left wrist, a bruised right arm and shoulder, and the left leg broken just below the knee. I am in a cast, and shall

---

12. On August 28, 1935, the *Guntersville Advertiser* reported the following: "William Nabors, Southern poet and writer, who with Ralph Adimari owned the Columbia Book Service on W. 23rd St., was run down last week by a speeding auto and very badly broken up. He is at St. Vincent's Hospital. The above was clipped from the New York World Telegram's book news column. Mr. Nabors is slowly improving form his injuries and it will be sometime before the casts can be removed." "Wm. Nabors Slowly Improving," *Guntersville Advertiser*, August 28, 1935. Nabors and Adimari opened the bookstore in late 1927. The editor has been unable to discern whether they closed or sold it before this accident. The Columbia Book Service was located at 131 W. 23rd Street in Manhattan. Advertisement, *Brooklyn Daily Eagle*, December 8, 1927; Advertisement, and *Brooklyn Daily Eagle*, December 11, 1927.

have to be for many long weeks. The doctors say my life was saved as though by a miracle: A metal pencil and fountain-pen which I had in my breast-pocket over the heart were broken completely in two on my ribs, so great was the force of the impact. And to make my situation a little more painful, if possible, they took me down to the cast room on my fourth day in the hospital, to put a "circular cast" on my leg, from the toes to the hip. And it was just my luck that a careless intern dropped my leg on the table; you could hear the bone crack clear across the room—and so they had to re-set it again! And that was just about the nearest I've ever come to fainting. I guess. It had already swollen.

But I mustn't talk too much about myself, for there are others here, and some of them very interesting characters, too.

My case, of course, was not an "emergency" one; and I was not made any happier when I awoke on my first morning in the emergency ward to find that I, Wm. Nabors from old Alabama, was lying between two "colored" brothers! But then I derived a little consolation from my plight by reflecting that our Savior, in His hour of agony, found Himself between two thieves.

From my window here on the fourth floor I can look out upon the roofs, the chimney-pots, the radio antennae and the clotheslines of Greenwich Village, with maybe a cozy little pent-house here and there to break the monotony of the dingy roofscape.

Saint Vincent's is, as the name implies, a Catholic institution and one of the world's largest hospitals. My ward is known as the St. Francis Ward; and I rather like that, for I remember having once read a life of St. Francis of Assisi, and I was very much impressed by that good Father's devout faith and martyrdom.

Shall I describe my ward for you?

It is about 30 feet wide by 70 long, with 16 beds in it, spaced at about 4 feet apart. There are 6 large windows on the south side of the ward, facing New York harbor and looking toward Wall Street and Battery Park. There are big, double doors at each end of the ward, one of which communicates with a sort of combination laboratory and medicine-room, and the other leads to an adjoining ward for medical cases. (We are all surgical cases in this ward.) Another big double-door opens out into the hall or corridor; and over this entrance is a legend to the effect that this ward was "furnished" by a Mrs. Joseph somebody, in honor of that worthy's father. While above one of the doors at the end of the ward is a cedar cross, with a likeness of Christ carved in ivory and hanging there-upon. This figure of Christ looks, from my bed, as if it might be the work of some old master. It is perhaps a foot in height; and as a work of art alone would be strangely fascinating.

Last week I composed a little poem in appreciation, to the Catholic Sister here on my floor, who is one of the kindest and most noble-hearted persons I've ever known. She was highly pleased with my little tribute in verse to her, and thought it very remarkable that one could compose a poem while in pain. But I told her that I only tried to express the simple sentiments of my heart. Sister Nielita (for this is her name) has been succoring the distressed, administering to the suffering and the dying for more than forty years.

And here follows the little poem to her:

Dear little Sister,
    so solicitous and kind,
Always so ready
    with hand or with mind

To console the sorrowing
    or encourage the weak;
An Angel of Mercy
    to the ailing and meek.

How oft, as I've lain
    on my pillow at night,
I've traced thy passage,
    like an Angel in flight.

On an errand of mercy
    for some poor soul;
Giving and doing,
    this is your role.

How petty and little
    are the things that we do
Compared, dear Sister,
    with a person like you!

It's Cotton-Pickin' Time at Home
September 18, 1935

In a most interesting and newsy letter from the South today I learned—and oh, how homesick it made me feel!—that the fields down home are white again with cotton. And reflecting upon the incomparable beauty, to one who has so long been away, of a field of newly opened cotton in the early autumn, I fell to thinking of those happy, carefree days at home, when the hand that traces these lines was out with the rising of the sun and busy filling and refilling the long old "pick-sack" with the soft fluffy staple that has often been the only source of livelihood to millions of us poor Southerners. And though the happy faces of many of my fellow pickers have been so dimmed and faded by the passage of time that I can no longer remember their names, I can still see the long white rows stretching out before me as I sit here by this window, an invalid looking out upon a Northern landscape through the deepening shadows of dusk. Yes, I can still see those long white rows, and the fading flowers of the last days of a lingering summer. Nothing can be lovelier than the last blossoms of a fading Southern summer, or than the delicate gaufred edges of the strawberry leaves embroidered with frost, while above them Arachne's delicate webs hang swaying in the green branches of the pines—little ball-rooms for the fairies, carpeted with powdered pearls, and kept in place by a thousand dewy strands, hanging from above like the chains of some magic lamp, and supporting them from below like the anchors of a vessel. Little airy edifices which have all the fantastic lightness of the elf-world, and all the vaporous freshness of dawn. Yes, I can see the old field, the old rail-fence, the little cotton shed under the old 'simmon tree and the whole familiar old scene again in all its humble detail. And what wouldn't I give just to go back there and resume the old pick-sack again, and be surrounded by the cheerful little companions of these twenty-five years gone by! Yes, I would gladly put on the same old pick-sack, even at the expense of reversing the sentiments of a certain little composition written in childhood. And here is the complaint which our poet indicted at the rebellious age of ten, against "pickin' cotton all the day:"

When the frost is on the pumpkins
    and the moonlight floods the hills,
And the world is wrapped in silence
    save the calls of whippoorwills,

It is then I lie a-dreamin' of the places far away,
  where my back would not be achin'
And my heart would not be breakin'
  at the thought of pickin' cotton all the day!

———•◦•———

Mussolini, Man or Devil?
October 16, 1935

Benito Mussolini, the strutting, swaggering, power-drunk tyrant who has Italy under the iron heel, and possibly the lives and fortunes of half of the human race in the grasping palm of his bloody hand—this same Mussolini, a greasy double-crosser who not only betrayed but murdered his own best "friend" in cold blood in order to climb to power; this insatiable monster in human form, this living embodiment of the Evil Power is perfectly willing to drench the earth in blood in order to achieve his pet ambition to become the modern Caesar.

The spark has already been struck that may possibly ignite and consume the whole world.

Defenseless women and children, a harmless primitive people who claim to be the only living descendants of King Solomon—these poor, ignorant, miserable wretches are today being killed and maimed by the thousands by cowardly invaders (for the "wops" are notorious cowards) who rain destruction down upon their defenseless heads from giant bombers miles up in the air. The "dago" flyers are so shockingly brutal that they actually dropped tons of bombs on a big red-cross hospital that was clearly marked by flags and signs, according to reports from the American correspondents in Ethiopia! This inhuman act alone, if it is true, is enough to condemn Mussolini forever in the eyes of all civilized human beings. And this, mind you, by a beat of a hypocrite who has the audacity to pretend to want to "civilize the poor benighted Abyssinians! Indeed, the only difference between Il Duce and Al Capone is that one murderer has a helpless, spineless nation (Italy) under his thumb, while the other cowardly murderer, Capone, was content to display his daring heroics by ordering his villainous henchman (as he actually did in Illinois) to pour gasoline over a helpless young American girl and burn her alive in an automobile, and all this merely because the unfortunate girl happened to be the daughter of a deputy sheriff who was trying to get Capone and his Italian gunmen who were plundering the country, controlling the politicians and waxing rich in our notoriously lax, and shameful Hoover era.

We are told by the Mussolini apologists that Italy is hopelessly over-popu-lated; that she (Italy) was tricked out of her "rightful share" of the spoils of the last war by the Versailles peace maneuvers, and that, in fact, all Mussolini wants (great altruist that he is!) is a chance to "civilize" the poor Ethiopians.

Let's examine some of these claims, or excuses, which our dear apologists put forth in defense of Mussolini's "policy," and see how they stand up.

First: as to Italy's over-population. If dear old sunny Italy is already over-crowded, as the great Musso vociferously claims, why in the name of common sanity is it that Mussolini is giving prizes in the form of money and property to the Italian women who bring the most babies into the world? Does that, by any stretch of the imagination, seem to be a logical or a reasonable or a rational thing to do, this hiring women to have babies (for it amounts to exactly that) when the country is already seething with its surplus millions that can't be fed or housed? Clearly it is not the sane or sensible thing to do under the circumstances.

What, then, is the big idea behind this urging the Italian women to pro-duce more babies? Obviously, war. Cannon-fodder. National expansion, at the expense of weaker nations. And for this delightful (!) process to continue, mind you, the mighty Mussolini should be ruling and dictating the world!

Secondly: As to Mussolini's wanting to "civilize" the Ethiope and "put an end to slavery."

Mussolini's "civilizing" business has been going on in Italy now for more than a decade; and with what results?

With these results, namely: that every Italian writer, poet, artist or profes-sional man with an atom of democracy or culture or decency or self-respect and dignity in his makeup—in short all intellectuals and teachers who refused to bow to Mussolini's fascistic goose-stepping were either exiled or imprisoned—that is except those thousands who fled to France, England and America.

And as to freeing the slaves in Ethiopia—why, the average man in Italy today is worse than a slave! No less than forty percent of everything he earns, if he should have a job, goes toward building up Mussolini's war-machine. And in Italy today no man's time is his own: he goes and comes when and whither he is told to go, as in Soviet Russia.

And as to Italy's being "tricked" in the division of the German colonies after the war—why, did not Italy herself betray Germany and the Central Powers, with which she had an alliance at the outbreak of the World War?

Mussolini is whining about Italy's lack of natural resources as if that could excuse a plundering expedition into a weaker country! So are Norway, Denmark and Sweden deficient in natural resources. But yet these three little countries somehow manage to keep their populations within reasonable bounds, and to buy what they need by the fruits of their thrift and industry. And yet Norway, Sweden and Denmark rank very high among the civilized nations of the earth; with Norway possessing perhaps the most perfect and ideal social system in the world.

Yes, Mussolini's African venture is a land-grabbing scheme of the most brutal and cynical sort. If he were the only lunatic in high place with imperial ambitions the world situation today would not be so grave; for the powerful British Empire could settle his hash quite easily. But unfortunately for the peace of the world, there are other lunatics in high places who fancy that the Finger of Destiny has touched their foreheads. Hitler, for instance, is only awaiting the moment when he can loose his legions of goose-steppers to wreak havoc on Europe. Nobody knows what secret plans and understandings there may be between Hitler and Japan. And it does not require much imagination to foresee the results of a combination like that! Whether we should like it or not, we would have to go to England's assistance in that event, in order to protect ourselves.

This is a truly forbidding thing to contemplate. And may God spare us this horror of horrors!

Our Neglected Poets
November 6, 1935

Edgar Lee Masters, the Midwestern poet and writer who abandoned law for literature, has recently published a biography of the late Vachel Lindsay, one of our beloved but most shamefully neglected poets.[13]

Masters truly observes that Vachel Lindsay was neglected and ignored during those last miserable years that the poet lived in New York, simply because he was a true American who sang and wrote of America, instead of devoting his talent and genius to propagating foreign ideas and propaganda, as so many misguided American poets and writers are doing today.

I shall never forget the night, a few years since, that Edwin Markham, the dean of American letters and our unofficial Poet Laureate, Vachel Lindsay and myself sat in a cheap New York cafeteria till the wee small hours of morning,

---

13. On Masters, see Chapter 1, Footnote 19. On Lindsay, see Chapter 1, Footnote, 20.

while the gifted Lindsay entertained us with his inimitable stories of adventure while tramping it through the mountains of the South and through the West.[14] He used to stop along at the farm-houses and mountain cabins and offer to work a few hours for a meal, or to exchange a poem for a night's lodging. And he was particularly eloquent in his enthusiastic praise of the kindhearted old mountaineers in Tennessee and Kentucky, many of whom begged the migrant minstrel to remain among them.

The road of the modern troubadour, the Knight-errant and wandering singer is certainly not strewn with roses, but rather is lined with thorns—a lonely and uncertain trail that often terminates in the dreary wastes of Potter's Field.

Masters is outspoken in his condemnation of the Philistines in power in America for not making a place for a poet like Lindsay to earn a decent living. At least he could have been given a chair in one of our Universities or Colleges, as Sidney Lanier was in his last struggling years at Baltimore. But the fact that few poets have the patience to waste, as they see it, precious years in the dreadful and tedious process of acquiring a formal education, with its red tape and certifying degrees, this unfortunately makes it often difficult for the self-educated writers—many of whom are among the world's very greatest—to find their rightful places in society as it is constituted today, when money and material possessions take precedence over the intellect and things spiritual.

Anyone with any literary discrimination and appreciation at all who reads Vachel Lindsay, whether his prose or his poetry, will instantly perceive that he was far superior to the average pundit who holds sway in the dismal literary and English departments of our Colleges. They simply have nothing in them, except what has been stuffed there by other drudges like themselves. While a man like Lindsay was spontaneous, original, creative, and withal a most charming and likable human being; as unostentatious and simple as a child, and yet, like all genuine poets, surprisingly subtle at times.

I have not seen Edgar Lee Masters, the brilliant author of the Spoon River Anthology, and writer on Lincoln—I have not seen him since Lindsay's death. He came into my bookshop on Twenty-third Street one morning a few years ago, in search of an illustrated copy of Omar Khayyam's "Rubaiyat." When I asked him what translation of that famous poem he preferred, I was surprised at his ignorance and amused by his cocksure retort that there was "only one

---

14. On Markham, see Chapter 1, Footnote 20.

translation." I knew that he referred to the great and well-known Fitzgerald translation; but when I showed him an earlier, though inferior, translation of the "Rubaiyat," I will never forget the sudden transformation of his features, and the lawyer-like give-and-take with which he, the famous poet and scholar, thereafter deferred to my humble knowledge.

Yes: Masters has written a fine life of the unfortunate Lindsay, and one which every American should read. Masters the lawyer has penned a brilliant, an eloquent defense of a gifted, unaggressive, defenseless and much-abused poet; but it is the noble resentment of Masters, the impassioned poet, that really grips one.

But Edgar Lee Masters has written other fine works, too. I heard his great poem "Beethoven's Ninth Symphony and the King Cobra" recited once by an old bewhiskered poet-seaman while we were cruising leisurely under a big yellow moon off Bahia Honda, after having just escaped a fearfully thrilling typhoon.

Whether it was the John Masefield setting in which the dramatic old salt recited the great poem that inscribed it indelibly in my memory, I do not know; but I do know that I was greatly impressed by it. And months later, when we reached New York, I went to the Public Library to look the poem up, and found that it still retained its peculiar power to grip the imagination. And that, after all, is one of the chief functions of really great poetry—to exalt, to inspire, to lift up and enrich as well as to entertain us.

Wm. Nabors A Hotel Manager
November 20, 1935

There is a certain big hotel just off Fifth Avenue on Thirty-third Street in New York City which your humble correspondent never passes without a blush or shame suffusing his countenance.

A couple of years ago a friend of mine, who was night manager of this celebrated hostelry, asked me if I would hold his position for him while he made a few-months' trip to Europe. My first reaction, of course, was one of surprise and incredulity: I was surprised that he should seriously suggest such a thing to me, who had never worked in a hotel in my life, and knew next to nothing about the management of such complicated institutions as great modern hotels. However, after much flattering reassurance he finally persuaded me into believing that I was eminently qualified to fill just such a responsible position, and so I consented to become the night manager of a big thirteen-story midtown hotel, one block from the towering Empire State Building and two blocks from Mr. J.P. Morgan's great private library and rambling old brownstone mansion.

I arrived on the appointed hour at the big hotel, with my bag and a very knowing air, and you can well imagine my consternation when I suddenly found myself in the bewildering midst of much dashing about of elevator operators, porters, clerks, telegraph operators, waiters, waitresses, telegram boys, messengers and whatnot, and with not the faintest idea of what to do, or even what to say, for my friend was nowhere in sight, and I felt that every eye in that great, confused and terrifying place was focused upon my extremely self-conscience and rapidly wilting person, that everybody could plainly see that I was never hardly in a big hotel before, much less being capable of managing one!

While I stood thus stupidly trying to comprehend the meaning of the busy scene before me, a busybody bell-hop made off with my bag, taking the hesitating stranger to be a new guest. And in my great embarrassment and burning confusion (For my face felt as if it was blistering!) I didn't know whether to grab my bag and make a frantic dash for the big revolving doors, or to approach the great busy desk and timidly ask for "a room," pretending to be a "guest." But at this tragic juncture in my great extremity whom should I spy but my friend, the retiring night manager, coming out of his private office as cool and collected as a cucumber, if cucumbers could be said to be cool and collected.

I instinctively dashed toward him for safety, somewhat as a puppy might dash for his master when he finds that his loud barking has got him into trouble.

My friend obviously discerned my distress in my face, for he immediately led me to a big downy chair, and dispatched one of my tormenters for a glass of water. Of course, he was anxious to know what on earth had happened to so upset me, as we had been talking by phone hardly an hour before. I pretended that I thought I had eaten some poisoned food or something, whereupon he called for a doctor at once! Fortunately for me, the house doctor happened to be busy just then, and in desperation I suggested to my friend that the fresh air of the street (the carbon-monoxide from a million automobiles!) was just the antidote for food-poisoning. And so, the good fellow very obligingly took my arm, and with tender solicitude escorted me out into the "fresh air of the street,"—for he, poor man, had great faith in suggestions.

My friend, who happened to be a great book-worm and a worshipper of writers, remained at the hotel with me for a few nights, showing me around and sort of breaking me in on my new duties. And by the time he sailed on his long-anticipated vacation I was as much at home in the manager's office as if I had been an old hand at the game.

Needless to say, there is no better place for a writer to study character and humanity than a big metropolitan hotel. There you have a cross-section, as it were, of the genus homo sapien. Actors (and actresses), doctors, lawyers, business people, professional folk, big-time gamblers, rich idlers, shady creatures of the night, promoters of every species, agents of companies, corporations and governments, representative specimens of every known form of human activity go to compose the variously composite personality of a great hotel. But the life (of a hotel executive), while perhaps rather trying at times, is certainly interesting, not to say fascinating, and never dull. Next to writing, I think hotel work is the most interesting employment that one could "follow."

The Curse of Drink
November 27, 1935

A minister or a professional moralist would not need to go far in the streets of New York in order to find the requisite materials with which to point their morals or to illustrate their sermons. Nor would a dramatist or a satirist find it difficult to procure the necessary elements, buttressed with cold facts, to create a scorching indictment of our so-called modern civilization.

I was never more struck by the utter incongruity, the callous indifference of New York's civic life than when I stood on a street corner on Fourteenth Street the other day and counted no less than four saloons within two hundred feet of a public school! It was really a painful picture to contemplate. School children were running to and fro up and down the sidewalks, while drunken sots were weaving their erratic and uncertain ways amongst them, cursing at those who were slow to get out of their way! While all the time a policeman stands directing traffic, not a half-block away! It is the sort of scene that one might expect to find in a mad-house. And no doubt it may partly explain the eternal and fearful crime problem that New York has to face.

It is a common sight, since the saloons came back, to see ragged little boys and girls coming out of vile grimy, smoke-filled saloons with their little tin buckets of beer, which their fond parents have sent them to bring!

If you can walk two blocks along the Bowery south of Houston Street without having to step over or go around a drunk sprawled out on the sidewalk, then you will be lucky! And nearly every doorway, especially in the evening when the shops are closed, contains its two or three besotted derelicts, usually too drunk to even get up out of the rain or snow.

The Bowery, like Limehouse Street in London, West Madison St. in Chicago and Howard Street in San Francisco, is the last refuge of those hopeless and useless legions of human drift-wood whom Maxim Gorky has immortalized in his famous book "Creatures That Once Were Men."

If you would like to hear some interesting stories about the tragedies that have been caused by drink, then I suggest that you make the acquaintance and win the confidence of some old-time New York policemen. They can tell you some things—all true stories, too—that would freeze your blood to hear.

A likable old Irish cop told me that he was making his rounds on his beat one night around midnight. He was just passing by a dingy old brick house when a great crashing noise caused him to wheel about in his tracks. And he, though hardened old officer that he was, was shocked to see there in front of him on the sidewalk a smashed coffin, with a dead woman thrown half out of it! Naturally the poor old cop was not quite prepared for a thing of this sort; and so rather than go up into the dark old building alone to investigate, he called the station-house for help. To make a long story short, they found that a bunch of underworld characters had been holding a "wake" over the dead woman, and that, having all got drunk, they proceeded to brain one another with chairs and blackjacks and to cut each other's throats, not even neglecting the poor corpse in the carnage!

One night about five years ago I was coming from the old *New York World* building downtown, where I had been doing some writing. I had just turned off Park Row into China-town, and was swinging along rather briskly when my attention was attracted to a darkened door-way, where a pale-faced lad of perhaps sixteen or so was sitting with his elbow on his knee and his finger pointing at me in a strangely accusing way. I paused and looked at him a bit more closely, and concluded that he was just another dope addict who had been thrown out of some Chinese dive. But the peculiar look in his eyes, and the extreme pallor of his face sort of fascinated me, somewhat as one might be held by the gaze of a serpent. I asked what the trouble was; but, receiving no reply, I walked over and shook him by the shoulder. And you may well imagine my surprise when, as I let go of his shoulder, he toppled over backward, his feet coming up as he fell—for he was already stiff!

I had to walk several blocks before I found a patrolman. And I shall never forget his callous observation when I informed him of what I'd found. "Serves him right!" was his laconic retort. But even the cop was surprised when he saw that the lad had hardly begun to shave.

The youth, so the policeman surmised, had probably been working at a camp job somewhere and had come into the city with his money, which some crook had seen and made his acquaintance, later taking him into some dive and giving him "knock-out" drops in drink. Whatever it was, the lad had died suddenly while still accusing his murderer.

They never found out who he was or where he came from. Perhaps from the Middle West, or maybe from the South somewhere, for he looked like an American.

A Little Hero
December 11, 1935

His name was Joseph Smith, surely a not uncommon cognomen in the more American sections of our great country. But the truly heroic little character who bore that name and who was simply known as "Joe" among the fish-markets and the great produce houses of New York's lower East-side—the manly qualities that distinguished this brave little chap are certainly not as common as the name that identified him.

Little Joe was the victim of a cruel, vicious and wicked society that permits one person (a sort of human swine) to accumulate a fortune of a billion dollars while it forces another, little Joe, to suffer the most awful indignities, the most terrible deprivations and unbearable exposure, which were his sad lot in his brief but tragic sojourn amongst the unfeeling and sordid creatures that inhabit this uncertain old earth.

The big New York newspapers printed the simple story of little Joe's tragedy with the same impersonal and factual disinterestedness with which they might report the doings of a committee or a club.

Little Joe was eight years old. He had been supporting his crippled mother and tiny sister for two years. His father died when he was six; and it became little Joe's duty, as the only remaining able-bodied member of his family (for his little sister was only three)—it became Joe's duty to go out and find food to keep his ailing mother, his infant sister and himself alive. Every morning he would take his little basket and thread his way in and out amongst the great speeding vehicles in the streets and through the milling throngs of pedestrians on their way to work, until he finally came to the great open-air fish markets along the water-front, where his little ill-clad figure became a familiar one amongst the keepers of the fish-stalls and the proprietors of the produce markets, many of whom already knew his name, and the sad story behind his daily trips there. The fish-dealers would throw a few fish-heads, and occasionally a whole fish into his little basket, and the men in the great vegetable marts would give him the leavings from the previous days left-overs, and likewise a kind-hearted old German lady, who ran a little bakery, would give him a stale loaf or two each day. And in this way the poor family was kept going.

It seems that the unfortunate mother was slightly demented, and her exaggerated sense of pride had prevented her from asking the city for help. And so, the responsibility of keeping the miserable household going fell upon little Joe's frail shoulders.

This state of affairs continued for more than two years. Each morning, rain or shine, the ragged, puny little Joe would go forth with his little basket. He never knew what it was to have warm clothes to cover his shivering little frame, or light-hearted little companions to play with him and make his dreary existence a bit more cheerful. He never saw a book, and doubtless never knew what a school was. But he was faithful to his dependent mother and his bright-eyed little sister. He knew, small and ignorant though he was, that but for himself his little family should surely perish in their dark and dismal little flat which, thanks to the conscientious old man who owned the dilapidated old tenement, they were permitted to occupy rent-free.

On account of exposure the thinly clad little Joe fell ill during the extreme cold weather of last winter, when the thermometers were registering temperatures of 12 and 15 degrees below zero, or 45 below the freezing point! He was allowed to remain indoors for a few days; but when he had sufficiently recovered from his illness to crawl out of the heap of old rags which were his bed in the corner, he had to take the empty basket and brave the frigid blasts of the wind and snow-swept streets in search of something to keep body and soul together.

He reached the great long rows of deserted fish-markets along the icy water-front, but on account of the extreme cold weather they were all closed up and abandoned. And so, there was no chance of getting anything there for the hungry mother and little sister who awaited his return. After much (too much!) tramping about in the snow of the sub-zero weather the little fellow managed to get a handful of frozen vegetables and a little bread. But on his way back to the dreary hole which was their home, the poor little lad succumbed to the cold, and fell in the deserted street. When they found him, he was dead. The cold and blue little toes that protruded from his broken shoes would find their way to the fish-markets no more. The faithful little hand that had so long been the mainstay and only hope of the desolate "home" was found frozen to the handle of his little basket. Even the merciful numbness of death, which came to free the noble little spirit from its pathetic struggle, could not make the little fighter take his frozen hand from the handle of the basket which contained the food for his mother and little sister!

It is the likes of little Joe Smith who have been the real heroes of this awful depression. And when I read of our big international bankers and exploiting industrialists squawking about their income losses, I always think of little Joe who wasn't the squawking kind, though he lost his all. And there surely must be a better place somewhere for people like Joe!

Pleasant Memories
February 5, 1936

As we travel down life's uncertain road, what is so pleasant as the memories of those joyous and happy moments of the past, which sometimes come back as if by some divine providence to cheer us along our way?

The memory drapes its magic veil of tenderness over those precious moments, events and scenes which lie like beautiful oases in the desert of the past. And the cherished faces which we are privileged to look upon again through the soft and mellow light of memory are doubly precious for being gone from us. The pleasant smile, the sympathetic and understanding look, the warm and friendly clasp of one over whom the grave may long since have closed are ours still in memory. And how unbearably dreary and empty so much of our existence would often be without the blessing of reminiscence which enables us to escape the drab realities of the present by reverting to the more interesting and ideal points along the wayside behind us!

As I sit here by my lonely little window looking out upon the dismal and chilling scene before me, how utterly forlorn and desolate it all seems! The snow and slush on the streets and sidewalks below make it too dangerous for me to venture out on these miserable old crutches. And I know there will not be a soul come to see me this long, dreary, lonely Christmas Day! And nowhere within the range of my vision is there a single object to cheer or to warm the heart—a picture of more unutterable drabness it would be impossible to imagine! But oh, how different from this is the scene which memory brings back to me from across the years!

One spring about nine years ago Simeon H. Pickering, the well-known American painter, and I decided to go on a tramping trip up through the Adirondack mountains into Canada, and then travel north and east into the beautiful "Evangeline Country" of Nova Scotia, where the artist hoped to capture a few impressions for sketches, while our humble poet perhaps composed a fugitive verse or two.[15]

I shall never forget the grand sunny day that we were hiking leisurely along the north shore of the beautiful St. Lawrence River. The soft, whispering breezes which came up from the river like the sigh of some languorous beauty was redolent of the most fragrant and delightfully indefinable odors; and everywhere the peaceful scene scintillated with the most exquisite and affecting beauty. The tender green of the Thousand Islands lay strung out upon the bosom of the river like a gorgeous necklace of rare emeralds, with here and there a blushing maple to accentuate the vernal beauty of the scene. Our admiring eyes had hardly quitted the beauty of this natural vision when they lit upon another yet more lovely and fair to behold.

As we rounded a little promontory or point in the river, what should we see but a trim little canoe, as light and graceful as a fairy's slipper, come shimmering across the limpid surface of the river and glide to a perfect landing on the pebble-strewn beach almost at our feet! The pilot of the delightful barque was a young lady of decided beauty, with a "spice-of-Amazonian spirit." She was rather slender and very straight, with a jaunty little hat and feather perched a bit coquettishly atop her pretty dark brown head, as if she had been the true descendant of some proud aboriginal princess of these shores. Her complexion was clear; her eyes as blue as the river horizon beyond her, and spanned by sharp, characteristic brows; her mouth small and decisive; the soft curves of her cheeks flushed by a faint ruddiness, like the velvety surface of a half-ripe peach, and her whole cast of features indicative of quick talent and independence.

On the seat in the other end of the canoe reclined a bewitching little dream in a white lace dress, with the indolent composure of a pondlily. This one was fairer than the first, having one of those beautiful English complexions of mingled rose and snow, and a dash of gold-dust in her hair when the sun touched it. Her eyes, however, were dark hazel and full of fire, shaded and intensified by

---

15. On Pickering, see Chapter 1, Footnote 16.

these long, sweeping lashes. Her mouth, ah, how can so poor a poet do justice to that mouth, other than by kissing it! —her mouth was a rosebud, and her chin and throat faultless in the delicious curve of these lines. In a word, she was somewhat of the Venus de Milo type; while her companion was more of a Diana. Both easy to look at, and easier to dream about!

And so, to end our little memory-story, the painter and the poet met and admired the Venus and Diana. And as a memento of so unexpected and happy a meeting, we all carved our names, with the date, on a great spreading old beech-tree, which shall surely never again shelter four young hearts so light and so gay.

O memory! What were life without thee?

Roosevelt or Ruin (Part I)
August 12, 1936

In an article in these columns a few months ago your correspondent prognosticated concerning the vast volumes of hot air, with which the hordes of opportunistic loudspeakers are now endeavoring to inflate the electorate throughout the land. Of course, I did not then foresee the emergence of Lemke's third party to commingle its volumes of agitated vocables with the execrable vituperation, the fisher-wife excoriation which is emitted in great gaseous clouds whenever the shameless Romanish demagogue (Father Coughlin) feels the pain to exorcise himself of the Capitalist devils that fain would devour him alive.[16] (What stomachs they must have!)

Another one of these voluble vultures who exploit the misery and discontent of the disinherited for their own selfish purposes is the Rev. Gerald L.K. Smith of Louisiana.[17] This reverend gentleman has ambitions to take up where the late unlamented Huey Long left off. Huey Long's secretary, one Earle Christenberry, charged in a public speech the other day that this Rev. Mr. Smith

---

16. William Lemke (1878–1950) was a U.S. Representative for North Dakota. In 1936 presidential election, he ran as a third-party candidate on the Union Party ticket. See, Edward Blackorby, *Prairie Rebel: The Public Life of William Lemke* (Lincoln: University of Nebraska Press, 1963). Father Charles Coughlin had his own radio program and frequently criticized President Franklin D. Roosevelt and the New Deal. See, Donald Warren, *Radio Priest: Charles Coughlin, The Father of Hate Radio* (New York: Free Press, 1996).

17. Originally from Wisconsin, Reverend Gerald Lyman Kenneth Smith (1898–1976) worked as an organizer for Huey Long's Share Our Wealth Society. After Long's assassination in 1935, Smith helped form the Union Party with Dr. Francis E. Townsend and Father Charles Coughlin. Smith was known for being incredibly anti-Semitic. See, for example, Glen Jeansonne, *Gerald L.K. Smith: Minister of Hate* (Baton Rouge: Louisiana State University Press, 1997); and "Gerald Lyman Kenneth Smith," *Encyclopedia of Arkansas*, https://encyclopediaofarkansas.net/entries/gerald-lyman-kenneth-smith-1767/ (Accessed April 8, 2020).

was actually receiving no less than six hundred dollars a week for his pious efforts on behalf of the Share-our-Wealth movement. One hundred a day! Not so bad, eh, for a Northern faker who parades himself as a Southern minister, and who would turn the land of the South, which our fathers fought and died for, over to the rank and filth of the Communist party, and the mongrel rabble of carpet-baggers that are misled by them. These are the charlatans, mountebanks, demagogic fakers and political monstrosities that are making the most noise in their several campaigns to defeat Franklin D. Roosevelt, one of the strongest, most courageous and noblest Presidents we've ever had.

Father Coughlin (to revert again to this foreign-born harpy) has already made over a million dollars for himself out of his holy efforts to inflate the currency and flood our country with worthless money! This is the same Judas Iscariot that had unexampled effrontery, the disgustingly low taste to employ the public platform and the radio to vilify and calumniate our great President. Yes, this windy, vulgar Roman priest even stooped to hurl the ugly epithet, "liar," at our President, whose gracious hospitality he had accepted but a few months before at the White House!

Besides these rank opportunists there are others yet more powerful and unscrupulous who are out to defeat the President and the people. William Randolph Hearst, the world's richest man and its biggest publisher, is at present carrying on the most vicious and vitriolic campaigns of his foul career in order to defeat Franklin D. Roosevelt. This same Hearst is now supporting Landon for the presidency, on the flimsy pretext that he (Landon) will save our country from communism.[18] Nothing could be more laughable than the thought of William Randolph Hearst (who cannot even set foot in France today)—nothing, I say, could be funnier than the spectacle of the great fascist Hearst pretending to want to preserve the freedom of our American institutions! Why it's precisely the ruthless land-grabbers and money barons like "imperialist Hearst" that bring about revolutions in countries.

I will tell a little story about this cynical false-prophet Hearst which exemplifies and illustrates the man's character and his unbelievable hypocrisy. For personal reasons Hearst was carrying one of his cowardly campaigns in some of his big New York papers against a certain shop-owner, a small manufacturer who employed girls in his little factory at twelve dollars a week. Mr. Hearst, so

---

18. Alf Landon (1887–1987) served as governor of Kansas from 1933–1937. See, Frederick Palmer, *This Man Landon: The Record and Career of Governor Alfred M. Landon of Kansas* (New York: Dodd, Mead & Co., 1936).

the story goes, ordered his editors to hound this particular shop owner out of business by publicizing the poor wretch as a cruel heartless sweatshop owner who worked his slaves for starvation wages. And here is the gist of the story: The poor shop owner paid his girls twelve dollars for their week's work; while the young woman reporter whom Hearst had assigned to get the story spent almost a week in obtaining the desired information; and as she was only getting space-rates, her week's pay amounted to exactly eight dollars! So, who was the slave-driver—Hearst or the poor man who he ruined?

Roosevelt or Ruin (Part II)
September 9, 1936

In the initial or introductory article of this series of what might be called political articles, I attempted to reveal the mercenary motives that inspire the raucous philippics and poisonous diatribes against President Roosevelt by his picayune and pettifogging critics (priest Coughlin and "Rev." Smith); as well as to ridicule and explode the argumentum and absurdum concerning communism which is being so vociferously spouted forth by the yellow Hearst press in whooping it up for the big oil man Landon. If I may have seemed unduly intemperate in some of my characterizations, it should be remembered that fire sometimes has to be fought with fire.

In this article I shall confine myself to a few pithy remarks from the fiery and colorful old General Hugh S. Johnson concerning President Roosevelt as a statesman and student of foreign affairs.[19]

"For the last twenty years," writes the General, "we have been taken for one almost uninterrupted buggy-ride by the Big Butter and Egg Men. They ballyhooed us into a war, short-changed us in paying for it, panhandled us into financing their recovery from it, used the effects of it to wipe out most of our foreign trade, vamped us into sinking part of our navy and abandoning our defensive ocean outposts, while they kept and expanded theirs; repudiated every agreement to which we were a party, and, as a result of all the foregoing maneuvered us into a forced dollar devaluation which gave them a 40 percent discount below prices to our own people for the purchase of our goods and

---

19. Brigadier General Hugh S. Johnson (1882–1942) was a member of President Roosevelt's Brain Trust and director of the National Recovery Administration. He was also a prolific speech writer and journalist. See, John Kennedy Ohl, *Hugh S. Johnson and the New Deal* (DeKalb: Northern Illinois University Press, 1985).

business and the payment of all debts. It is an unexampled record of the most maladroit conduct of foreign relations in the history of our country."

"But recently," continues the General, "there has been a decided and remarkable improvement. Whatever may be said about some errors in domestic policy, there has been little to criticize in Franklin D. Roosevelt's conduct of America's affairs with all the cockeyed world. Every chancellery in Europe and Asia recognizes this—even if we don't. They know that they are at least up against as good a poker-player as they have in their own backrooms.

There are no more patronizing smiles on the subject of American diplomacy. "Good-time Charley" (the Republican incompetents, he means) "has gone back to Podunk, to be replaced by a hardboiled city representative."

At Peace With the World

"For the first time in many decades," continues the General, "there are no American marines or soldiers occupying foreign territory—except legation guards—and no tense or furtive situations anywhere. Throughout the whole world American relations are on a better basis than before 1914."

"Mr. Roosevelt," observes our General, "has been called a 'Navy' President. He has certainly put the navy in its most efficient condition. He has served notice on the whole world that it is to be second to none. But that does not mean that he has neglected the army. He has done more for it than any President since Wilson."

"Harding, Coolidge, and Hoover," notes the General, "treated the army as a stepchild. The President has strengthened it and straightened out its principal kinks, such as the promotion stagnation. He is equipping it with modern arms. He has increased the West Point output. He knows how to use its officers, both regular and reserve, in CCC and relief work of all kinds. The regular personnel is at its very highest standard during my lifetime, and reserve officers are now something more than civilians who own uniforms. Our Air Service—army, navy, and commercial—leads the world. In a word, this country is more nearly ready for efficient mobilization for defense by land, sea and air than it has ever been. I think it is sufficiently ready to preserve our peace."

Landon Totally Inexperienced

"Under Republican Presidents since Teddy Roosevelt," remarks the General, the policies of diplomacy and defense were just reversed. In both departments we slowly went to seed. All that Mr. Landon has said on the subjects is to point with pride to that dreary record. With civilization in turmoil, and a danger so deadly that it can hardly be exaggerated, there is a major and vital issue here—perhaps the principal issue. How could sanity so much as consider making a virtue out of total inexperience and put it in untrained hands? Nothing less than the destiny of an imperiled world. The reasons advanced are that Landon has balanced a budget—which, as Arthur Krock points out in the *New York Times*, is but a little larger than that of Schenectady, N.Y.—and that he is a plain pleasant, honest, frugal fellow, who is just like his neighbors. As for the former," concludes our analytical writer, "The more we learn about it the less significant it seems. As to the latter (Landon) there are some twenty-five million such men in the United States. If, with this dangerous situation in mind, we are to elect a President on these considerations, why not just draw one out of a hat and be done with it?"

A Great Statesman

I will conclude this article by quoting a few wise words from President Roosevelt's masterful speech delivered recently before an audience of 25,000 cheering people at Chautauqua, N.Y.

"I am not concerned," said the President, "and less cheerful about international world conditions than about our immediate domestic problems."

"The whole world now knows that the United States cherishes no predatory ambitions. We are strong, but less powerful nations know that they need not fear our strength. We seek no conquest. We stand for peace."

"Peace, like charity, begins at home; that is why we have begun at home. But peace in the Western World is not all we seek. It is our hope that knowledge of the practical application of the good neighbor policy in this hemisphere will be borne home to our neighbors across the sea."

"Permanent friendships between nations, as between men, can be sustained only by scrupulous respect for the pledged word."

"We are not isolationists except in so far as we seek to isolate ourselves completely from war."

"I have seen war. I have seen war on land and sea. I have seen blood running from the wounded. I have seen men coughing out their gassed lungs. I have seen the dead in the mud. I have seen cities destroyed. I have seen two hundred limping, exhausted men come out of a line—the survivors of a regiment of one thousand that went forward forty-eight hours before. I have seen children starving. I have seen the agony of mothers and wives. I hate war."

"The effective maintenance of American neutrality depends today, as in the past, on the wisdom and determination of whoever at the moment occupy the offices of President and Secretary of State."

"Industrial and agricultural production for war markets may give immense fortunes to a few men; for the nation as a whole it produces disaster."

"If we must face the choice of profits or peace, the nation will answer—must answer—we choose peace!"

"Let those who wish our friendship look us in the eye and take our hand."

These, surely, are the thoughtful and sincere observations of a great statesman and profound student of foreign affairs, and not merely an uninformed, superficial politician of the Harding-Coolidge-Hoover stamp.

Roosevelt or Ruin (Part III)
September 16, 1936

The Republican editors throughout the land, who are the logical apologists for the big budget and oil man, Landon, are just now strangely silent concerning the much-ballyhooed economy of the Kansas Coolidge.[20] It may be partly because they are sore at Hearst for stealing their show. But one suspects that there are other more cogent and patent reasons dictating this silence that aren't so golden. For instance, let's look at Landon's record of rigid economy, and see what we can find.

We find that the hospitals, insane asylums, orphans' homes and other institutions in Kansas have borne the brunt of Landon's dollar philosophy. Aroused over the unbelievable conditions, the State of Kansas is not preparing to embark on a building and replacement program—the cost of which will be borne by Gov. Landon's successors in office. But in the meantime, thousands of poor folks, insane people and orphans are suffering in great misery because the program has long been delayed.

Jails for the Insane

The deplorable situation was brought to a head this spring when a poor sixty-year-old farmer committed suicide. Like hundreds of other poor unfortunates, he cracked up, lost his mind as a consequence of the awful suffering he had endured during the depression; and they put the poor old fellow in jail!

---

20. On Landon, see Chapter 4, Footnote 18.

It was then revealed that in county after county, insane persons were held in jail because there was no room for them in the State institutions. Five Probate Judges indignantly condemned such shocking and inexcusable conditions. The *Kansas City Star*, a strong supporter of Gov. Landon, printed the following dispatch in one of its columns not long since: "The overcrowded conditions of the State's institutions for the mentally sick were descried by Judge Clyde M. Hudson, of Sedgwick County, as nothing short of barbaric in a letter to the State Board of Administration. Denouncing the practice of holding insane people in common jails, Judge Hudson said, "These persons are not common criminals. They deserve the utmost sympathy and the greatest care, that their minds may be restored to normal. Build more hospitals; enlarge those now in use; do anything to relieve the situation; but in the name of justice and human kindness do not force the pitiable human beings behind prison bars. It is imperative that the State lend assistance."

Judges Going Crazy

Similar statements were made by a number of other judges. The following recent article from the *Wichita* (Kan.) *Eagle* is typical: "Judge A.B. Leigh, of Hutchinson County, says that at present he has several patients who should be in the State Hospital, and he says, "If they don't give us more room soon for our present patients, they will have to build an addition somewhere for Probate judges, for the situation is running us crazy."

It should not be assumed that the people of Kansas are calloused or indifferent to the fate of insane folks, orphans, and the indigent poor. Like other farm-belt states Kansas suffered from twelve long years of depression under Republican rule. With falling revenues over a period of years, it was financially impossible for Kansas to embark on a building program.

Roosevelt Built Hospitals

But Gov. Landon had a chance to build them. New Deal policies revived Kansas and brought revenue flowing into the treasury. A building program was urged upon Gov. Landon, but he preferred to save money instead of human lives. As former Republican Gov. Clyde Reed said, "Alf Landon has been a good Governor; but he has been entirely too economical so far as hospital facilities are concerned."

President Roosevelt on the other hand, being a great statesman and humane man, and not just a money-hungry politician, quickly perceived and apprehended the demoralization which the depression had brought to hospitals, schools, orphan homes, and other institutions. And he accordingly sponsored a building program to relieve those institutions, and at the same time put money in circulation to accelerate recovery.

The School Situation

What has happened to the Kansas public schools and colleges under Landon's rigid economy? Let's see, nearly five-hundred schools were forced to close entirely. School teachers' salaries were sliced to as low as nine dollars a week! And the teachers in the higher institutions of learning in the great Sunkist state of Kansas are today, under tightwad Landon, the lowest paid of any in the entire country. And harken to this: Kansas under Landon has dropped from sixth to fourteenth place in literacy! And though Kansas has taken in from the Federal Government over forty-five million dollars, more than she has paid out, those outrageous conditions are still permitted to exist. Like all patronage-grabbing politicians who try to get their feet in the public trough, this ridiculous Wall Street stooge of a Landon recently sent a personal telegram to Harry L. Hopkins, panhandling him with no less than $150,000 of government money, to be used in rectifying one of his Kansas mistakes! Mr. Hopkins suggested that a State appropriation might be the more proper procedure in the matter.

Alf Landon has the third worst labor record of any governor in the country—being worsted only by the strike-breaking governors of Oklahoma and Indiana. No wonder organized labor will vote to a man for Franklin D. Roosevelt and so should you.

Wm. Nabors

—————•-•-—————

Roosevelt or Ruin (Part IV)
September 23, 1936

Our "economic royalists," as President Roosevelt so aptly termed them— the big industrial plutocrats and money czars who owned most, and plundered all, of our once proud country under the calamitous regimes of Harding-Coolidge-Hoover—these forty thieves in evening clothes are now shouting at us in chorus (some of it pretty coarse indeed!) about President Roosevelt's alleged "radicalism." If our President is such a dangerous radical, why is it that Senator Couzens, of Michigan, a millionaire Republican, has come out openly for Roosevelt?[21] Why is it, if our President is the radical that red-baiting Hearst claims he is—why is it, then, that Herbert S. Hoover, former publisher of the "World's Work," a life-long Republican who was one of the organizers of the United States Chamber of Commerce, is today supporting the candidacy of President Roosevelt? Why is it, if Roosevelt is a "red," that the Socialists and Communists will not support him? The answer is, Roosevelt is not a radical; he is a democratic American of the true Jeffersonian type—a statesman who puts the welfare of the many above the privilege of the few.

They say, those thieves in evening clothes, that the Roosevelt administration is spending so much money (money, you know is their god) that the tax-payers will be bearing the burden for generations to come. Let's examine and analyze some of these expenditures and compare them with those of the preceding Republican regimes.

According to a late book on the subject (Ernest K. Lindley's "Half Way with Roosevelt"), we find that the gross increase of our internal national debt under Hoover from December 1930 to March 1933, was almost five billion dollars. The gross increase under Roosevelt from March 1933 to June 1936 was approximately twelve and a half billion dollars, including the soldiers' bonus. But, deducting recoverable assets and the bonus, which was passed over the President's veto, the increase under the New Deal was but a little over five billion dollars, or about the same as the Hoover debt.

"This is the extent," says Mr. Lindley, "of the back-breaking load which has been imposed on ourselves and our children and grandchildren. It is about the same amount," continues the writer, "that we added to the Federal debt in five months of the World War—and we got nothing in return for our money." (Of course, we got nothing in return for our money: the Morgans, the Du Ponts and the Rockefellers, who are supporting Landon, got it all!)

While the national debt gross total rose a little over twelve and a half billion dollars under Roosevelt, stocks and bonds on the New York Exchange increased more than 43 billion dollars. In other words, the net Federal debt when Mr. Hoover left office was 48 percent of the national income for 1932. While on April 30, 1936, it was only 44 percent of that for 1935. Our national debt of 34 billion dollars in 1936, under Roosevelt, costs the tax-payers less than a debt of 20 billion dollars cost on June 30, 1924, when the country was

---

21. After serving as mayor of Detroit, Republican James J. Couzens (1872–1936) became a U.S. Senator in 1922. See, Harry Barnard, *Independent Man: The Life of Senator James Couzens* (Detroit: Wayne State University Press, 2002).

in the hands of the Coolidges and the Mellons, and nobody was worrying about the national debt!

We're back in the "black"

Now let us see what is and has been going on under the able guidance of President Roosevelt: We find that industrial activity has expanded phenomenally. According to the Federal Reserve's "index of industrial production for July, compiled from actual turnout in 15 or 16 major industries, we note the following significant figures: Based on the average output of the three years 1923–25 as 100, the seasonally adjusted average for July 1936, is placed at 108; in June it was 103. It is the highest percentage computed by the Reserve Board's statisticians for any month since Nov. 1929, and is in sharp contrast to 58 in July 1932, when the low level was reached under do-nothing Hoover.

What else do we find that gives credit to Roosevelt as a great leader? In an impressive list of gains, we find: A 59 percent rise in industrial production; 46 percent in the index of factory employment; 55 percent in factory payrolls. We also note a conversion from a deficit to a profit to the income accounts of corporations. There has been a 70 percent increase in automobile production; a 68 percent gain in steel output; a recovery of over 30 percent in farm prices. All this we find, and much more. The big so-called national magazines, such as the staid old "Saturday Evening Post" (most of the stock of which is owned by Wall St.)—though these publications are, naturally, supporting Mr. Landon, yet under the able stewardship of President Roosevelt their advertisement have increased in many instances more than 100 percent!

Statistics are rather bewildering and boring to some people. So, let's close this article with a few remarks on Mr. Landon

We have seen above that the burden of the public debt today in relation to the national income is actually less than it was in 1933, when Mr. Roosevelt assumed office. Yet the Hon. Moneybags Landon and his supporters would have us believe that our able President is leading us to economic perdition. He (Landon) howls and squawks about taxes; but what taxes would he repeal were he President? The only tax which Landon has said that he would repeal is the tax on the big corporations! Which last year brought in some 600 million dollars to the government, and which is helping to feed and clothe the hungry and destitute in Mr. Landon's impecunious Kansas! Yes, Landon loves the big corporations. And why shouldn't he—he's a big oil operator himself! But this fine gentleman, who now aspires to the highest office in our land, has no use for the poor and distressed, as we've seen in some of the previous articles of this series.

Landon Inconsistent

From the moment that Ogden Mills publicly endorsed Landon, as Gen. Johnson caustically remarked recently, he (Landon) changed from the most rabid of the New Dealers to an individualist with a hide so rugged as to make Hoover's seem the skin you'd love to touch!

Today Landon is against any interference in commodity production. He recently said, "It is clear that limitation is not to provide work." But in 1933 he said, "unrestricted production is economic chaos," and he accordingly endorsed restriction on the part of each farm crop which move to market! Taking his cue from his chief supporter and patron, jingoistic Willie Hearst, Landon today tell us that the "way of our fathers" is "being challenged." Yet only three years ago, this politically-minded gentleman referred scornfully to the "candle-light era," and said: "It is necessary to learn something new; and the only way to do it is by trial and error. We are departing farther and farther from parliamentary government. Democracy is on trial."

Today Landon is against monopolies. In 1933 he said, "The Sherman (anti-monopoly) laws should be repealed!"

Recently, while in the East, Landon took occasion to berate Congress for not fully debating all emergency legislation before accepting the President's "must" legislation. Yet in 1933 we find him saying, "The makers of the Constitution recognized that, in a great emergency, the country could not conduct business with a debating society . . . We have never felt it a confession of weakness in a Democracy to repose in our President the greatest powers of any government head in the world in time of war!"

Just what are the fixed principles and convictions, if any, of this political chameleon, it would be difficult indeed to ascertain from his public utterances. I hardly think that we American people are prepared to accept this critical juncture in our national affairs!

Roosevelt or Ruin (Part V)
September 30, 1936

It is truly gratifying to read the latest report from the Agriculture Department in Washington, election or no election. "U.S. Reports 8-Billion Farm Income in 1935," reads a headline in a big Republican New York paper.

Although the above figure, according to the statistical data which accompanied the encouraging report, is nearly three billion dollars short of the gross farm increase of 1929, it nevertheless represents an actual income of 2% more than for that year. The "real" income being figured by allowing for the difference in the level of prices paid by farmers for commodities purchased for the family's living.

The tabulation was announced after months of intensive work on 78 different crops and 13 livestock products with all the variable factors of prices and supplies. The gross farm income was reckoned as 17% higher than for the year 1934; and 59% higher than for the year 1932, the last (let's hope!) miserable year of the Republican regime, when we are hearing so much about "Prosperity is just around the corner"—"Two chickens in every pot" (for the politicians)—"Two cars in every garage" (for the bankers)—"The full dinner-pail" (yes, with 20 million unemployed workers facing the distressing prospect of having to subsist on public handouts!)

Yet despite the encouraging report of the Agriculture Department concerning the increase in our farm income, we are told by the windy megalomaniac who is running (wild?) for the Vice-Presidency on the Republican ticket, that Roosevelt is retarding prosperity. What was it Hoover said about "grass growing in the streets" if Roosevelt should become President? Yet Mr. Knox's big Chicago newspaper tells the world in banner headlines that "Chicago Leads the World in Recovery!!"[22]

If you'll pardon the pun, I think the old Republican machine has developed some awful Knox. At least it has developed enough Knox that, unless muffled, will prevent their selling it to the not-so-dumb Mr. John Q. Public!

When these fine gentlemen start their little song-and-dance set about Republican prosperity, you and I are immediately reminded of those dark days not so long ago, when hogs fell to two dollars a hundred-weight (1932); when corn dropped down to 12 cents a bushel, and cotton to 4 cents a pound; while mortgages ran as high as (depending on the section of the country) $150 to $200 an acre; when the tens of thousands of farmers were forced to give up their farms altogether, and become tenants or day-laborers. (I saw the once-prosperous farmers of Iowa and Kansas wearing clothing made of flour-sacks, and their sockless feet in shoes that were held together with wire!)

When these fine Wall Street gentlemen start talking their brand of prosperity to us—the Republican brand—you and I recall the terrible days not so long since when more than three hundred thousand homeless children, young boys

22. Newspaperman Frank Knox (1874–1944) ran as Alf Landon's running mate in the 1936 presidential election. He was part owner of the *Chicago Daily News*. Norman Beasley, *Frank Knox, American: A Short Biography* (New York: Doubleday, 1936).

and girls that ranged in age from 9 to 18 years—we saw them, poor, starving, hopeless little creatures, wandering in rags and tatters up and down the highways of the country, and "riding the rails" on freight-trains by the thousands. Their poor parents had "gone into the wall," lost everything, including their God-given right to work for a living (for there was no work to be had), and the awful consequence was, just what I've described above—more than a quarter of a million children wandering homeless and starving through the land. Honest, but poor parents committed suicide by the thousands (twenty thousand in one year!) rather than see their children starve before their helpless eyes.

Thank God for Franklin D. Roosevelt, a noble soul whose philosophy has ever been—human beings above dollars. President Roosevelt ordered CCC and various transient camps established all over the United States, in order, as he said, to see that "no man, woman or child goes hungry in this rich country."

And what do you suppose Mr. Do-Nothing Hoover would have done under similar circumstances? He would have said, "Let them go to the Salvation Army." But if you'd really like to know what Hoover might have said, then read a book called "Herbert Hoover Under Two Flags," and you'll soon find out. You will also discover, if you don't already know it, just how Mr. Do-Nothing Hoover made all his millions. He made some of it working poor Chinese slaves 18 hours a day and paying them 20 cents a day for their back-breaking toil!

Do we, the American people, who have boasted of our freedom and equality for 150 years—do we the free voters of one of the last surviving democracies in the world,—do we want to elect a gang of plutocratic Tories to wield the whip of economic serfdom over us, and mayhaps force us into a bloody revolution that would terminate in Communism, or some other form of "totalitarian" ism, in which all decency and humanity (see Italy and Germany, not to mention Russia!) is subordinated to "expediency"? I don't think so!

If you are willing to break your back producing 4-cent cotton for the Wall Street bankers and speculators who control the Republican Party, that is your business. But I must confess that I wouldn't think very highly of such a business! If you are willing that your wife and children should slave in the fields and factories from morning till night in order that Mr. J. Pickpocket Morgan should have a few more million dollar yachts to cruise around the world in, when the U.S. government gets after him for defrauding the Treasury out of 30 million dollars in taxes (in one year)—if you are such a supine and spineless jellyfish as to let them get away with it, while all you get away with are the callouses you acquire in the process, then you are surely a fit subject for a Hitler or a

Stalin or Mussolini, and by voting for the Republican Tories you are making the first step in that direction! But if, as I know you to be—for I've bent my back over the "pick-sack" in the cotton fields with you—if you are the God-fearing Southerner who loved his family and his country, who respects the rights of his fellow man and scorns to profit at the price of conscience, then you, like your fathers before you, will do your share toward perpetuating the Democracy that came to us, not like Manna fallen from Heaven, but through blood and heroic sacrifice. Then vote for Franklin D. Roosevelt, and you will have made another step in the right direction.

Roosevelt or Ruin (Part VI)
October 7, 1936

I will preface this our sixth article on the Presidential campaign with a few trenchant remarks, pungent observations from a recent interview in New York with Gen. Hugh S. Johnson, one of the most brilliant and devastating wits of our time.[23]

"The Republican platform," said Johnson, "is just a sickly sister of the New Deal. Real Republican progressives like William Allen White made the Republicans keep Hooverism out of the platform.[24] But where are Bill White and all the Republican progressives now? They're in the Landon dog-house, and Herbert Hoover has the key." What does this mean? If Hooverism was the answer to our worst, then Hooverism is the answer they are cooking up for us now. That isn't a guess; that has been the Old Guard belief for 14 years. They (the Old Guards) say that for the Federal government to try to do anything to control economic forces is unconstitutional, immoral and obscene. "Those forces," continued the General, "can throw 13 million people out of jobs, reduce agriculture to medieval peonage, leave 50 million people destitute, let 300 thousand children roam the woods like abandoned gods in a famine in the Dark Ages, wipe out half the wealth and half the income accumulated in America since Christopher Columbus, double the burden of private debt, threaten the dispossession of 5 million homes, wipe out the people's savings of life-times, crowd our streets with bread-lines of thousands of men, women and children

---

23. On Johnson, see Chapter 4, Footnote 19.

24. William Allen White (1868–1944), owner of the *Emporia Gazette* and was known for his passionate editorials. See, Sally Foreman Griffith, *Home Town News: William Allen White and the Emporia Gazette* (New York: Oxford University Press, 1989).

staggering from hunger, fill our public places with unsightly 'Hoovervilles' for miserable sufferers in shacks that would disgrace a hobo or a Hotten-tot, destroy courage and obliterate hope—but the Hoover Old Guard say 'Let it alone'!"

This last sentence—rather a long one, to be sure—contains one of the most scathing indictments of human greed to be found outside of the Bible.

And now, by way of supplementing and substantiating General Johnson's withering indictment, I will here quote a brief passage from one of the recent windy speeches of Col. Knox, the Presidential candidate on the Republican ticket.[25]

Shouts Col. Knox: "Our economic system cures its own diseases, and if left alone it will end a depression. What we need for permanent recovery is for the government to take its hands entirely off business. Give American businessmen assurance that there will be no further violent and unexpected interferences with the vital processes of individual enterprise, and our whole economic life will burst into an activity never known before!"

Pretty awful stuff, isn't it, when we recall how, not so long ago, the high and mighty tycoons of finance and industry, were trembling in their pirates' boots and only too happy to have Mr. Roosevelt come to the rescue of their crumbling enterprises!

Our Rugged Individualists

When the corruption of the Harding administration was succeeded by the stupidity of the Coolidge-Hoover era—when more than 11,000 banks were allowed to topple, bringing appalling losses and ruin to millions of investors; when the R.F.C. was finally set up by Hoover in his pathetic effort to end the depression—yes, Hoover's wonderful idea of ending the depression was to make an immediate loan of some 90 million dollars to the Dawes bank in Chicago! And Uncle Sam is now taking a loss of more than 24 million dollars on that one Hoover effort to "end the depression!" When these vociferous ragged individualists were haunted with the thoughts of becoming ragged individuals, they weren't so violently obstreperous in defense of their exploded philosophy! No: they were as meek and docile as so many little lambs when utter chaos threatened to overwhelm us during those last dark days of the Hoover dynasty.

The essence of the Republican Tory's philosophy has always been: Give industry the freedom to slash prices, cut wages, and sell wherever and however

---

25. On Knox, see Chapter 4, Footnote 22.

it can, and we'll all benefit. This idea, as some editor recently pointed out, has a long and interesting history. Adam Smith (he of "The Wealth of Nations" opus), about the time of our Revolution, formulated his doctrine of free trade and free competition. Expanded by the Manchester (England) school of economic thinking, this doctrine came to be accepted by almost everybody as fundamental—that it was impossible to cheat the iron law of supply and demand in the long run, and simply dangerous and expensive to try.

Yes, industry according to this (the Republican) school of economic and social philosophy, must sell as high and buy as low as it can, including labor costs. If the government, for instance, does anything about minimum wages or child labor, that is contrary to the eternal economic law.

No Such Law

But as a matter of fact, there is no such eternal economic law. There have been other social systems besides capitalism; and some of them have worked better, in some ways, than has capitalism. Long before Christ came to the world with his beautiful and humane religious philosophy of the brotherhood of man, there had been social systems founded upon altruism and selfless service instead of selfishness and private gain.

These two social and economic philosophies are as old as the history of man. One of the first clashes between them in our country was the bitter and violent campaign between Thomas Jefferson and Alexander Hamilton in 1800. Jefferson (who, by the way, though called "atheist," was one of the first men in the world to write the sayings of Jesus, in his famous "Jefferson's Bible")— Jefferson, like our own Roosevelt, stood for the good of the many as opposed to the privilege of the few. And, like Roosevelt, Jefferson was accused by the Liberty League of his day (the Federalists) of being a red—a Jacobin—who was out to subvert and destroy the Constitution! And in the midst of his campaign, the "Baltimore American" of that day (the counterpart of Mr. Hearst's New York American of today!) came out with the report that Jefferson was dead. These Federalists thereupon had three days of rejoicing before it was proved that the great Father of Democracy was very much alive indeed!

Other Great Leaders

We have had other great leaders who fought for the inalienable rights of the people against the depredations of the predatory few. Andrew Jackson was a brilliant example of this school of thought, despite the fact that the "spoils system" has been charged to him by the Republicans. Lincoln was another leader of great vision and spirit. But during the last several years—before the rise of Franklin D. Roosevelt to take his place with Jefferson, Jackson and Lincoln as a great national leader—our two major political parties have admittedly degenerated to an appalling level. Yes, we must confess it—our Democratic leaders have been a pretty mediocre lot for the past couple of generations. But the spirit of the people today is being quickened and aroused by one sent as if by divine decree to vivify and resuscitate a once-noble institution—the Democratic party. And let us—you and I—be thankful for the opportunity to do our little bit in helping a great leader to make this a better world.

Roosevelt or Ruin (Part VII)
October 14, 1936

Seven is considered by some to be a "lucky" number. And so, in concluding this series of articles on the Presidential campaign, let us stop on number seven—and may it bring us luck.

Some few days hence you will have the opportunity to go to the polls and exercise your prerogative as a free-born American citizen in choosing the person whom you would have direct the destiny of your country during the next crucial four years of its history. And the decision you render on that occasion will be a momentous one indeed.

On your decision may hang the fate of civilization as we know it today. In any event, the choice you exercise will have more reaching consequences than you could possibly imagine, though you had the imagination of a Shakespeare. One subject alone will suffice to suggest the importance of your decision at the polls on Nov. 3rd—the subject of foreign or international relations. National isolation as exemplified by the Stimson Doctrine during the Hoover regime might well precipitate us into a universal holocaust that would make the last world war look like the Ethiopian Affair! The so-called "splendid isolation" advocated by the chauvinistic Hearsts and the selfish exploiters who seek to hide their sinister purposes in the folds of the flag—this species of isolation, if pursued to its logical conclusion, can result in but one thing—war.

While on the other hand, the "good neighbor" policy of President Roosevelt makes for peace, prosperity, and international amity. It at least is a move in the right direction; and if pursued by succeeding administrations will go far in dissipating the suspicion and distrust which have been engendered in the hearts of our less powerful neighbors by the asinine blunders of our Hardings-Coolidges-Hoovers.

We—mankind—have reached the stage in our political and social evolution where the old law of the tooth and the claw will no longer suffice as a philosophy by which to live. Many things have brought this about; chiefly among which are the myriad inventions that have accelerated the tempo of life. The speed and facility with which knowledge—once the possession and privilege of the few—can in this marvelous age of scientific wonders be disseminated amongst the masses of mankind—these and other things have brought and are bringing about a change in our concept of, and our attitude toward life.

There are too many instruments of destruction—infernal and diabolical contrivances that we "know not of"—in the hands of ambitious creatures in the world today for any one nation, be it ever so powerful, to court destruction by raising a wall of self-sufficiency around itself.

So, we can see, for instance, nothing further by way of example, how it is decidedly possible that your choice at the polls on November 3rd may spell the difference between Armageddon and Millennium! When we consider, with David, how fearfully and how wonderfully we're made, our responsibility to posterity is surely not a thing to be taken lightly; else why should we have been endowed with a conscience and a knowledge of "right and wrong."

If this may read to you more like a sermon than a political article, then just stop to reflect that both are seriously concerned with and vitally affect the processes of life. And whether you wear the garb of an undertaker or of a clown, you are a part of the long parade down life's eternal road. And as an integral part of this "numerous caravan," we should play our little pieces as well as our feeble lights will permit. And so, to end this little contribution to Mr. Roosevelt's campaign with the words of another William! (Shakespeare): "Unto thine own self be true, and will follow, as the night the day, that thou can'st not then be false to any man." Yes, unto thine own self be true—and vote for Roosevelt!

A Literary Renaissance in the South
November 18, 1936

Mr. William Allen White, the famous Kansas editor, who is himself a literary personage of considerable stature, remarked or, more properly lamented to a group of Boston reporters the other day the sad fact that the Middle West, and especially his section of the country, was not producing any writers or literature to speak of today.[26] Though expressing regrets at the deficiency in this depart-ment of Kansas's cultural progress, Mr. White took occasion to point out, what most of us already know, the intensive literary activity that is going on today in the Deep South. He named some half dozen of our authors who are, compara-tively speaking, new comers to the literary scene—Allen Tate, Mrs. Mitchell (of "Gone With the Wind"), Thomas Wolfe, William Faulkner, Erskine Caldwell, Hamilton Basso, Andrew Lytle, et. al., all of whom are doing outstanding writ-ing today.[27] And Mr. White is quite right. The above-mentioned authors are capable of holding their own in any literary company—that is, any contem-porary group in America or abroad. Of course, there are a few individuals here and there—Shaw, Wells, Yeats, Huxley, Sinclair Lewis, Dreiser, etc.—who have done greater things than perhaps our younger authors have yet achieved; but give them time!

I recall that some philosopher—Kropotkin, I believe—wrote some time ago that our South was the most likely section of the earth to next produce a living, organic, vital culture. He offered many reasons in justification of his prophecy; one of which was that we of the South haven't been totally corrupted and spiritually bankrupt by eternally thinking of nothing but wealth, position, power, and the rest of it, as our materialistic brothers of the North are generally supposed to do. Another reason was, of course, our Southern heritage, both racially and spiritually speaking. Be that as it may, the South is certainly pro-ducing, consistently better-quality literature today than any other section of our country. What a company of literary folk the South can now boast! If we include—and we must, for they're Southern born—such literary stars as Upton Sinclair (this famous socialist author and pamphleteer, who came very nearly being governor of California, was born South of the Mason-Dixon line!) if we consider the penetrating and brilliant critic and agnostic H.L. Mencken—of Maryland, suh!—if we list such justly famous artists as James Branch Cabell,

---

26. On White, see Chapter 4, Footnote 24.

27. Allen Tate (1899–1979) was Poet Laureate from 1943–1944. See, Radcliffe Squires, *Allen Tate: A Literary Biography* (Pegasus, 1971). Thomas Wolfe (1900–1938) gained fame as a novelist with works like *Look Homeward, Angel* (1929) and *Of Time and the River* (1935). See, Elizabeth Nowell, *Thomas Wolfe: A Biography* (Praeger, 1973). Novelist Hamilton Basso (1904–1964) wrote an array of books like *Cinnamon Seed* (1934) and *In Their Own Image* (1935), but is best known for *The View from Pompey's Head* (1954). See, Inez Hollander Lake, *The Road from Pompey's Head: The Life and Works of Hamilton Basso* (Baton Rouge: Louisiana State University Press, 1999). Andrew Lytle (1902–1995) grew up in Tennessee and later, on a farm near Guntersville, Alabama. A member of the Agrarian movement, he opposed modernism. Lytle wrote plays, biographies, novels, and essays. He taught at the University of Florida and at the University of the South. See, Foster Dickson, "Andrew Lytle," *Encyclopedia of Alabama*, http://www.encyclopediaofala-bama.org/article/h-3943 (Accessed April 8, 2020).

and Stark Young—and oh, how many others!—what section can rival us in literary honor?[28] None!

And still the Southern writer is more or less without honor in his own country, so to speak. But it has always been thus. Edgar Allan Poe lamented this peculiar trait in Southern character nearly a century ago. I've often wondered just why it is. It cannot be that we are a mean and miserly-spirited people; for we are certainly known for our "Southern hospitality," our generous impulses, and our noble disregard of the wealth. It is true that we are inclined to be a modest, a shy and retiring lot, unlike (thank heavens!) our Northern sensation mongers. It is also true that we do not read as many books, magazines, and papers as our Northern brothers do. Our poverty, and the limited circles of our culture at present prevent this. Our deplorably high rating in illiteracy also mili-tates against our writers, poets, and novelists receiving the notice which they're justly entitled to from their own people. An ambitious demagogue, like Huey Long or "Reverend Smith," or Gene Talmadge, can command the attention of people who should know better. But when a really outstanding literary artist rises amongst us, he is almost completely ignored, as if there were a conspiracy against real culture extant in our section of the country!

I'll bet that you can count on one hand the number of persons in Marshall County that are familiar with Mr. Andrew Lytle's fine works.[29] And this rising literary star is a product of our own county. He is a thousand times better known in New York, or Boston, or Philadelphia, or in Mr. White's Kansas than he is in Guntersville! And still there is no reason for this—that is, no valid reason. Surely there must be literally scores of school-teachers in Marshall County who like to read and develop their minds, and at least familiarize themselves with what is being done in their own country? Of course, I appreciate the fact that many teachers have little time to devote to much reading outside of their work, and I also realize that many do not have the money with which to purchase the books which they might like to read. But this is beside the point: the point I'm making, or trying to make, is, even those who do not have the leisure and

---

28. Originally from Baltimore, journalist and author Upton Sinclair is known primarily for authoring *The Jungle* (1906), an expose on the meatpacking industry. While a socialist, he ran as a Democrat when he strove to win the 1934 California governor's race. See, Lauren Coodley, *Upton Sinclair: California Socialist, Celebrity Intellectual* (Lincoln: Bison Books, 2013). James Branch Cabell (1879–1958) wrote an array of novels but is best known for his risqué work *Jurgen* (1919). See, Edgar E. MacDonald, *James Branch Cabell and Richmond-In-Virginia* (Jackson: University Press of Mississippi, 1993). Stark Young (1881–1963) was known as a playwright and novelist. See, "Stark Young," *Mississippi Encyclopedia*, https://mississippiencyclo pedia.org/entries/stark-young/ (Accessed April 8, 2020). On Mencken, see Footnote 68.

29. On Lytle, see Chapter 4, Footnote 27.

the funds to acquire a degree of culture are rather apt to spend them in pursuit of—but, oh, what's the use? The South will always be like that!

The Unknown World
December 9, 1936

It's funny how one's taste and interests in literature and life seem to change as the years roll by. I like to flatter myself that my developing new tastes in literature from time to time is a sign of progressive intellectual evolution, if you'll pardon the redundancy.

Of late years, for instance, I seem to be losing some of my youthful love of poetry and romantic fiction, and to have developed or acquired instead an insatiable curiosity concerning such complex and mystifying subjects as psychology and psychic phenomena in general—that is, the study of the mind and human personality.

A most singular and amazing experience which occurred to me some few weeks since has only served to heighten my interest in the human mind and its possibilities both as a passive instrument for unknown external forces to play upon and as a positive internal creative force. Of course, when I say "mind" I do not necessarily mean the brain, but rather the thought-processes that go on in it. And here is the story of my weird experience (ordeal is perhaps a better term!) in clairvoyance or provision, or crypt-aesthesia, or telepathy or whatever it might possibly have been.

I had left my place of abode for a couple of days and gone to help a friend with some writing in another section of the city. About midnight of the second night at his apartment I was awakened from a most terrifying and frightening dream, which had affected me so that a cold sweat had already broken out on my forehead when I awoke.

In the dream—if, indeed, dream it was, for it somehow didn't seem like a dream, it was vividly realistic—I saw a very charming little friend of mine, an elderly lady composer whom I have known for several years—I saw her in the dream chattering like an idiot and coming toward me with positively the most awful, the most hideous face that I have ever seen. Her teeth were gone and her mouth was drawn up under her nose in that peculiar way that we are wont to associate with witches, hags, and suchlike forbidding creatures. Her eyes were supernaturally bright, and one of them was turned in toward the nose and fairly blazed with an insane, unearthly light, which made one quake to behold. Her fingers were gnarled and drawn in knots, as if she were going to clutch or tear something to pieces. Her whole body looked taut and tense with demonical intent, as though she were crouching to leap upon me with some evil purpose. As she cautiously approached me, with the stealth of a cat, I noted that her mouth was dripping with slobber at both corners. Perhaps fortunately for me, at this juncture in the fiendish nightmare I awoke, sprang out of bed and dashed out of the room, a thing I have never done before in my life after waking from a mere nightmare. I rushed into my friend's room, and startled the poor fellow out of both his sleep and his wits. He flashed on the light, and appeared almost as frightened as myself. When he had sufficiently collected himself, however, he exclaimed, "My God! What on earth has happened? You look like a corpse." I sat down upon the side of the bed, and it was some several seconds before I could utter an articulate sound. When the paralyzing effects of the fright had sufficiently subsided to permit speech, I related, incoherently and in gasps, my horrifying experience of the dream. My friend was too much affected and impressed by my looks and the thing I described to laugh at me. He suggested, rather, that I was perhaps nervous from overwork and too much coffee. He poured me out a strong stimulant to soothe my nerves, and we sat for an hour or so discussing the mysteries of the subconscious or dream part of the mind. And, though I'm not usually a coward when awake, I refused to return to that detestable room that night! I felt as if I had been in the presence of some indescribable unearthly influence.

The next day I returned to my own quarters; and the clerk at the desk informed me that a man had been 'phoning me at intervals all night and imploring me to come at once, that my friend, the little lady composer, was seriously ill. It was then mid-afternoon, and I rushed at once to her address. And what I found upon entering my friend's room almost froze my blood: Instead of the charming, smiling, cultured little lady whom I knew so well, a babbling horrible idiot stood facing me near the center of the room—positively the exact replica of the paralyzing picture I had seen in the nightmare—eyes, mouth, hands, all! I called to a Negro maid who was working down the hall. She ran to the door, and upon looking into the room almost fell back in my arms with a "Lawdy! Lawdy!" I then shouted for the landlord, who, knowing of the lady's illness, rushed upstairs and into the room. But by this time, she had fallen to the floor in a convulsive fit. An ambulance was called and she was taken to the psychopathic ward at Bellevue Hospital, where she lay for three days and nights in a profound slumber, from which she could not be aroused. She was some three weeks recovering sufficiently to leave the hospital. All the doctors would say was that it was "some sort of seizure," which was an honest confession of their ignorance; for the medical profession knows as yet very little concerning the workings of the human mind and the mysteries of life.

Since then I have read perhaps a dozen works on psychology, psychic phenomena and kindred subjects. And I was surprised to learn that my strange experience has been paralleled by hundreds of others, some of which are even more remarkable.

Maurice Maeterlinck's great work, "The Silent Guest," is replete with case-histories of such phenomena. So is Dr. Thos. J. Hudson's fine book, "The Law of Psychic Phenomena," as well as Sir Oliver Lodge's "The Unseen World," Camille Flammarion's "The Unknown," and Dr. Frederic Myers's monumental psychical researches called "Human Personality."

If you can explain how I saw with what some call the "subliminal" mind, my little friend some fifteen hours before the event occurred, then you know more than any living scientist knows today! It is perhaps possible that there is no such thing as "time" as we know it today? I do not pretend to know. However, it might be interesting to note here that a group of distinguished scientists at Duke University are now carrying on extensive research into this little-known field; and some of their results are amazing indeed—but entirely unexplainable!

Regarding Success
February 17, 1937

The Biblical injunction, "Thou shalt earn thy bread by the sweat of thy brow" seems to have but few adherents in these hectic days of fast travel, fast, loose, and high living.

The chief ambition, the main objective and goal of nine out of every ten youngsters ground out by our hundreds of so-called "educational" mills today is to become a number (more often a mere cipher), a cog in the wheel of High Finance, a white-collar nonentity to be cooped up at starvation wages in dirty, ill-smelling, over-crowded, health-destroying cities.

It seems to be the burning, the all-consuming dream of most of our ambitious boys and girls today to desert the old homestead as soon as they become old enough (one would think!) to know better, and to head for the great teeming human bee-hives, and there to be at the beck-and-call, at the mercy of every whim and caprice of heartless exploiters, cold-blooded employers, many of whom can hardly speak a word of our language, and who care nothing for our American backgrounds, our standards of living or anything else about our country, except how to gouge and thieve and sweat money out of it.

Hundreds of thousands of intelligent American boys and girls flock into the great industrial centers annually, hoping to find the rainbow of "success" at the foot of the skyscraper. And how often the eagerly-sought rainbow turns out to be a sad mirage, the Siren's call, a bitter disappointment which not infrequently ends in sin or suicide.

More than a hundred thousand young women, mostly in their teens, are sent home from New York every year by the various welfare, social, and charitable agencies. They are lured here by false and fake advertisements which the six hundred employment agencies (mostly controlled by crooked and unscrupulous foreigners), who seek to draw the innocents into their hellish spiderwebs in order to supply the big industrialists with cheap labor. However, the newspapers throughout the country, and the Federal government itself, have engaged in a campaign of publicity in order to break up this form of racketeering.

How many beautiful girls who came from honest but poor homes in quest of social betterment wind up in cheap, shady dance-halls, taverns, and houses of ill-repute? One meets the pathetic little creatures in nearly every street in the city in which one chances to stroll late at night. Nothing can be sadder to a sensitive or reflective person than to think of all these potential little American mothers being hopelessly wrecked and ruined by the foreign blood-suckers who roll through our streets in their gaudy limousines and their loud, vulgar clothes, each diamond shirt-stud of which was bought with a girl's soul.

Years ago, when I was writing "script" of the movies in California, I wrote a scenario for a movie, based upon the tragedies which I had known of in which young and lovely girls who had come out to Hollywood "to go in the movies," ended their pathetic careers in disgrace or suicide. But not a motion-picture magnate would touch it!

Today Los Angeles is known as a "woman's town," as nearly all the jobs there are held by women. Most all the restaurant work, the dishwashing, and the scrubbing is done today by pathetic little drudges who left, many of them, good homes "to go in the movies." Greedy employers, realizing that the city was full of young women, drawn there by the magic of Hollywood, soon began to slash wages to the starvation level, to discharge their male employees and hire the starving young women to fill their places!

Here in New York nine of every ten young Southerners I meet are either without employment of any kind and at the mercy of charitable institutions, or are slaving at a mere pittance, usually no more than what they could have earned on a farm in the South. And what do they have here to compensate for the absence of friends and loved ones, for the awful loneliness in which they must eat out their hearts? Bitter thoughts, empty pockets, hungry stomachs, insults, sometimes even the prison!

Though I have wandered over a considerable part of the globe, working in dozens of great cities at various occupations; though I have known the romance of mining gold in the deserts and barren mountains of the great Southwest; though I have experienced the thrills of danger in the oil fields from Oklahoma to Mexico; have worked in the lumber camps of the great Northwest; have adventured with fishermen in Alaska; have labored in the harvest fields of the Middle West; have gone to sea as a sailor and hauled bananas aboard in the moonlight of the Tropics; though I have taught English and traveled as a salesman, and tramped it and roughed it; though I am an editor today in my thirties, how gladly I would trade it all for the peace, the happiness and the friends that might have been mine had I stayed on that sunny Southern farm where I have known the only real happiness of my life!

How good it would be to sit down again to the old oil-cloth covered table that groaned under the inviting load of good old Southern-cooked food, to be able to reach out and spear that coveted old drumstick which has been browned in thicken' gravy, and which makes the mouth water after these twenty years! To get out on the hillsides and whoop and holler, and romp and cut up and throw rocks, and hunt rabbits' beds and eat persimmons, and climb the highest tree and go 'possum huntin' with Uncle Ad, who let you tote the lantern and feel important and talk loud and "cuss" if you "stumped" your toe and not tell your ma on you![30]

As I sit here at this desk on the twentieth floor of a New York skyscraper, I can see the moon coming up over Brooklyn Bridge. But it somehow doesn't have the same look it used to have when its silvery beams sparkled on the frosty boughs of the old 'simmon tree down in the pasture yonder, a thousand miles and twenty years ago.

---

30. Adler Hulsey (1886–1970) was the brother of Lucinda Nabors, William's mother. U.S., Find a Grave Index, 1600s-Current; and Nabors Private Collection.

The Human Soul
April 7, 1937

Before assuming to write upon such mooted topic as the soul, perhaps it is best to devote a few speculative words to the definition of this ancient term.

What do we mean when we say "soul?"

Edgar Allan Poe, who was as profound an analyst as he was a critic, and as great a critic as he was a poet, defined art as being nature interpreted through the medium of the soul. But, though an original interpretation of art, it does not tell us what the soul is. Another inspired poet sang: "I am the Captain of my soul," but neglected to tell us what the "I" or the "soul" was. Such metaphorical declarations are apt to conceal more than they reveal.

If we despair of the poets, who are fond of pursuing their Muse on the "winged soul," and refer to the dictionary for a definition, we find: "soul, n. the spiritual and immortal part of man; reason or intellect; conscience."

Thus if Mr. Webster is correct and reason and intellect are the soul, then the soul has already been photographed for us: An English scientist—Dr. E. D. Adrian, Nobel prize winner of the Cambridge Laboratory—recently succeeded in transforming into light rays the electrical impulses of the brain set in motion by thought, and photographed them!

If reason or intellect is the soul, then animals possess souls, for some of them—such as horses, dogs, etc.—possess the faculties of thought, and are capable of reasoning to a surprising degree. Dogs have been known to rescue children from drowning, from burning houses, from the path of speeding trains and autos. And if they didn't reflect or reason upon the situation, why did they risk their own lives in rushing to the rescue?

Modern psychologists (Psychology means science of the mind. The word psyche in Greek means soul. But scientists use it now in referring to the mind, for most scientists today deny the existence of the "soul")—to repeat, most psychologists, pathologists, and physiologists concern themselves only with the mind, which they consider to be a development of the brain, which in turn, with the nervous system, is a part of the body, which is a product of inheritance and environment. In other words, a purely materialistic conception of life. According to this philosophy, the mind grows with infancy, develops with adolescence, matures with maturity, decays with senility and ends with death.

The problem of how things so disparate or different as mind and body can have any relation to each other at all, has been the subject of endless conjecture, theory, and speculation. According to science we may trace the various ramifications of the chains of sensory neurons (nerve cells) from the periphery or terminal extremities (fingers, eyes, etc.) to the sensory centers of the cerebral cortex, and we may understand how these centers became related one to another through the great association areas; we may even suppose that all the pathways by which sense-impressions of "sensations" finally converge to some hypothecated center wherein the complex sensory impulses undergo some form of physiological fusion correlative with the physical (mental) fusion revealed in introspection. But no elaboration of histological or physiological methods will help us to bridge the mysterious gap which separates physico-chemical processes of knowing and feeling and willing; and no refinement of psychological investigation will reveal to us how these conscious states come to have any relations to the actions and reactions which take place between the bodily organism and the outside world.

Yet the common sense of mankind has always held that there is a very close relation between mind and body. It accepts without question the casual nature of the relation. It maintains that states of mind are caused by states of body, and that states of body, especially bodily movements, are caused by the states of mind. Common-sense holds that mind and body interact, one with another, and in all our conduct this is tacitly assumed, else all our laws were founded upon error.

I believe that man has a soul, and that the soul is superior to the mind; that the mind is an instrument of the soul, as the body is of the mind. If you ask me what the soul is, I must decline to attempt a metaphysical definition. But, briefly, I feel that the soul is the sum total, the very quintessence of human personality, the quality of conscience which directs our reactions to external stimuli; it is that which colors our thoughts and approves, or disapproves, of our acts.

I recently attended a lecture by one of the much-prated materialists on the subject of the soul. And I came away a sadder but not, alas, a wiser man. It saddened me to think a fellow mortal, blessed with image (but none of the wisdom) of his Maker, would waste so much time and energy in acquiring a doctorate only in order to shout from a rostrum that he had no soul. It was like that other brilliant light in the old Chinese story who carried water from a great distance in order to prove that he could fill a bottomless tub! This fine exhumed Hume, descanted upon Kant and volunteered with Voltaire to deprive us about all that we have left—our hopes, and in a way that would have pained even Paine! His feeble and second-hand thoughts wriggled and tortured their ways (and the audience) through endless linguistic contortions, to finally thrust forth their little heads from the murky surface of an obviously shallow mind, like so many serpents, only without the serpent's subtlety.

He proved, to his own satisfaction, that we are a sort of forked worm, with no more soul than a frog has feathers. This low-born "lecturer" bristled with cheap jibes and sophistical vulgarisms like a porcupine does of quills. He uhm-ed through one nostril and uh-ed through the other for sixty dreary minutes. He was so inflated with vanity, and the verbosity which expressed it, that one almost expected him to go sailing off in the air like the big air bubble that he was. And one felt at times like applauding him when he said he had no soul. But he was so successful as a mass hypnotist that half of his auditors were asleep within five minutes. However, he twanged his verbose way to the bitter end, and when he finally sank back exhausted (he had exhausted his vocabulary) into the chair, the house echoed to the rafters with thunderous applause, not at what he'd said, but because he had stopped!

Call me a mystic if you wish, and a dreamer, but as I see it all physical life is but the expression of unseen force, of the Eternal Elixir Vitae. We cannot see what turns the earth over in its appointed course through the heavens. But we know his mighty unseen Power which is whirling our great life-globe down its road of destiny at such dazzling speed is the same Power that guides the reins of gravity, and that paints the blush of beauty on the sinless face of the rose. We do not behold the Hand, but only the perfection and the beauties of its handiwork. Our eyes are too worldly, too finite and imperfect to behold the creative hand of Infinite Perfection. It is surely faster than the lightning, brighter than light, mightier than force, older than time, yet younger than tomorrow. It is harder than adamant, and yet softer than the sweetest thoughts.

The hand that weaves the moon beams which played in my sweetheart's hair is the Hand that cups the dark waves of the ocean which took her away from me.

This hand surely never misses what it reaches for. And when it reaches out to lead us across the Dark Valley at the end of life's journey, we can be sure, if our hands are clean enough to grasp That Hand, that it shall not leave us wandering lost and forgotten in the night of eternal oblivion.

A Close Call
May 19, 1937

It has long been a truism that you can't find a policeman in New York after midnight. Where all the cops disappear to in the after-theatre hours is indeed something of a mystery. But it's true that one can walk for blocks even on such busy thoroughfares as Broadway after midnight without encountering a bluecoat.

I have ample reason for lamenting this strange fact. On Monday night, May 10th, I had left the New York Public Library at the closing hour (ten o'clock); and stopped into an automat cafeteria for a late snack and a glance through the morning paper (which, in New York, comes out around nine in the evening) before going "home." After the culinary and journalistic repast, I boarded a downtown Broadway bus, which took me to within a few blocks of my lodgings. While walking along Houston Street, through a district inhabited mostly by Italians, I suddenly realized that I was lying on the sidewalk, and that two dark-looking figures were hitting me in the face and about the head. Though momentarily stunned by the blow that felled me, I was not knocked unconscious, and I knew they were robbing me.

"My God!" I pleaded," don't kill me: the money's in my side coat-pocket." At this one of the thugs jerked my topcoat open, taking every button in that gentle operation, and tore the pocket out of my coat, while the other hoodlum put the finishing touch, the coup de grace to their manly performance by knocking out all the teeth on the left side of my mouth!

When they had extracted my poor wallet (which contained about nine dollars!), they ran in opposite directions. I spit the teeth out—the ones I hadn't swallowed—and pulled myself to my feet, but quickly fell again, for I was too giddy to stand. Strangely enough, I felt no pain in the face, but by this time I felt a stinging sensation on my head, and a ringing in my ears, as though I had been boxed violently over the ears. By this time my eyes were so swollen that I could scarcely see (I was in the middle of a rather dark block), and I felt as if I was going to faint. I called out, for the first time, for help; but my lips were so swollen and the tongue so cut to pieces that I could hardly utter an audible cry. However, someone must have heard me, for a man came from somewhere, and helped me to my feet with a "Good God, man! What's happened?"

As the good Samaritan led me toward the street-lamp at the corner I discovered that I was drenched with blood from head to foot, a most disgusting and unsightly spectacle, which did not ameliorate my misery. A medic at a nearby drugstore patched me up and took me home, and advised me to keep to my bed for a couple of days at least.

All the police could find in the case was a bloody sock with a doorknob tied up in it; which is about the usual old story: "Robbery was the motive." But the thugs are usually several hours ahead of "New York's finest," which perhaps accounts for the two or three murders a day in New York!

Of course, what happened to me is liable to happen to anyone who lives in a large metropolis which is full of American-hating foreigners who would kill us for a dollar.

The last time I was robbed was one night about twelve years ago, when I was returning to the ship on the waterfront at Vancouver, British Columbia. But on that occasion, it was a white man who did it, and he merely covered me with a gun and went through my pockets. He had something of the old Westerner about him, for he handed me back a dollar before leaving me.

One night in San Francisco, in 1923, I was awakened by feeling a hand under my pillow. By the streetlight which came in at the widow I could see a giant Negro standing over me, with a weapon of some sort in his hand. I lay perfectly still until he had left the room through the window. When I got up and turned on the light, I found my trousers missing. I saw them on the fire-escape a couple of flights down. He got nothing but my watch, for I was too wise to the ways of waterfront hotels to carry money into a room—I had left it with the clerk, who gave me a receipt for it. But I shudder to think what might have happened had that burglar thought I was awake!

Being robbed is just another experience—in this instance a rather painful one—to be added to one's repertoire of stories.

Seeing Without Eyes
June 30, 1937

For the past few years, I have immersed myself in the subject of psychic phenomena, studying all the treatises on hypnotism, all the literature on abnormal psychology which I consider of genuine scientific value and worth studying. But perhaps the most interesting, and multiplying, work that I have come across on the subject is a book which was written by the Rev. W.G. Mitchell, of Athens, Ala., in 1876, entitled "The Sleeping Preacher of North Alabama."

In the book Rev. Dr. Mitchell describes, in detail, the remarkable mental feats of one Rev. C. B. Sanders, who lived in the vicinity of Huntsville, Alabama, for many years prior to, and after, the Civil War. This Rev. Sanders (of whom you may have heard) was the unhappy victim of a most baffling affliction, a strange malady which so swelled the poor man's brain that his skull parted on top of his head to the extent that one could almost lay a finger in the fissure. And during these singular attacks (the physicians of the time admitted that they were completely stumped, both as to cause and cure)—during these mystifying strokes or seizures, or whatever it was, the poor man, though suffering horribly, was thrown into a sort of somnambulistic (sleep walking) or clairvoyant state, at which times he was able to "see" things at great distance, sometimes for hundreds of miles away, and could foretell events that were going to happen, even down to the minutest detail.

While possessed by this unknown power Rev. Sanders could tell people where to find lost objects, such as money, keys, etc. On one occasion he told a man where to find a gold coin which had been lost for several years, and after the rains and storms had buried it beneath several inches of mud and sand! He could read the contents of letters before they arrived; and at one time he "saw" an officer of the Confederate Army falling dead, though the officer was several hundred miles away at the time it happened!

Some of the most remarkable and amazing things imaginable were done while under the influence of this rare psychic or spiritual power: The percipient or seer, at such times, could read foreign languages with which he was absolutely unfamiliar when in the normal state of mind. And he astonished his physician by evincing knowledge of medicine and pharmaceutics which only a trained doctor could have known. (The Rev. Sanders was ordinary, a comparatively ignorant country preacher, with but little schooling).

Scientists came from far and near to witness these singular manifestations of occult or unknown power. And the press of that day, even as far away as Cincinnati, carried long stories about it. Another baffling feature of the Sanders case was the fact that the unlettered country preacher could, when in one of his "spells," not only read Latin and foreign languages, but could diagnose medical cases without ever seeing the ailing person. A University president out in California, having heard of the wonderful and apparently miraculous things the poor preacher was doing, wrote the miracle-worker a letter, begging him to tell the educator what was wrong with him as he had been undergoing treatment from the best doctors for years, and grew continually worse. While in one of his "spells," Rev. Sanders told a friend to write the great educator and inform him that he had a "stone in his bladder" (this was long before the advent of the X-ray and scientific diagnostics); and it proved to be correct, and the educator was soon a well man!

Another peculiar and inexplicable thing about the "possessed" Sanders was that distance didn't seem to make the slightest difference in his visions. He even once cried out, while under the strange influence, that an awful catastrophe was taking place that very moment on one of the greatest planets, millions of miles away! Of course, it may be a hundred years yet before this can be verified; but who knows? It may be true.

It would thus seem, from pondering over these mysterious phenomena, that the human soul possesses some as yet undeveloped faculties which recognize neither time nor space—something genuinely spiritual, perhaps; universal, cosmic, eternal.

The Sanders case has been vouched for by eminent doctors, prominent judges, and well-known ministers who actually witnessed the things that happened.

The South in the Movies
August 4, 1937

That the Southland has contributed more than its share of talent (and pulchritude) to the movies, is adequately confirmed by scanning the biographies of America's leading moving picture "stars."

Recently, while engaged in some research writing for a motion picture publication, I had access to certain secret information and private data to which the general public and the so-called movie magazines are denied. And it was while scanning through some of the biographical sketches of the various movie stars that I first began to appreciate the part which the South plays in this field of entertainment.

Of course, a column-length article is entirely too short to more than touch upon the subject; but here follows some of the facts concerning Southerners of the screen world.

Richard Arlen was born at Charlottesville, Virginia, in 1899. His real name being Richard Van Mattimore.

Madge Bellamy hails from the little town of Hillsboro, Texas, where she was born about 37 years ago.

John Boles, another Texan, was born at Greenville, in 1900. He graduated from the University of Texas as a physician, but the World War cut short his career in the field of medicine.

Olive Borden, though of Irish descent, is a little flower of "Ole Virginie," having been born at Norfolk in 1906.

Evelyn Brent, was born at Tampa, Fla., in 1899. She studied to be a school marm, but Fate evidently decreed otherwise.

Mary Brian— "The sweetest girl in Hollywood"—comes from Corsicana, Texas, where she was ushered into this vale of tears in 1909.

John Mack Brown—the "Dothan Flash"—is, suh, a product of old Alabam, at the seat of learning of which proud state he honored himself, and his state, by a most envious gridiron record. He was born at Dothan in 1904.

Corinne Griffith was born at Texarkana, Texas, in 1897.

William Haines was born at Staunton, Va., in 1900. He comes from an old and prominent Virginia family.

James Hall is from Dallas, Tex., where he was born in 1900. His father was Clinton F. Brown, the famous artist. Young Brown ran away to New York when a mere boy, and was informally adopted by the Halls of theatrical fame.

Leatrice Joy was born of a socially prominent old New Orleans family. She abandoned society for a movie career, and of course became famous.

Arthur Lake was born at Corbin, Ky., in 1905.

Jacqueline Logan first saw the light of day in San Antonio, Texas, where she was born in 1902.

Bessie Love's father was a famous old Texas Ranger. She was born at Midland, Texas, in 1898, and her real name is Juanita Horton.

Sharon Lynn comes from Weatherford, Texas, where she was born about 30 years ago. Ken Maynard, another native of the Lone Star state, was born at Mission, Tex., in 1895.

Thomas Edwin Mix (Tom Mix) was born at El Paso, Texas, in time to serve in the Spanish-American War!

Mary Nolan was born in Louisville, Ky., in 1905.

Joan Crawford (she was christened Lucille LeSueur) was born in San Antonio, Texas, in 1906.

Bebe Daniels was born of a Spanish mother and a Scotch father, at Dallas, Texas, in 1901.

Mary Duncan was born at Luttrellville, Va., in 1905. She is a "college-bred" woman, having studied in Virginia and in New York.

Kay Francis, to whom unlucky numbers mean but little, was born in Oklahoma City, on Friday 13th, in the 13th month of her mother's marriage!

Jobyna Ralston comes from South Pittsburgh, Tennessee.

Dorothy Sebastian was born in Birmingham, Ala., in 1905. She studied dramatics in New York, and finally got a "break" in the movies.

Of course, everyone knows that Miss Tallulah Bankhead is the charming and talented daughter of an Alabama legislator.

Nothing better illustrates the fact that America is a land of opportunity than the biographies of some of the screen's greatest stars. For instance, Douglas Fairbanks (his real name is Rudolph Ullman) once sold papers on the street corners of Denver, Colo., where he was born. He also worked as a waiter in Denver restaurants. He married Mary Pickford—"America's Sweetheart"—who was plain Mary Smith in Canada, where she was born!

Gary Cooper, who is today one of the highest-salaried persons in the movies, had not eaten for three days when he landed his first job in the movies! The same could be said, perhaps, of many others who are too proud now to let the world know it.

There are many other Southerners in the movies; but space does not permit expanding further on the subject.

War by Wm. Nabors
October 6, 1937

Nearby half a million American Legionnaires paraded in one of the largest parades in New York's history the other day. It was estimated that the parade was witnessed by more than two-million people. The big show started about nine in the morning, and was still going strong long past midnight. The contingent marched up the confetti-strewn, flag-bedecked canyon that is Fifth Avenue.

Most of the paraders, now middle-aged citizens of a country at peace with the world, marched up the same old avenue some nineteen years ago as young soldiers just returning home from "over there."

Although pacifism was the burden of their collective public utterances and, no doubt, of their individual private sentiments; though resolutions of neutrality were approved and adopted almost unanimously by the Legion assembled in convention, yet these desiderata, commendable though they may be, may avail us naught, to judge by the portentous signs of the times—What with war raging on two sides of the earth already, and with land-hungry dictators glaring at each other and at the democratic countries which they hate with a fury born of envy and covetousness; with these conditions obtaining it isn't likely that resolutions or anything else will stay the spread of the deadly flame once it is loosed. The dreams of empire that animate Mussolini and Hitler today will probably be the nightmares that will agitate democracies tomorrow. Italy, already inflated with pride and self-importance on account of her quick and easy acquisition of Ethiopia, will not rest content with even that sizeable slice of north Africa to exploit. Japan, in one of the most ferocious and vicious exhibitions of barbarism the world has ever seen, is now in the process of carving out an empire on the Asiatic mainland. And if she is not circumvented in her "scheme of destiny" it may well spell the beginning of the end of Western civilization, as Spengler foresaw in his famous book on the decline of Western civilization.

Germany has not yet made her plunge, for the simple reason that she is not quite ready. But the long-dreaded explosion may come now at any moment. The British statesmen are now trying desperately to keep their balance on a diplomatic tight rope; and with every gust of the political wind their tenure becomes more precarious, their disequilibrium more patent. The United States is the only power that can save the British Empire. And if these two great democracies do not hang together, they may, to use the Marxian phrase, hang separately. Indeed, it is quite possible that we who are now living today may witness the breaking up of the world's greatest empire, the destruction of the earth's most civilizing influence—For the Clique of military dictators who now rule Germany, Japan, Italy, and Russia have nothing but scorn and contempt for the cultural norms and institutions which form the bulwark of free democracies. Force, not reason, is the power by which dictators rule. And in countries where they hold sway the still small voice of reason, the pitiful cries for justice are crushed beneath the iron heel of a relentless despotism.

"Give us guns, not butter!" shouts fanatical little Hitler. For he knows that guns make widows and orphans; guns speak with the voice of death; they despoil mankind of its flower; they depopulate cities and destroy the handiwork of civilized artisans. Allow us to arm today, say the dictators to the world's democracies, and we shall make slaves of you tomorrow; we will deprive you of the freedom to worship according to the dictates of your own conscious, and we will destroy forever your ridiculous concepts of liberty, your puerile notions of freedom. Give us guns, say they, and we'll give you the freedom of the concentration camps; your feeble torch of knowledge will be displaced by the fagot of fanaticism, and the ballot of democracy will give way to the bigot of authoritarianism. All that you cherish and hold dear we condemn and despise. Yours, they shout, is a decadent and outmoded system of society; our is a vigorous, virile organism.

Indeed! So is cancer a virile organism and, like Nazism, fascism, communism, and militarism, unless effectively scotched, will bring about sure and complete destruction.

We Poor Whites
December 1, 1937

Erskine Caldwell, the professional labor faker and anti-Southern ranter who is becoming famous (or is it notorious?) for his infamous libels on the South, has just emerged from another one of his muckraking sallies into the deep South, to rush into print with a book which purports to depict the deplorable conditions under which the persecuted share-cropper is forced to exist today in the South.

Not content with words only, Mr. Caldwell has this time managed to have his text illustrated by pictures of ragged and illiterate starvelings at the mercy of merciless Simon Legrees who, we are informed, sweat every penny out of the poor wretches that it's possible to sweat.

It will be remembered that this Erskine Caldwell is the same unprejudiced (!) uplifter who wrote two or three years since, in Mr. David Stern's Socialistic *New York Evening Post*, that babies in parts of the South are suckled by dogs! (The writer sent the editors of this paper Mr. Caldwell's article about the Southern babies and their dog nurses.)

It is a rather popular past-time with certain rather dull and unimaginative Northern writers to go into "the Bible belt" as they call the South, and snoop around for material with which to buttress their communistic-tracts and propagandistic effusions which pass for novels with the hyphenated American illuminati of the North.

We all know, especially we who have been brought up in the South, that there are more poor people than there are rich people, or even moderately well-off people, in that section. But this is not necessarily the fault of those who happen to be in better circumstances although there are no doubt cases of peonage—people who have become enslaved through debt by systematic robbery on the part of their betters, the landowners and bosses who control the instruments of production. But I suspect that most of us in the South are poor because of the simple fact that there isn't enough wealth to go around, and that those who are long on brains and short on scruples are rather apt to be among the "haves" than the "have-nots." But with human nature being what it is (but few homo sapiens have as yet evolved to the molting stage and become angels!)—mankind being what it is, I know of no practicable way where the goods of this world could be divided to each according to his needs, instead of to each according to his deserts. Even the tight and rigorous doctrine of communism seems to bow to the teachings of old Alma Mammy Nature when it comes to practicing the gentle art of politics. The hardboiled realists in charge of Moscow have no traffic with such ideological tomfoolery as "to each according to his needs." Instead they reward Stakhanoffism and the stretch-out system of production, and thereby differing no whit from Capitalism which they profess to despise![31]

But let me get back to our poor whites and the reason thereof. When I said a little while ago that there wasn't enough wealth to go around and make everybody well-off in the South, I was only repeating a truism. According to Professor Webb of the University of Texas, the North (meaning most of the big New York bankers) owns more than $80 of each $100 in the banks in the country. Furthermore, these same financiers regulate some 90 percent of the national income; they own and control, through interlocking directorates, some 200 large corporations which now produce 95 per cent of the country's advertised consumer goods, as well as controlling 95% of all the country's life insurance; they also hold more than 90 per cent of the country's outstanding corporate securities, as well as pay 80 per cent of the country's income tax, and benefit from 80 percent of all philanthropic gifts!

And yet I wonder if Mr. Caldwell and his ilk who delight to write of the South's "Tobacco Road"—one wonders whether these scribblewits realize that one out of every seven persons in New York is forced to live on charity! In the South, at least the South of 20 years ago, we were taught that any kind of poverty, be it ever so abject, was preferable and more honorable than to accept charity. Yet millions of foreign-born Northerners not only gladly accept charity as a way of life, but even advertise the fact by organizing into clamorous and noisy and shameless "marches" and strikes and public parades and otherwise succeed in making nuisances of themselves.

---

31. The Stakhanovite Movement, named after Ukrainian coal miner Aleksei G. Stakhanov, was a Soviet initiative involving laborers working harder to produce more than necessary. Those who participated received recognition and perhaps higher pay. Serge Schmemann, "In Soviet, Eager Beaver's Legend Works Overtime," *New York Times*, August 31, 1985.

Yes, the South is poor— "poor but proud." And we think it's better to be poor and proud than be poor and without pride. Although it has been truly said that "pride goeth before a fall;" yet the very poor cannot very well fall any lower, economically; and besides pride is so nearly akin to decency that without pride there would be but little decency—though pride of this sort should not be confused with vanity, for the excessively vain are seldom very decent, and always vulgar. And Mr. Erskine Caldwell is excessively vain or nothing or both!

The Home Paper
December 15, 1937

Only those who have been away from home for years on end, so to speak, can really appreciate the home paper and its items of local news. To us whose fate it is to spend our lives away from the place in which we were brought up, and with which we naturally associate the happiest days of our lives; we alone can know the heart-hunger with which every little item and crumb of news or local gossip is devoured. The deaths, births, weddings; the goings and the comings, the doings and the accomplishments of those whom once it was our pleasure to know—these things to us are as food to the hungry, water to the thirsty, love to the affectionate.

We are shocked and grieved when, as in the course of life we sometimes must—when we read of the death of an old friend or an acquaintance of whom we perhaps had not thought of in years. And when we read of such and such young lady or young man being graduated from college, or engaged to be married, or just become a father or a mother, we are also shocked to realize that they, whom we last saw as mere babes, are now grown to maturity. And we can hardly realize that so many years have come and gone since the yesterday we left there!!! We somehow do not seem to realize that they are now men and women whom we saw last as babes twenty years ago! Such thoughts are repugnant to the mind which likes to regain in its memory the images of the past in all their sacred entirety.

We who are living in great teeming metropolises, where thousands upon thousands of new faces impress their images upon our minds daily, and where things happen so fast that amazing events follow, astounding happenings in almost unbroken sequence—the human mind, in trying to adjust itself to such tempo, inevitably loses much of its freshness and its capacity for retaining the memories of faced scenes and events. And this probably is why that most rural folks have "better memories" than city people: they do have so many things to recollect! We have all seen those amazing individuals in country places who could remember even the day of the week that such-and-such thing occurred on twenty-five years ago! But had these same people been transferred to a great city in youth or childhood, it's doubtful whether they'd have the same retentive faculties. Personally, I can hardly remember my own birthday. And to save my life, I couldn't tell you where or with whom I spent Christmas five years ago! Such is the price we pay for being cooped up in a kaleidoscope too long.

But to get back to our home paper. I often wonder why it is that more interesting people don't write for the local paper. For instance, the lady who recently wrote the fine little piece in regarding the "memoirs" of her kitchen garden. Whoever she is, she can write. And it's too bad that persons with such natural talents do not choose to exercise them more, thereby amusing themselves while entertaining us. But I suspect that cacoethes scribendi (the itch to write) is a sort of disease that afflicts only the weak and the feeble-minded, who in turn take it out on the public!

The home paper is not only a faithful chronicle of our desires, aspirations, achievements, pleasures, tragedies, comedies, successes and failures, it is in somewhat a record of our lives here, and often the only testament to our existence. And its (the paper's) files that shall sooner or later become the repository in which shall repose in transcript the remains of many of us who otherwise shall have ceased to be. And, who knows? Perhaps fifty years hence, when some enterprising researcher is perusing this column, he will wonder what matter of person this quaint individual was who signed himself Wm. Nabors!

The Old Covered Bridge
December 22, 1937

It was with a heavy heart that I learned, only recently, the old covered bridge at Nabors Mill had been torn down to make way for a more modern structure.

The old covered bridge was an integral part of the landscape thereabouts when I was a boy. And many are the moonlit nights that we children of the neighborhood played hide-and-seek within its spooky shadows. And how many times did I risk my foolish young neck by diving from its little windows into the shallow old millpond below! And oh, how often have I sat under its friendly protection on rainy days, with my fishin'-pole and the little can of bait by my side! And the little fellows who shared these pleasures with me—where are they?

Some in Texas, some in Oklahoma; others are in California, and perhaps points North and East. Such are the roads of destiny.

It seems somehow such a shame to tear down our old covered bridges. They were not only quaint and picturesque architectural productions, but they were one of the last visible links that connected us with the South of our fathers—the South of romance, of hospitality, and friendly, unhurrying dreamers. I have a "sentimental attachment" for old covered bridges. And if I should ever, by some miracle, become fabulously rich, like Mr. Henry Ford, I think I should buy up all the old covered bridges and put them in a museum!

Travel wherever you will today, you will not likely cross a covered bridge. There are perhaps a scattered few in the mountainous regions of the South and in the remoter sections of New England. (Although I don't recall having crossed a single covered bridge between New York and Montreal the last time I was up there.) I believe there are still a few old covered bridges in the Blue Ridge country of Virginia. At least I recall having crossed one or two down there a few years since. But even they may be no more.

Change, of course, is in the order of Nature; and deplore it how we will, we must bow to the inevitable! The picturesque old wooden structures of the horse-and-buggy period would probably be unsafe today, with our big, heavy machines and their terrific vibrations. Yet, personally, I, for one, prefer the old way, with its leisurely, friendly gait rather than the breathless, maddening tempo of this present dehumanizing machine age. Steel and iron are perhaps safer than wood or bridges; but wood seems somehow warmer, more friendly than steel or iron.

CHAPTER 5

Pensive Essayist, 1938-1941

"It is nothing to die; it is dreadful not to live."
—Jean Valjean in Victor Hugo's *Les Misérables*

Christmas in New York
January 12, 1938

While walking through the fashionable Gramercy Park section of New York City on Christmas Eve, the writer counted no less than 86 Christmas-trees, some of the swankier houses boasting two trees at their front entrance, besides the ones inside! And what a wonderfully pretty, fairyland picture they made, with all their thousands of rainbow lights sparkling and glowing amid the glitter of tinsel and the aromatic greenery of the beautiful little trees.

Gramercy Square is a private little park with pretty artificial fountains and benches and ancient, well-groomed trees and shrubbery, all enclosed within a high iron fence and kept under lock-and-key. Only the privileged families who have keys, and their friends are allowed to enter this park. Of course, the maids, the butlers or the chauffeurs (all in livery) are permitted to walk their masters' dogs within these sacred precincts of an evening. But the ragged little urchins who live in the dark and squalid tenements over on Third Avenue, two blocks away, are not allowed the privilege accorded the rich man's dogs!

I like to stroll through this little paradise of the wealthy during the evenings of Christmas week, for the little trees with their cascades of color are so beautiful to see.

Three or four blocks South of Gramercy Square in Irving Place stands the little old red-brick house in which Washington Irving is said to have lived and wrote some of his works. Across the street, opposite to the historic old landmark, is the great Washington Irving High School, with a huge bronze bust of its famous namesake to inspire the thousands of pupils who enter its enlightened portals.

Every Christmas week I go, if I can, up to the old cemetery at 129th Street and Broadway, to spend a few respectful minutes at the grave of Clement Moore, the beloved children's poet who composed the little classic "'Twas The Night Before Christmas." And, incidentally, not far from the poet's grave is another tomb in which lies the remains of a son of the immortal Charles Dickens. And I regret to say that young Dickens's grave is shamefully neglected. One would think that, in a great city like New York, where there are thousands of well-to-do people who have been entertained and enlightened by the great Dickens, that at least some of them would have the goodness to lay a wreath upon the grave in memory of him who wrote "A Christmas Carol."

As I walked back down Broadway, meditating upon the thoughtlessness and ingratitude of mankind, I was stopped by a poorly-dressed Negro woman, who had a babe in her arms and two frightened little tots clinging to her skirts and crying.

"Mistah, can yo-all tell me where 'at place is whar dey give out dem boxes fo' de po' folkes?" she enquired as she shifted the barefoot baby from one arm to the other, and tried to stop the crying of the two who were tugging at her skirts.

I couldn't help wondering at the contrast the two scenes presented. The one near the old cemetery was a picture of abject misery and sad destitution. Christmas Eve found the pitiful mother with three barefoot and ragged babes, and not a penny in the world or a soul to help her. If only, I thought, one of those bejeweled dowagers in Gramercy Square could be persuaded to donate just one of their dozens of diamonds or rubies or pearls, this poor, harassed, distressed creature could look forward to a shelter and food for herself and babies at Christmas.

What a Christmas! Surely this is not the widowed and the orphaned whose birthday the Christian world professes to celebrate with drinking and dining and merry-making!

The Ghosts of the Ozarks
January 19, 1938

While reading H.G. Wells's eerie, creepy ghost-story of the haunted old rooming-house last evening I was reminded of an experience that befell a fellow traveler and myself while hiking through a desolate and remote part of the Ozark Mountains in northwestern Arkansas, several years ago.

My companion was a young Texan, a barber, who, like myself, was smitten with the wanderlust—the irrepressible desire to know what is on the other side of the hill.

We were two days' journey out of De Queen, and our destination was the Seminole Country in the Indian Territory of Oklahoma, one of the wild and rugged hideouts of the notorious bank and train robbers of the Southwest. We were in a very wild and lonesome section of the mountains, where one walked for miles without seeing any human habitation. And the few log-cabins we did see were occupied by Indians and fierce-looking moonshining mountaineers who were definitely unfriendly to strange wanderers. And it was like taking your life in your hands to pass those inhospitable habitations. From the Indian cabins especially packs of gaunt, howling dogs came tearing at you like so many ferocious wolves. And had it not been for our heavy hickory walking sticks we should certainly have been torn to pieces, for their Indian owners were coldly indifferent to our plight, raising not a voice to deter the vicious animals from their murderous intentions!

We had left the last cabin miles behind us, and the ominous rumblings of an impending storm told us that, lest we quickly reached another house, we were in for a miserable night of it. But fortunately for the forlorn wayfarers, just as nightfall was enshrouding, we saw a long, lean double-jointed scarecrow coming down the mountain road in a calico shirt and pair of pants that, like the darkey's coat, looked as if they'd been cut off three times and were still too short. He hadn't had a shave since the woods burnt, and was carrying a rifle with a barrel so long that he probably saved ammunition by just poking the squirrels out of the trees with it! He had a pair of beady eyes that bored right into your heart and gave us the uncomfortable feeling of being caught in a lie.

When we had satisfied this curious individual as to who we were and where we were heading for, he condescended to tell us how to reach an abandoned old two-story log house that stood about a half-mile from the road. But in a final burst of confidence he warned us that the old house was haunted, and that nobody has dared to live in it since the Whitlow family had all been murdered there in a feud years before. We thanked him most obsequiously, and set off as per directions.

We found the old house just as he'd described it: Two giant cedars almost obscured it from view; its old split-board roof had long since fallen in here and there; two large chimneys supported each end, while a "dog-trot" or "hall" divided it into two box-like compartments.

We chose the end with the soundest roof, and set about finding the requisite pine-knots and wood to furnish the light and heat for an otherwise cheerless night. A plentiful supply of fuel was soon had from the hillside above the old spring. And we had scarcely established ourselves in our dilapidated refuge when the storm broke upon us with a fury as of vengeance. With a bright fire roaring in the huge old fireplace and a dark storm roaring without, we sat upon the floor and devoured our last two sandwiches. And with the reception we were getting from the denizens of that God-forsaken region it looked as though that might be our last food for some time to come! When we had finished our cigarettes by way of dessert, we stretched our weary lengths out upon the floor in front of the old fireplace and, with the monotonous patter of rain upon the old room, were soon lulled into sweet repose.

We had hardly slept ten minutes when we were awakened by a noise, as if something was falling on the floor upstairs just over our heads. We both rose to a sitting position simultaneously, and cast questioning looks at each other.

"Did you hear that," whispered the barber, as he grabbed my arm. "Yes, it's the ghosts!" I said derisively, as I threw some fresh pine-knots on the fire and lit a cigarette. But perceiving that my young friend was inclined to be a bit superstitious, I suggested that perhaps a hanging branch of one of the great cedars had been flapping against the roof by the wind. The logic of this explanation, with my pretended indifference, seemed to reassure him, and we were soon dozing off again.

We had scarcely fallen asleep, however, when we were startled by the same, or a similar falling sort of noise upstairs! We both sat up again and both lit cigarettes; perhaps instinctively feeling that Lady Nicotine would help to dissipate our nervousness.

"You know," whispered Tex—for men of the road are usually called by the name of their state— "I don't like that noise—it sounds funny to me."

"Aw, it's nothing!" I scoffed, "unless," I added thoughtfully—"unless it's a trap we've been led into."

"What'cha think we'd better do?" asked the alarmed Tex, as he inched closer to my side and looked anxiously in the direction of the door.

"Stay here!" I said rather emphatically, "for it'd be plain foolish to go out into this storm in these strange mountains in the dead of night."

"Gee, I wish we had a gun," lamented the unhappy tonsorialist.

"Throw some food on the fire!" I commanded in a none-too-gentle tone—for I sensed that Tex was becoming unnerved— "You're acting like a frightened old maid." I chided, as I lighted another cigarette and secretly wished that we were where we weren't.

Perhaps an hour had elapsed from the time of the above pleasant dialogue. The storm had passed on down the mountain and all was quiet as the grave, and just about as cheerful. We each sat smoking and staring into the fire. Neither of us spoke; but both were silently praying for day to come.

"Looks as though your ghosts rode away on the storm, Tex," I laughingly remarked as I stretched myself out for a pretended nap. But as if to mock my words, the whole upstairs above us suddenly came alive, as if many persons were dancing or jumping about over the floor. If Tex had been scared before, it was nothing compared to the hysterical panic or fright that seized him now! His teeth chattered like a race horse on a concrete track, and his eyes were endeavoring to abandon their sockets in a most undignified manner, while every hair on his head was standing up for its rights, or something. And to tell the unflattering truth, old Alabama himself felt just as weak as a New Year's resolution, and about as happy as a one-legged man at a kicking match!

"Oh, Lordy! Lordy! What'll we do," cried poor Tex, grabbing my arm as if it were the one straw in his ocean of despair.

"Get your walking-stick! Come with me!" I commanded as I grabbed a blazing pine-knot from the fire and started for the rotten old stairway.

"Good God! You-you ain't agoin' up there, are you?" he pleaded, as he pointed up to the source of his awful agony.

"All right-stay here," I sneered, as I started with the club and torch for the stairs.

The suggested alternative was altogether unacceptable; and poor Tex clung to my coat-tail like a Negro at a baptizing. When, by careful maneuvering, we had negotiated the old unreliable stairs and gained the landing above, all was still and quiet as the tomb. I held the bambeau [*sic*] above my head and peered through the almost impenetrable mass of cobwebs which suspended from the old rafters into the dark blackness of the room. Not a thing to be seen.

But as I turned to peer into the other end of the old house the irrepressible Tex let out a yell like a Comanche Indian.

"God a'mighty!" he shrieked somewhat ungrammatically, "A arm is a hittin' at you without no body to it—it just missed your head!"

I could feel my very blood freezing in my veins, for I, too, had glimpsed the thing as it swished like a flash past my head. Almost at the same instance I heard something like a heavy footstep on the floor by my side. Lowering the torch in order to see better to peer into the darkness, I was horrified to see a monstrous reptile coiling its deadly length not three feet from where I stood. And as I leaped back out of its reach, I saw that the floor was literally alive with rattlesnakes!

The heat and smoke from the old fireplace had probably roused the snakes from their places of hibernation about the old chimney, and while crawling about over the old rafters they would fall to the floor. Needless to say, we slept no more that night.

Why He Quit Drinking
February 2, 1938

The following little story was told to the writer by the famous Dan O'Brien, the "King of the hoboes" who, it is claimed, "beat" his way around the world three times, hoboing over every important railway on earth.[1]

As the world-famous hobo modestly observes, the word "king" as used above has no regal significance, for royalty is not recognized in Vagabonia. The title, rather, is synonymous with "Ace," or "No. 1," and was conferred upon him by his migratory admirers, who consider him Patriarch Emeritus of the open road, a tried and true son of the wanderlust.

The silver-haired Dan is now nearing his eightieth year, and is considered to be something of a scholar and philosopher as well as a wanderer and dreamer. He has been the subject of innumerable articles and editorials, and is himself associate editor of that witty little journal, the "Hobo News."[2] Personally, he

---

1. On O'Brien, see Chapter 1, Footnote 1.
2. Ex-hobo Patrick Mulkern started the *Hobo News* at a little place in New York City on West 17th Street in August 1934. Eventually, he moved the operation to 105 West 52nd St. In 1944, he bought a building at 119 West 52nd St. and it became the home of the *Hobo News*. He enlisted hoboes to sell the paper and they did so, nationwide. He also paid hoboes who submitted poems (50 cents), cartoons ($1), or stories ($2–3). By 1945, he paid $2 for poems and $10 for stories. Harry Baronian, who later edited the *Bowery News*, worked for Mulkern as a publishing editor but eventually resigned over a salary dispute. Jack Harris, "An Informal History of the Hobo News," *Collier's*, October 6, 1945. This *Hobo News* is not to be confused with the one that operated out of St. Louis, Missouri.

is a witty, enlightened, sympathetic and charming fellow to know. In him are blended Plato's idealism, Rabelais' humor, and Baron Munchausen's ineffable romancing. The unconquerable Irish courage, the adventurous spirit which successfully carried him through the "school of hard knocks," though now tempered with the mellowness of age, still gives him that indefinable touch of glamour which people associate with adventurous cosmopolitan.

Though I cannot relate this story with the picturesque imagery and gusto with which the colorful old raconteur always embellishes his narrations. I will simply try to give you the essentials of the yarn as retold to me, and depend upon your own imagination to supply the "local color," if any.

A motley assortment of hoboes—those plain and fancy "Knights of the road" whom one can see perching upon the station platforms and atop the piles of railroad ties at most any desert water-tank along the Southern Pacific Railroad west of El Paso—a small group of this picturesque (and picaresque) brotherhood was reclining lazily in the shade of a palm tree in southern Arizona, looking out across the shimmering sands of the desert and swapping tall-tales of the road while waiting for a West-bound freight train.

An ancient derelict was holding forth on the virtues of strong drink, and, if a rubescent nose is any criterion in such matters, he is undoubtedly a connoisseur of what he declaimed, for the bulbous appendage that dominated his countenance was redder than the Russian flag! In fact, his face looked like nothing so much as a hairbrush with a beet stuck in it. And his pants were fuller of patches than Joseph's coat was of colors. But as a master of the fascinating art of declamation—well. Cicero and Demosthenes were only splutting gas-merchants, windy tyros.

His auditors, all battle-scarred veterans of many a ribald bout with old John Barleycorn, were agreed that strong men should take strong drink, and that teetotaler was merely a synonym for sissy. All agreed, that is, except one sheepish-looking tatterdemalion who rose to exercise his privilege as a free man; for he was free in every sense of the world—free of property, free of ideas, free of food and almost free of clothes!

This dissenting member boasted that he had once loved his toddy as well as the next one, but that Providence, or Fate, or Destiny, something, had decreed that he, Jake Bottlechaser, should walk, or ride, in the unblurred path of sobriety for at least a little of the way down life's unpaved road.

The open confession of abstinence exploded like a bomb upon the assembled "jungle buzzards," and Jake's standing in the rheumatic fraternity was consequently lowered by several degrees thereby. A great chorus of raucous voices went up in depreciation of his backsliding, with each member clamoring to know the cause thereof. In the vernacular of the road, his fellow nomads were giving the abstemious Ishmaelite the "'r' nose-laugh."

"Well," commenced Jake in a decidedly apologetic manner, "it all happened twenty years ago this fall. I was working—yes, that was before I went on the road—I was working as station-agent in a microscopic tank-town on the Union Pacific. One day a barrel of liquor was shipped out there from St. Louis to a Mr. Richard Roe, freight prepaid. Nobody in the hamlet knew this Mr. Roe or had ever heard of him."

"Well, the barrel of whiskey set in the freight-room for several months, and still no one came to claim it or to ask about it. So, one day, feeling a little thirsty for a drink, I decided to bore a little hole in the top of the barrel and steal a little drink through a quill. Well, sir, that was the finest liquor that ever pickled a tonsil! And every day I'd sneak in there when nobody was around and just help myself to Mr. Roe's whiskey. This kept up for several months, and still nobody came to call for Roe's liquor."

"One day the superintendent of the road got off there at Grainfield to inspect the station, and sort of check up, you know. Well, one of the first things he wanted to know was what the terrible odor was that he smelled when he came into the depot. Of course, I couldn't tell him what it was, for I hadn't been feeling well for a few days and another man had been working in my place. I figured that whiskey was sort of giving me stomach trouble or something, for I got to where I was having awful heartburn and indigestion."

"Well, the old man—the superintendent—had to hold his handkerchief to his nose, the smell was so bad. He went around cussing and raving, and swore that he'd tear the blooming station down to find out what it was! We hunted high and low, and I even crawled under the floor, looking for a dead rat. But we couldn't find a thing. Finally, the old man hollered for me to come into the baggage-room where he was as the odor seemed to be worse in there. I went in and we looked around till he came to the liquor barrel, then he stopped in his tracks. 'What's in that barrel?' he bellowed. I told him what it was. 'That's not liquor in that barrel!' he snorted, taking a whiff at the top of it. He then made me bring an axe and knock the barrelhead in. But when I looked in the barrel, I dropped the axe and fainted! Yes, sir, just fainted away like a woman."

"What was in it?" all the hoboes asked at once.

"A dead man with a derby pushed down over his ears! They said he must have been killed by gangsters in St. Louis and shipped out there in the barrel of liquor, so that the alcohol would keep him from smelling."

"Nope, I ain't touched a drop since," sighed the reformed station agent as his unregenerate audience scrambled to its ill-shod feet and shuffled off in the direction of the water-tank in obedience to the "call of the road;" for the sound of the whistle down the tracks betokened a change of scenery.

The Power of Faith
March 2, 1938

There is something beautiful and sustaining in the power of faith, a mystic kind of something that defies our feeble attempts at analysis, "rationalize" them how he will. And a cheerful mind is a fruit of faith, as truly as goodness is a quality of wisdom.

How touchingly beautiful, how strangely sustaining has often been the power of faith, when all else was gone! And He surely possessed Divine Wisdom Who uttered the gentle reproof, "O ye of little faith!" For without faith we could do absolutely nothing; our will-power would be utterly paralyzed. You couldn't even move your finger without faith in your ability to do so. Without the will to do, we should be as helpless as plants. And if you do not think so, you should observe the actions of one under the influence of hypnotism, where the will-power is in obeyance or completely controlled by the hypnotist. If the hypnotist, for instance, raises the arm of the person hypnotized and tells him that he can't lower it he simply cannot do so—that is, if he is really hypnotized. The counter-suggestion of their own secret wish, and determination not to be hypnotized perhaps renders them impervious to the hypnotist's power of suggestion. And, in the final analysis, suggestion is really all there is to hypnotism, for the mysterious passes employed by hypnotists are only for the purpose of impression.

It might surprise you to know that some people are so susceptible to the power of suggestibility that even major operations can be performed upon them without the use of anesthetics, by merely inducing a deep hypnotic sleep in the patients! As a matter of fact, many doctors and psychiatrists now treat certain forms of nervous disorders by first hypnotizing the patients and then suggesting to them that, from a certain time onward, their troubles will disappear. And some surprising results are obtained, some remarkable cures effected by this method of mental treatment. It therefore seems that science is merely taking a leaf from the faith-healer's book when it suggests that the subconscious or sleeping part of the mind has the power to cure its own hysterical disturbance.

But let us not stray off too far into the fascinating field of mental phenomena, and thereby trespass upon the precincts of science.

The power of faith, when exercised devotionally and in righteous causes, is truly a wonderful thing to contemplate. But to discourse upon such a sacred topic is perhaps infringing the rights and prerogatives of the preacher and the spiritual teacher, for this field is the proper province of the minister. So, what I'm trying to write about here is not so much beatitudes and beauties of religious faith, but rather the abuse of the will to believe as concerns things material.

High-pressure confidence men—these suave bunco artists who literally talk people out of hundreds of millions of hard-earned dollars every year—these glib swindlers are natural psychologists. And none, perhaps, realize this unfortunate fact better than do newspaper men.

While working on Mr. Cornelius Vanderbilt's Los Angeles "Illustrated Daily News" several years ago I was assigned to interview a retired Iowan who had been "hornswoggled" by a slick confidence man, who had taken him to the "cleaners" for the tidy sum of a thousand dollars. The victim had been so successful as a farmer back in Iowa that he had retired and come to Los Angeles with his wad, hoping to spend his remaining days amongst Southern California's flowers, oranges and movie stars.

I soon found, to my surprise, that this man was none of your ignorant one-gallus farmers, but an intelligent body who had studied scientific farming at one of the agricultural colleges in the Middle West. And yet the crafty city slicker had somehow managed to insinuate himself into the retired farmer's confidence, and had actually sold him, for a thousand dollars cash in hand, an ordinary street-car, such as you can see in any large city!

The old farmer had jotted down the number of what he naively supposed was his trolly-car, and decided to take a ride on it. So, when it came along again, he boarded it with an air of great importance, and when the conductor asked for the fare the new "owner" threw out his chest and displayed his "receipt," with great putting on of airs and much-to-do. But strangely enough, the conductor was singularly unimpressed by all his show of pomp and circumstances, and even had the audacity to suggest, where all within earshot could hear, that his "new boss" was either drunk or crazy or both.

The brilliant investor, of course, was full of what he considered righteous indignation at his employee's unmitigated gall, and so rushed off in a mighty huff to the nearest police station, where the upstart conductor's outrageous conduct toward the new traction magnate was duly laid before the desk-sergeant for the proper action in such important matters. All the police did, however, was to laugh the gullible rustle out of his countenance and pass the story on to the newspaper.

People with more money than brains have been "sold" everything in New York from the Woolworth Building to the Brooklyn Bridge, and this is a fact! A smart confidence man actually "sold" a rich old duffer one of the famous city parks for twenty thousand dollars in cash! The old man hired a bunch of laborers and went into the park to remove the benches preparatory to commencing a big real estate development, when an inquisitive patrolman came along and demanded to know the whereof and the whyfore of all the activity. When the old bargain-hunter confided the secret of his good fortune in acquiring the marvelous property, the policeman could hardly believe his ears. Concluding that the old boy was slightly touched in the head, the cop took him down to the stationhouse, where he repeated his amazing story to the police Captain. And when informed of his awful folly, the old man was so stunned, so completely and profoundly bewildered, that he couldn't even describe the clever swindler.

These glib bunco men and jip artists usually stay in the smartest hotels. They affect Chesterfieldean manners, are lavish spenders, and very apt to be the very last word in fashion. But to a detective or a trained newspaper man they have "fake" written all over theme in box-car letters, for very few of them are really educated or possess genuine culture. But so potent is the magic of suggestibility that some people would believe them, even if they were trying to peddle the moon!

You would think, wouldn't you, that a person intelligent and industrious enough to make a sizeable fortune would have better sense than to believe that ten thousand dollars would increase to twenty thousand by merely letting a Gypsy fortune-teller tie it up in a piece of brown paper and mumble a few unintelligent words over it? Well, that's exactly in New York last week!

A well-to-do woman suddenly decided, for no good reason at all, that she would like to take a peep into the future. So, she went to have the fortune-teller—a frowsy, dirty, ignorant vagabond of a Gypsy— "read" her palm. But the gypsy quickly read the curious visitor's mind instead, and saw that it wasn't exactly overburdened with wisdom. So, after telling the foolish one how delightfully happy and how tremendously wealthy she would soon be, the fortune-teller, for some wonderful reason, generously confided her own secret formula for making money quickly. She had the lady wrap five dollars in a piece of "magic" paper, whereupon she (the gypsy) made a few mysterious passes over it with her hands, and then bade the lady take it home with her and sleep with it under her pillow, but not, under any circumstances to look in it till a certain specific time on the morrow, when she should find that the money had, during the night, doubled in amount. The good fairy Gypsy also, as a sort of second though, further confided that she would be only too happy to work her wonders with even larger sums.

With the most implicit and complete trust, her superstitious visitor graciously complied with her suggestion. And upon looking into the packet the next day, why, lo and behold, her money had actually doubled in amount! To make a long story short, the lady drew ten thousand dollars from her bank and dashed deliriously back to the good-fairy with it. The same rigmarole of course was repeated, but with this slight difference: When the expectant lady looked in the magic paper the next day she found—an old dirty sock instead of huge roll of bills! The good fairy, like her good money, had vanished in the night.

Books and Writers
March 23, 1938

You can very nearly tell when spring has come to New York, by strolling along Fourth Avenue south of Fourteenth Street. Here is located one of the most famous book marts in the Western Hemisphere, if not in all the world. And on balmy spring days hundreds, yea, thousands of book-lovers—poets, artists, musicians, writers, dramatists, professors and just ordinary readers—can be seen gathered in little clusters about the second-hand book-stalls on the sidewalk in front of the dozens of old and new book shops along there.

Hundreds of thousands of books by most all writers, dead or living, and on every conceivable subject under the sun are jumbled together here in heterogeneous disarray.

The Prophets and the Apostles here rub shoulders, as it were, with vicious slanderers and venomous calumniators. Sacred and devotional literature is here mixed indiscriminately with the rankest pornography. And the frivolous joke-smith or the veriest punster may be found in juxta-position to the wisest sage or the most profoundly erudite scholar. The vicissitudes of fortune, the ravages of time have made dusty bedfellows of them all. It is truly saddening to reflect that a fine work, in which a great genius may have poured out his very soul, should come to rest beside the trashy effusions of superficial vulgarians. But Fate, like Nature, plays no favorites. Gold is mixed with dross; diamonds in common clay are found.

To the old book-shops, the struggling poor scholars and the impecunious authors (and what writer is seldom free from pecuniary worries?) come to collect the tomes of information or learning necessary to their calling. And in truth, a really comprehensive library can here be acquired at very little cost, if one knows how to select the valuable from the worthless books. Many a good book have I picked up from these secondhand bookstands for a few cents each. And if one knows books—how to distinguish a first edition or a collector's item, say—it is possible to occasionally pick up really valuable books from these old stalls. Some people do nothing but search them for rare old first editions of famous writers, which they in turn sell to wealthy professional collectors for as high as thousands of dollars each!

There is the story of the starving old scholar who went into one of the old book-shops one evening just at closing time with a few old "volumes of forgotten lore" under his arm, to sell for whatever he could get. The book-seller (they are mostly Jews who are not above resorting to sharp practices) gave the poor old book-lover only a few cents for the precious old volumes which had so long been his only companions and friends in his humble, solitary retreat. When the old fellow had departed with the meagre sum to find a bit of food somewhere (for hunger will drive people to part with their most cherished possessions)—when the sad-hearted old gentleman had gone, the mercenary, unfeeling and inhuman Jew book dealer fairly danced with joy. The starving old scholar, through ignorance of its commercial value, had sold the heartless Jew a rare old first edition of Edgar Allan Poe's first printed poems, which was valued as a collector's item at seventeen thousand dollars! Such, it seems, is sometimes the irony of life.

In the collector's catalogues are listed hundreds of old first editions of great American writers, which are in great demand because of their scarcity. And many book dealers now send their agents into the old cultural centers of New England and to the older cities and towns in the South—such as Richmond, Charleston, Savannah, Mobile, etc.—which were seats of culture in the Old South. And there they snoop and gumshoe around, looking for chances to buy up old libraries in the hope of finding a few valuable first editions amongst them. In other words, these uncultured (unprincipled is perhaps the better word?) foreign-born book dealers, with the morals and feelings of pawn-brokers, seek to rob the Americans, not only of their heritage of freedom and decency, but of their most cherished and valuable possessions as well! Such grasping, unpatriotic parasites can do only one thing for a country—hurt it. Some of them would even sell their grandmothers if only there were a market for them!

(P.S.—Thanks, Dream Girl of Eddy, for the pretty compliments. And why shouldn't they be pretty, when "Dream Girl" is such a pretty name? I am tempted to tell you—if Mr. Burke, the editor, will only walk away where he can't hear us!—that my grandfather Nabors donated the land for the first school-house there at Eddy. And years ago—I won't say how many, for you might think I'm impossibly old! —I went to school there, to a Mr. Alfred—or was it Albert? —Thompson. And I'm sure that I should have been a wiser and a happier young man had some knowing little fairy whispered to me to stay there instead of making this big wide world my home! My present address is 16 Rivington St., New York, N.Y.

Those Old Sweet Songs
August 3, 1938

It has been nineteen years this summer since I left Alabama. And in all that time—yes, I say it with shame—I have only been back there once, and that was more than twelve years ago. How swiftly the years have come and gone! And, upon reflection, how little they seem to have brought one.

If you are one of those rare, sweet-tempered souls who are long on patience and not easily bored by tedious trifles, I will talk to you for a while, via Mr. Burke's splendid little paper, about a very dull subject—myself.

If you should ask me why I have chosen to live in this great, seething melting pot in the North, often under trying circumstances, and usually among inhospitable and uncongenial people—noisy, ignorant foreigners for the most part; clannish, self-centered, suspicious and small-souled creatures—if, I say, you should ask me why I live in this polyglot abomination called New York, I could not honestly tell you, for the very good reason that I do not know. But I suppose life is like that. Fate deals the cards—which so often seem to be stacked against us—and we must play them. One becomes a minister, another a murderer; one must subsist on a beggarly dole while another wallows in effeminating luxury. What is the meaning of it all? What the purpose? 'Tis but a farce, scoffs Voltaire; a tragedy, says Shakespeare; a *Divine Comedy* avers Dante. "Vanity, all is vanity," thus soliloquized the aged Solomon. And a man who had squired a thousand women must surely have been an authority on Vanity!

But what has all this to do with the title of our little chat—Those Old Sweet Songs? I do not quite know, except that I was in just this sort of musing cast of mind last evening while strolling leisurely through an unfamiliar section of this eternally strange and bewildering city, when the haunting strains of a sweet old song caused me to stop short in my tracks—if one can be said to make "tracks" on feet-killing concrete. As the beautiful words, "leaning on the everlasting arms," faded away on the evening breeze blowing gently up from the Hudson River I was, on that fleeting precious moment, back home again at "prayer meetin'" in the little Sweet Home church near Nabors Mill.[3] The years and cares had fallen from my shoulders in the magic of the moment. And how ineffably happy I felt, only those can know who have spent long, lonely years far from home. How carefree and happy and companionable we all were! We were always that way at home—all so young and jolly together. Our parents, Lord bless them, seemed somehow different from other parents, more like brothers and sisters than parents. I wonder if the years have changed them. I truly hope not, for the young in heart are old in love.

When the words of the sweet old hymn had melted away, I was surprised to discover tears coursing down my worldly cheeks, so entranced had I been by the beauty of its spell. And as I walked slowly away, and for many blocks thereafter, I was living again in the blessed days of childhood. How like a kaleidoscope the old scenes and events came back! Days in the cotton fields, happy days with favorite little pals, some of whom, alas, I may never see again. Picking berries—fishing—swimming—going to school—going to the "revival meetings" and flirting with the little cuties instead of lending an attentive ear to the good preacher, as I should have done. Then came those dear, delightful days so happily, and usefully, spent on the hill there at Guntersville, absorbing knowledge under the able tutelage of Professor Horton, and tumbling about over the terraced hillsides with Minor Woodall, Neely Henry, Timmons Jordan and the other little chaps my age and size.[4] And how I idolized, from a shy and respectable distance, the bevy of pretty little misses whose cheerful smiles so

---

3. Sweet Home Baptist Church, located on Union Grove Road, still exists. The facility offers Sunday services, life groups, and Bible Study. www.sweethomechurch.org (Accessed April 8, 2020).

4. Minor Woodall, Sr. (1902–1986), a prominent Guntersville businessman, operated retail stores including the largest clothing store, a flower shop, gin, and 14 greenhouses. Smith, 85; "Obituary," Advertiser-Gleam, March 8, 1986; and U.S., Find a Grave, 1600s-Current. Electrical engineer Neely Henry (1904–1973) became executive vice-president of the Alabama Power Company. U.S. City Directories, 1822–1995; and "Obituary," *Advertiser-Gleam*, June 28, 1973. Timmons Jordan Sr. (1903–1988) owned a farm and the Gulf gasoline distributorship in Guntersville. William Nabors lived at the home of Jordan's parents, when attending school. "Obituary," *Advertiser-Gleam*, June 25, 1988. On Horton, see Footnote 120.

brightened my class and filled my dreams there in that memorable autumn of 1916. How like yesterday it all seems! But ah, how many yesterdays have come and gone since then—twenty-two years of them! I wonder if I shall ever grow up. I suppose you are impatiently hoping so!

A Cold Ride (Part I)
August 24, 1938

The *Saturday Evening Post* is publishing, currently, a series of most interesting biographical stories of Jack London by Irving Stone. And while reading some of Jack London's experiences on the road in his tramping days, I was reminded of a rather painful experience which I myself underwent once while hoboing it over the Santa Fe Railroad in Northwestern Arizona many years ago.

Another young chap—who, by the way, is now an officer in the Marine Corps—and myself had been "ditched" (put off) from a freight train in Skull Valley, Arizona, a wild, God-forsaken place in the Silver Range mountains about a hundred miles north of the Mexican border—a rugged, dismal, terrifying place, if ever there was one! For two long, agonizing days we waited at the desert waterstop in what seemed vain hopes for a train that might stop there for water or maybe slow down enough in making the hairpin curve to allow us to catch it "on the fly," a very dangerous business, to say the least of it. The slightest error in calculating speed or distance when grabbing for a speeding train is apt to spell disaster. For if you grab on to the ladder-irons when the train is moving too fast she will fling you like a wet rag so hard against the side of the car (if you can hold on at all!) that it's liable to break your ribs, or even your legs. And if you can't hold on (how many poor wretches don't!) the chances are about nine to one that the speed of the train will throw you under the wheels. I had the sickening experience of seeing a twelve-year-old lad lose both his legs in this dreadful manner at Abilene, Texas, one night.

Skull Valley was aptly named, for look in whatever direction one would, the blanched bones and skulls of cattle and sheep that had perished on the desert there for the lack of water lay grinning their awful warnings to whoever might venture into the blistering sands of that desolate inferno. The only sign of human habitation in all that dreary region, except for the shack occupied by the Mexican water-tender, was a deserted miner's cabin about a half-mile up on the side of the mountain from the water tank. And nailed to the door of that inhospitable abode was a crudely penciled warning in the form of cross-bones and skull, with a legend scrawled beneath advising any stranded wanderer to enter therein at his peril! Needless to say, we did not tarry long in the immediate vicinity of that cabin!

At night the timber wolves and desert coyotes howled around us in packs, and occasionally a mountain lion could be heard making his sinister way across the rugged mountainside. The mountain lions in that region are almost as large as the African lions, and will kill horses and cattle wherever they find them. I saw Zane Grey, the famous novelist, who is also a great sportsman, with the carcass of a mountain lion latched to the running-board of his car in Arizona which weighed over two hundred pounds![5]

For two interminable days and nights we had nothing but cigarettes with which to keep up our flagging spirits, as there was no food to be had thereabouts. And as nightfall enshrouded our prison fastness we would climb to the top of the lonely water-tank and take time about sleeping. At least the wolves and lions couldn't stalk us there! In those days, I was something of a daredevil adventurer, and had literally flirted with death on more occasions than one, having worked for some two years as derrickman in the tops of the dangerous 112 foot oil derricks throughout Texas and Oklahoma, disdaining to even put on the life-belts, and where one false move meant death. I had a large, hundred horse-power steam boiler to literally blow up within ten feet of where I stood in Oklahoma, and the only injuries I received were third-degree burns from the scalding steam! I've been, at different times and places, shot, stabbed, slugged and run over by a speeding hit-and-run car and dragged for a half-block while the broken bones crunched in my body and my helpless head bounced up and down on the pavement as if my very brains were being spilled. But withal I seem to bear a charmed life, and if the true story of my strange career could be written, I'm sure it'd read stranger than fiction. But I shall never forget those awful hours at Skull Valley!

Along toward sunset on our second day at the desert stop, a long freight train came puffing in from the east and stopped to take on water for its two powerful locomotives. The big double-headers were pulling a string of some forty refrigerator cars, mostly empties going back into California for fruit, melons, lettuce, flowers, etc. for the great Eastern markets. My pal and I hid ourselves behind a big boulder just off the right-of-way, and lay there waiting for the long, alkali-covered train to get under way again for its slow, hard grind

---

5. On Grey, see Chapter 1, Footnote 2.

up the snow-capped mountains to Prescott, Arizona, which is over a mile above sea level and, at that time of winter, apt to be buried under several feet of snow.

As the engineer gave the two short blasts on his whistle which signified that they were on their way again, our hearts were beating like triphammers and pounding so against our ribs that they felt as if they were almost in our throats, we were that excited! For we knew that the next few seconds would tell whether both of us were safely aboard the long freight-train and on our way out of that lonesome death-trap, or whether one of us mayhaps had made the fatal slip and fallen under the merciless wheels. We ran for it before she should start picking up too much speed, and caught her, one of us at the front end of a refrigerator car and the other at the rear end of the same car. We climbed atop and walked over the tops of the moving cars until we came to a ventilator (the iceboxes at the end of the cars) that was open, and down into this "vent" or icebox we climbed. There were several rather large chunks of ice in one end of this "vent," making it a cold, wet, and extremely disagreeable place in which to steal a ride. But we were already down in there, and by then the train was hitting it along at a pretty high speed around dangerous curves, through deep canyons and gorges, making it too risky to venture out of our hiding-place in quest of a drier ventilator. And so, we lit our cigarettes (I smoked in those days) and huddled close together in one corner, in order to keep warm.

We had been on the train for perhaps thirty or forty minutes, and were congratulating ourselves upon our good luck in escaping from starvation in the desert, when suddenly the door of the icebox above our heads crashed down over us with a frightful bang. And there we were, locked inside a refrigerator car on a train that was taking us higher up into the mountains every minute, and with the temperature falling at a most alarming rate! A brakeman, coming over the train, had slammed the door down upon us without looking in to see if anyone was in it below! We, naturally, started shouting and hollering at the top of our lungs in order to attract the thoughtless trainman's attention. But what with the rattle and roar of the train and the airtightness of the refrigerator, we had as well been shouting at the man in the moon. The door was perhaps three feet higher than a man's head, and so we couldn't quite reach it in order to push it up. I, being slightly larger and stronger than my companion, let him climb up on my shoulders and try to raise the door that way. But the big, heavy, metal-lined door was too much for him, and so he couldn't make it.

"My God!" groaned Harold, the lad with whom I was hoboing on that never-to-be-forgotten trip, "what on earth'll we do?"

"Keep calm," I admonished, "and quit smoking for this thing is air-tight, and we shall surely die of suffocation if we don't quit filling it with smoke." I then suggested that he let me try the door from his shoulders. But the little chap was so weak from hunger and fatigue that the first time I attempted to heave back the heavy door his knees buckled under him and down we went, with heads and faces crashing into the bruising old chunks of ice piled up in the other end of the eight-foot ice-box (it was 8 feet long, 3 feet wide and 7 feet dep—a veritable grave). We disengaged our fingers from each other's eyes, ears and mouths and scrambled to our feet to strike matches and see how badly hurt we were, for it was black as pitch in that grave on wheels. Our injuries consisted for the most part of a gashed temple for me and a broken tooth for him. But these were trifling annoyances compared to our extreme mental anguish, for it was getting colder by the minute, and already our feet and hands were becoming numb. We knew neither what time it was nor where we were, for neither of us boasted a watch. But I remembered, vaguely, of having noticed on one of the railposts at Skull Valley that it was 82 miles to Prescott and as every foot of it was upgrade, it meant that we should be lucky to make ten miles an hour, and luckier still if we were not caught in the dreaded snowdrifts, for it often happens during the winter in that altitude that trains are caught in the great drifts and held up for days! These unpleasant forebodings were flitting like dark shadows across my mind, but I hadn't the heart to add to poor Harold's pathetic distress by acquainting him with these dread possibilities. So, on we rode, higher and colder with every turn of the bumpy old wheels, and not even daring to light a cigarette.

A Cold Ride (Part II)
August 31, 1938

For the first hour or so after the trainman had unknowingly locked us in the ice-box of the "reefer" (refrigerator car), my young companion and I were in a state of acute mental agony, superinduced partly by the realization of our imminent prospects of freezing to death—a horror not to be lightly dismissed!—and partly because we were weak from hunger, not having tasted food in over forty-eight hours. And as our long prison train chugged its dreary way up and ever upwards into the land of perpetual snow, a thousand dark thoughts presented themselves to our gloomy contemplation.

We reasoned, and rightly, that we had but one and only one slim chance of being rescued alive from our terrifying predicament, and that was the all too unlikely probability of attracting attention to us by shouting at intervals as loudly as we could and knocking on the sides of the metal-lined ice-box with the chunks of ice. The possibility of our cutting our way out was nullified by the distressing fact that neither of us had a pocket-knife!

I tried again to push the heavy door open by standing on my little buddy's frail shoulders, but all efforts in this direction were now futile, for he was becoming so weak that he could no longer sustain even my own weight, much less that of the heavy door. And to make matters worse, he by then had begun to fancy that it was getting warmer, although his hands and feet had long since become numb, and I realized the horrible fact that he was beginning to freeze! I rubbed his face and hands as best I could with ice, for I had read somewhere that the best thing to do when one is freezing is to rub the body vigorously with snow. And here I made another most disconcerting discovery: My own hands had become so numb from the cold that I couldn't even feel the ice! And so all seemed hopeless and lost. I had kept stomping and jumping around as best I could in order to keep my feet from freezing to the bottom of the wet car; but when you've gone without food for nearly three days, you haven't the strength to jump about and pound your chest like a gorilla in order to keep warm.

My little pal was now rapidly freezing. That sad fact was only too obvious. He mumbled a few incoherent words, but his tongue was so thick that I couldn't make out what he was trying to say, and slumped down in the corner and became quiet and still. I put my cheek against his face—for my hands were now quite useless—and it felt colder than any corpse could feel. He no longer heard, or at least responded to my encouraging words, and appeared to have fallen into a deep sleep. Though his overcoat was heavier than mine, I somehow managed to struggle out of my own old coat, and by holding it in my teeth and between my arms I wrapped it as best I could around his head, hoping that his breath and the remaining heat from his body would maybe keep him from freezing to death. And then for the first time in my life I fell, yes, literally fell on my knees and seriously prayed, not for myself but for him. The tears actually froze on my face as I remembered how we had agreed, hardly an hour before, to write each other's folks if worse came to worst and one of us should manage to survive. How utterly wretched, how inexpressibly distraught and forlorn I felt in that awful moment no mortal can know who has not—God forbid! —experienced such a dreadful thing.

On and on the creaking old train rolled and rocked, higher and higher in the land of eternal frost. As dark and silent as the tomb was the cold prison in which I now rode mile after mile alone, for my poor little friend was beyond the call of my voice. And soon, I began fancying that Death was blowing his cold breath on my own shivering cheeks, and a thousand terrors gripped my soul. A pale, greyish something in human figure seemed to be standing over the cold, still form of my little pal. "A ghost! A ghost!" I shrieked in frantic fright. I tried in vain to shout, to sing, to curse—anything to drive that hideous grinning specter away, for now it was unmistakably the dead image—yes, that was it, dead image—of my dying little friend! But I could not shout, I could not sing nor curse nor form any articulate sound whatever, for my jaws had become set and immovable. How nightmarish all now became! I fancied that I was losing my mind, that someone was calling to me, someone with a divinely sweet and musical voice. I tried vainly to rise from my knees and go find the sweet voice; but alas, I could not rise, for my by then insensate knees were frozen hard to the floor! Ice, ice, all the world had suddenly become ice, and I thought, of all the silly things, ice cream! And then I remembered how hungry I was and how long since I'd eaten. Maybe I was starving, and all this horrible ice was only a delirious dream; maybe there was no ice—maybe there was no me, even! Maybe . . .

I did not know whether it was because of the prayer or of the physical reactions which the emotion may have brought about, but suddenly a sweet and soothing warmth seemed to envelope me from head to foot, and in that delightful state my eyelids, so heavy with anxiety and fatigue, closed in blissful forgetfulness, and the icy world, the terror-haunted prison in which we were so hopelessly trapped, vanished from consciousness like dew in the sun.

How long we rode thus, I do not know, for the next thing I remembered was a little patch of flickering white light which I lay gazing at intently, like a baby, and trying to make out what it was. Slowly, very slowly I became conscience of the surprising fact that it was I myself who was lying there looking at the fascinating flicker on the wall. This tiny spark of consciousness which had been attracted by the flickering point of light was all of me there was, for I couldn't tell in what direction my feet lay, nor where my hands and arms were, if, indeed, I had any at all! I wondered where I was, and if maybe I was dead or something—a disembodied spirit. Then soon I became conscience of voices around me, but they sounded faint and far away, too indistinct to make sense of. A bit later, I became vaguely aware that I was not a soul without a body, for I began to experience what at first felt like a sort of dull, tingling sensation, somewhat as the hand or foot sometimes feels when it "goes to sleep," but this rapidly grew into very painful stinging, as if a million needles were being thrust into the body from every direction. And then the sickening realization that I had been frozen in the refrigerator car dawned upon me with a shock, and I, of course, wondered what had become of my fellow adventurer.

When they went to re-ice the refrigerator cars at the ice-shed in Prescott they found us, frozen almost stiff and quite unconscious. They carried us over to a nearby locomotive and laid us in the warm cab, meanwhile massaging us with snow in order to stimulate the circulation, and then wrapped us in warm, heavy clothes and poured brandy down us. And it was while lying in the cab of the locomotive that I regained consciousness.

Needless to say, it took us many months in California's sunshine to completely recover from the effects of our harrowing experience. And I carry to this day, as an unpleasant reminder thereof, a gapped left ear, which was nearly frozen off, and an ugly scar on my left knee, which I call my "prayer scar," for I got it when I dropped to my knees to pray when all seemed lost.

The Old House in Charleston: A Symbolic Fantasy
September 7, 1938

One moon-lit evening in late summer a few years since a young seaman set his heavy duffle-bag on the sidewalk and paused to rest for a moment in front of the aristocratic old mansions that lend such quiet dignity and grace to narrow old Church Street in Charleston, S.C.

The youthful marine had just disembarked from an old tramp steamer in the harbor there after many months of wandering over the seven seas. And how good it felt to be back in one's own country again and to feel the solid earth under one's feet for a change!

Fleecy little clouds that looked no larger than the hand were scurrying across the silvery-pale face of the ghastly-looking moon like fleeing witches astride their brooms. Scarcely, two blocks away still stood the infamous old auction-blocks—now Charleston's fishmarket—from which so many black people were sold into slavery when these rambling old mansions were in the heyday of their glory. But how unspeakably gloomy, how deserted and helpless-looking the old houses looked now, especially the one of which our young sea-farer had paused to rest. Its pristine beauty had vanished with the snows of yesteryear, for it had long since fallen prey to the eternal elements, its once snow-white colonnades now grimy with the dust of ages and its forsaken walls, scarred with patches of stucco, had dropped away. Its very decrepitude was eloquent attestation of a glorious past.

The rank shrubbery in the spacious grounds that surrounded the old mansion was now grown quite wild, and matted with the aromatic vines that hung in luxuriant masses everywhere. Even the two proud old magnolias which had once towered in regal majesty above song and laughter and gaiety now seemed bowed with gentile sorrow over the decadent reminder of a happier past. And from the graceful cucumber tree that stood like a faithful sentinel at one corner of the galleried old mansion came the dismal hosts of the lonely screech-owl that haunted its shadowy boughs, the only tenant left, it seemed.

"How sad," thought the poor but warm-hearted young Southerner wanderer as he slung his duffle-bag over his shoulder and started to move on— "how sad to see such a beautiful old house deserted and gone to ruin. It seems folks don't care no more what becomes of our old landmarks. Too busy makin' money, I reckon."

The young mariner was interrupted in the midst of this same reflection by the creaking of an old French window as it opened in the second story above his head. And he was so completely surprised, so utterly dumb-founded to see such signs of life in the darkened old house that his gear slid from his shoulder and fell unnoticed at his feet, and his eyes and mouth flew open in a startled wonder as he stood stark still and gazed up at the now open window.

He had scarcely noticed the details of the strange scene above him when a little old lady in black with a delicate lace collar and a little heart-shaped lavalliere at her neck appeared at the easement and stood smiling good-naturedly at the young seaman below. Her face, though unusually pale and sad-looking, was strangely fascinating to look upon.

When he had sufficiently recovered his wits from this succession of surprises, the young mariner closed his mouth, gulped embarrassingly, and removed his cap. It had all happened so suddenly and so strangely that he seemed undecided as to what to do, and in the confusing uncertainty he stopped to pick up his duffle-bag, when the little lady at the window addressed him thus:

"Pardon me, my dear young man, but are you perhaps returning from the war?"

This question appeared as strange as the little old lady who asked it, and before he could frame an answer she continued:

"But of course, you are returning from the war—how stupid of me! —I should have known by your soldier's kit that you've been in the service."

"Why, er—no, madam," stammered the mystified young seaman, "I ain't been to no war; I'm a sailor just gettin' off ship—just right now gittin' off ship. This here duffle-bag ain't no soldier's kit; it's my gear."

"Your ge—your what?"

"My gear, madam, my clothes and things; the sailors call it gear."

"Lord bless you! That you're in the Confederate Navy? Do tell me," she continued, without waiting to be corrected—"did you witness the sinking of the *Alabama*?"

"No, ma'am, I ain't in no navy neither," the young mariner replied truthfully, if somewhat ungrammatically. "They ain't no war again on now, I reckon—none that I've heard tell of lately," only the World War, and that was before I was old enough to . . ."

"Ha, ha, ha! Ho, ho, ho! He, he, he!" she tittered derisively. "My dear young man," she again became serious, "how pitifully innocent you are of knowledge! But then I suppose you're from the backwoods some place where they don't even know the war between the States is going on."

"The war betw-oh, yes, I know about that: read it in the history books, and my grandpappy was in it hisself. But that was way back in '65. I think it was."

"Back in '65! Why you poor, deluded child, don't you know it's only the summer of 1862 now, and that we here in Charleston are expecting to hear news of victory most any day? Ha, ha! Ho, ho! He, he!" she cackled mirthfully as she reached out with a long, thin white hand to close the tall old French window. But as she leaned forward to reach for the window a protruding vine knocked off the little lace dust-cap she was wearing, and a cold shudder swept over the young mariner, for he was horrified to see only a grinning skull where the face should be been!

"Law, mistah," came a childish voice from across the street, causing the sailor to straighten up quickly and look in the direction of the speaker. He saw a wide-eyed, ragged little piccaninny carrying a kerosene can with a small potato stuck over the spout. "Law, mistah," reported the kerosene carrier, "Yo-all ber not stan' ovah dah, kase dat ole house she nuff hanted, an' dat's de true fack."

Tiny fleecy clouds were scurrying across the pale face of the old moon like witches astride their brooms as the young mariner shouldered his duffle-bag and walked rapidly, very rapidly, in the direction of the Seaman's Institute. But then sailors, they say, are superstitious people.

———•••———

Going Home
October 5, 1938

In the hour of twilight today your nostalgic correspondent stood upon a knoll deep in Central Park, "far from the maddening crowd," and gazed somewhat wistfully at a flock of wild geese winging its way southward over a distant hill on the Jersey side of the Hudson River. And as he followed, with envious eyes, the course of the vanishing little "V" across the misty horizon he, too, was suddenly thrilled to find himself being transported on magic wings over the snow-white cotton fields and sleepy Piney hills of his beloved and long unseen Southland. And the sad, depressing thoughts engendered by all the deaths and destruction wrought by the terrible hurricane which swept great tidal waves over large estates of this region yesterday—these unpleasant thoughts were happily displaced by the light and airy fancies called up by following, in mind's eye, the flight of the wild geese back to the land of Old Black Joe and childhood.

As the dusk of evening settled like a dreamy veil over the face of the peaceful landscape, the tinkling of cowbells could be heard far across the fields, and the fresh, sweet autumn air was laden with odors of ripening corn, or frosty persimmons and delicious fall apples, of yellowing pumpkins and juicy wild-grapes, all delightfully comingled with the smell of burning "broom-sage" and pine needles. And as the dusty shadows deepened into night, the evening lamplights could be seen like fireflies, twinkling their friendly welcome from the windows here and there in the neighborhood, as if to say, "Why don't you come over for a while?"

But alas, such is the perversity of our gregarious kind, some nosy busybody is always trying to take the pleasures out of life, as the bee takes the honey from the flower; and the moment's precious bucolic enchantment was rudely shattered by an obtruding policeman with his harsh New York-ese. "Come awn, Mister: Ye'll haft git oot; yer not allowed to stay up here after darrak. 'Tis the new ruling, ye know, and it's too dangerous, with all the robberies and killings agoin on in the parks now."

"Even the wild-geese have better sense than I have," was the bitter reflection of your homesick correspondent as he betook his lonely way back to the crowded avenues and streets of the great metropolis. "For they at least know enough to go South for the winter, while I stay up here and shiver my heart out in forgotten loneliness." And if you think one can't get dreadfully lonely in the midst of a great sea of strange faces, then you simply haven't lived alone very long in a big northern city. If you can imagine a roaring mighty metropolis more than twenty times larger than Birmingham; a monstrous city that sprawls over five counties and contains more people than Alabama, Arizona, Idaho, Nevada, Utah, Wyoming, Montana, and New Mexico all put together! An indescribably polyglot center of seething humanity, where untold millions of restless mortals from every clime and country on earth surge like tides through its noisy, nerve-shattering, soul-frightening canyons for twenty-four hours a day without cease; as large in population as Chicago, Detroit, St. Louis, Boston and Los Angeles combined—if you can visualize such a mind-staggering aggregation of mankind, then you can form some faint conception of what New York City is like.

No wonder one feels so little—so microscopically small and inconsequential in such a bewildering place, like a drop of oil on a turbulent ocean. Not a policeman in all New York (and there are nearly twenty thousand police in the city!) is familiar with its perplexing maze of serpentine streets, even those old-timers who were born and reared here. Surely such an eternally strange and unknown metropolis is an alien place for a nature-loving Southern farm boy to find himself imprisoned in for year after lonely year—and for what? Don't ask me, for I couldn't tell you! But I suppose it's the great libraries, the wonderful museums and fine educational institutions that attract one to this unsurpassed world-center of culture and refinement as well as ignorance and vulgarity.

Jack London Confession
April 26, 1939

Those who are not familiar with at least some of the vast and comprehensive literature on the subject of spiritualism, so-called, might be surprised to know that there are literally hundreds of works upon the subject, books and studies by great writers, renowned artists, famous composers, medical doctors, college professors and, perhaps strangest of all, by even some of the world's greatest so-called physical scientists. Sir Arthur Conan Doyle, the famous author who wrote "Sherlock Holmes" and many other interesting and valuable books, became, like Sir Oliver Lodge, Sir James Barrett, Sir Wm. Crookes and Sir Arthur Thomson (all scientists of note), a confirmed believer in spiritualism, that is, the survival of human personality after death, and the possibility of communicating with those who have passed on.

To those who are seriously seeking truth and light in such matters, and not merely interested in satisfying a vain and idle curiosity in such things, I can think of perhaps no better work to recommend than Sir Arthur Conan Doyle's most interesting and instructive book on the subject entitled "The Edge of the Unknown." This work is written for the average layman with a common, ordinary education, and can thus be read and understood without a scientific education or a knowledge of the technical phraseology and jargon usually employed in such works by academic investigators.

But before proceeding to quote the interesting passages which follow, perhaps it might be best to explain, in a word or two, just how I came to be interested in spiritistic phenomena or "spiritualism," as it is commonly called. I must confess, to begin with, that I had to unlearn, as it were, many things which I had earlier been taught in regard to the subject; for up until a few years ago I was densely ignorant, yea, amazingly so, concerning the subject, and my skepticism and disbelief were quite as large and as vocal as my ignorance was deep. In a word, I was "conceited in my ignorance" and dogmatic on the question to a most absurd degree, as I now look back at myself.

My first contact with Spiritism (as the subject is more properly designated) occurred some sixteen years or so ago. I was working as a reporter on a Los Angeles paper at the time, and got an assignment to cover a séance, which was to be held at the private home of a well-known local spiritualist "medium." Of course, like most self-satisfied and ludicrously vain young newspaper writers who think they know it all, and who have no hesitancy in letting the world know the high opinion they have of themselves, I donned my most fashionable "society brand" salt-and-pepper suit, with walking-stick and everything, and took a taxi out to the specified address, assuming a superior worldly air and affecting great boredom withal. I rang the doorbell and presented my beautifully engraved calling-card with all the hauteur of Lord Chesterfield himself! I was admitted by a kindly and gracious little lady with snow-white hair and one of the sweetest, most innocent and motherly little faces I have ever seen. When I bowed (alas, too stiffly and too coldly!) and handed her my card, she glanced at it and opened wide the door with a most gracious and friendly gesture and with a graceful sweep of her slender little arm, she motioned me in. "I'm so glad they've sent someone who looks intelligent and truthful," she said; "for," she then added, "we are trying to do serious and important work here, and the people from the press who usually come to write about our experiments nearly always go away and print dreadful things about us and make us all appear to be odious fakers."

I blush with shame now as I recall that I, too, went away and wrote of the séance in a vein of ridicule and worldly levity, not even designating to take their honest efforts at all seriously, but tried rather to "prove," by what I then thought was very clever reasoning, that the light phenomena seen at the séance (for dim outlines did actually appear) could be produced by the clever manipulation of certain phosphoretted materials, etc. And I thus dismissed the whole séance as being only a crude exhibitor of humbuggery. But alas! it was I who was impossibly crude and a humbug, for had I been any sort of experienced psychologist at all, I could not possibly have mistaken the sweet and gentle and cultured little lady for a rank imposter and vulgar faker, such as most professional mediums and nearly all "fortune tellers" obviously are. But then we all make mistakes; we "live and learn." And (though yet so little!) since those early days amongst the make-believe and commercialized fakery of Hollywood.

But to return to Jack London: It is well known that Jack London, the great adventure-story writer and socialist, was a confirmed materialist, and believed that when the body died the soul perished with it. At the end of his life Jack London became a heavy drinker, in fact a drunkard. And it is said that his death resulted from an over-dose of a sleeping potion; but as he took the whole, evidently in a drunken stupor, it was hinted that he had committed suicide. But the spirit-medium in San Francisco who received the alleged spirit-messages from him by means of the "Ouija-board" discloses that his death was the result of his drunken condition, and not from suicide. Sir Arthur Conan Doyle journeyed all the way from London to San Francisco in order to investigate a so-called "medium" through whom the spirit-messages had come. And he was convinced of her sincerity and genuineness, and as he had known Jack London well in this life, he immediately recognized his style of writing, from his short, staccato sentences in which he usually wrote. (Sir Arthur exposed many false mediums.) And besides, the medium was a comparatively ignorant house-wife and not a professional "psychic" at all: she had read none of London's works, and didn't know a paragraph from a semi-colon! For the benefit of those who may not know of this form of "post-humous literature," as it is called, permit me to say that it is much more common than is generally known; and there are dozens of social works purported to have been written through mediums by dis-embodied spirits. (A spirit, as Swedenborg and others who have written on the subject tell us, can only see through the eyes of mortals here who are in visions or the trance state, and they can only materialize by using some as yet unknown subtle form of matter which living bodies throw off. Thus, when you see a phantom or a "han't" it has, according to those who are supposed to know, formed its "body" out of your own!)

I herewith quote the following passages from Sir Arthur Conan Doyle's "The Edge of the Unknown." "Death has taught me" (it is supposed to be Jack London writing) "what earth held from me. My spirit is plunging forward with more vigor than wisdom, as in my earth days. But I know the way and the life. Oh, I have much, much that I must undo. My soul, though I knew it not, was dyspeptic with the materialistic fodder I crammed into it. Death caught me unaware. He snapped me up when my face was not turned his way. I almost regret this. I believe it made my transition harder."

When asked what it was like when he "came to" in the spirit world he replied: "I awoke. Dreaming? I was sure of it! I dreamed on and on. I dreamed myself into eternity. My powers slowly returned. I could think. I hailed my old mind like a returned friend. I fumbled and groped. My earth-blindness was still on me. It hazed me about. I fought my way through it. I had no goal. I had already passed the only goal I had ever admitted. I was now on the other side of it. I struggle to seize the correct term. I try vainly to translate the expression into terms of earth which has no utterance for it."

At this juncture in the "automatic" or subconscious writing, the force which was controlling the medium's hand grew weak and trailed off into indistinguishable and confused scribbling. But shortly after, as if sufficiently recovered to go on, it continued: "I died. I am looking at death from the other side now—the tame, friendly side of him. And life is indestructible . . . I see man face his destiny as I saw him on earth. I see him fall. I see him rise and go on. He fights his way, and when his place is ready here, he comes. There are no catastrophes. All is in order."

After another brief pause as if to rest, the writer continued: "That which was my truth of yesterday, which I hugged to be as the quintessence of my distilled thought, becomes a volatile poison to me here, and I must . . . distill a new thought out of the fires of my previous experience, and by this thought shall I rise. Renaissance of soul is a labor shot with pains of remembrance, held by fetters of past error which are burst with a sweated toil while the heart strains with propulsion . . . I feel that I have got right with God—I am no longer worshipping myself."

When asked what specific work he, the great novelist, was doing on the other side he answered "I have to direct those lost or bewildered, as I was when I came. I labor to show them the way I would not take!"

He then said that his time was up and that he could write no more till another time, and he closed his message with the terribly pitiful and inexpressibly sad (though not altogether hopeless) declaration: "God! I am annihilated!" he cried; "my earth-life is stamped out, blotted from time by these passages. I can't puzzle it out. My hand fumbles. Did he steal the very face of me, that those who knew me there now see me here strange, feeble, pitiful? Who or what has cut the tap-root of my power? I am befogged."

"This message," he said, "comes from Jack London, the damned soul, struggling out of his own hell of gross materialism. But there is light ahead, and I must persevere. I am a soldier on the eternal march."

Thus, you have read words if true (and Sir Arthur Conan Doyle, Sir Oliver Lodge and other great geniuses believe they are true), which came from "beyond the veil," and which were thought by a mind that had no physical brain!

Days That Are Gone
June 7, 1939

As I sat in Battery Park this lovely Sunday afternoon watching the great ocean-going liners coming in and going out of New York's ever busy harbor, and thinking of all the strange and far-away places and foreign ports I had been in, I was suddenly aroused from my pleasant reverie by a tall and suntanned stranger who sat down beside me on the bench and gently tapped me on the shoulder in order to attract my attention from one of the world's largest liners, which was slowly plowing her way out toward the open sea. I turned and found myself looking into a dark but not unhandsome face, a friendly enough countenance, in whose rugged features there appeared to be something vaguely familiar.

"Don't remember me, do you?" queried the acquaintance of other days. I confessed that I didn't. "Do you by any chance recall where you were ten years ago today?" asked the amused stranger. "Good Lord, no! I couldn't tell you where I was ten days ago today," I admitted. The tall stranger then extended his hand and chuckled good-naturedly as he reminded me that he and I had once been "ship-mates together," and that on the last Sunday in May 1929, we had gone in swimming in the Panama Canal while our ship was tied up there awaiting her clearance papers.

It was a most pleasant surprise, meeting this old ship-mate of other days, whose very name I had long since forgotten, and I probably would never have thought of him again, had he not appeared before me there suddenly, like a phantom out of the mist. It was the first time I'd been down to the waterfront in a year, and I certainly didn't expect to see anyone I knew among the water-front loungers and hangers-on, as a whole decade had passed since I "graduated" from the life of a seafarer. But one thing about my old sailor buddy struck me rather forcefully (but of course I did not mention this to him!), and that was the obvious fact that he was pretty much the same old happy-go-lucky, Devil-may-care sort of fellow who still had his same old vices and who was still immersed in his same old slough of ignorance. Obviously, life's lessons had passed him by, for he had in nowise improved, morally or intellectually, in the ten long years since I'd known him. And our unexpected meeting furnished me with a valuable object-lesson in spiritual and intellectual evolution, or growth, to wit: that "there are no royal roads to knowledge," no easy ways to self-improvement, or short-cuts to wisdom; and that the higher and better things of life do not come of their own accord, but rather are as delicate plants that grow and develop only by hopeful and patient and diligent cultivation and care.

My old sailor pal suggested, in true sailor fashion, that we celebrate the occasion by repairing to some waterfront honky-tonk frequented by blond sirens and proceed to get gloriously drunk! And I noted the look of pained surprise that rippled across his sun-browned face when I told him that I neither drank nor smoked, and as for the blond sirens—well, they would have no worries about finding drinking companions in New York! I really felt a little sorry for the poor sap. He had meant to be sociable in his sailor's way, and he knew of nothing else which he might suggest to an old ex-salt as a sort of get-together party, than just to go out for a night of "whoopee" and general hell-raising. It would have been interesting to know his secret opinion of me as we parted! But then this type of fellow is not apt to be overly analytical when it comes to reasoning about their conclusions and the modus operandi of their thought-processes. They usually just dismiss the things they do not understand, with a shrug of the shoulders and a "oh, to-hell-with-it" attitude. And as I returned to my lodgings and my books (in our books we at least can choose superior companions), I reflected upon the terrible loneliness of those who, like myself, no longer find pleasure in the childish trumpers and vain inanities after which the world, or at least the largest part of it, is running day and night. A million dollars a night is spent in New York on things of pleasure, so-called!

But then I console myself with the reflections that in the ways of the lonely one, the dreamers, the mystics and the searchers for Truth, there are at least no painful disappointments and heart-breaking sorrows because of vain and unworthy things. And Manly P. Hall, in the introduction to this beautiful book "The Ways of The Lonely Ones," well expresses this in the following words:

"This life is not merely what it seems to be. Hidden from our eyes by the cloak of materiality is a world which only the eyes of the dreamer can see and the soul of the mystic comprehend. The stony walls of conventionalized thought and commercialized ideals shut from the view life's noble path. But as the ages pass, some see the greatness of the Divine Plan, and comprehend the glorious destiny of the human soul. Sorrow, suffering and loneliness are the great builders of character. Man never becomes truly great until his heart is broken. That is the supreme test. Those who are deepened and broadened by their experience rise triumphant from the ruins of their dreams, and pass on to a fuller destiny . . . There are theories which appeal to the reason, and there are truths which the mind can never know. Throughout the ages the emotion and the intellect have struggled with each other for dominion over the soul, and man has often foolishly allowed his servants (the emotion) to become his masters . . . Religion, however, is not merely intellectual—though it must be logical and reasonable. Religion, in order to unfold the spiritual nature, must be enshrined with the heart . . . Every individual who comes into the world is a Lonely One—a stranger in a strange land. At birth he begins a search which continues until he is laid away in earth—and probably even afterwards. Few can define the object they seek. If they only realize one thing, the quest would be ended: each searches only for himself . . . We live in a world of shadows. These phantoms are our not-selves, but most of us mistake them for the real self. Only periods of sorrow and suffering can bring the discrimination which shows us what is really worthwhile, and develops the determination which strengthens us for the greatest good."

And so it goes. I went down to the water-front to get a breath of fresh air and to spend a pleasant hour watching the big ships come and go, out past the Statue of Liberty. And I came away with a lesson in mental development and, incidentally, material for this article. And I am humbly grateful for all this beautiful day has brought to me.

On Being Painted
June 21, 1939

George Bernard Shaw, the world's greatest living dramatist, is said to have once remarked, apropos of having a bust study of himself made by the great French sculptor Rodin, that perhaps a thousand years hence he (Shaw) would only be known to the world as the subject of a study by Rodin. Though this flattering compliment to a famous sculptor from a more famous writer is very prettily expressed, one suspects that it is, for all that, just a pleasant bit of typical Shavian blarney; for obviously the great wit and playwright thought deep down in his proud Irish heart that it would be Rodin who would be referred to a thousand years from now only because he had the good fortune to make a statue of the immortal Shaw!

But, unlike Mr. Shaw, I can truthfully say of myself that I shall probably be known a hundred years from now, if at all, only as the unknown subject of a portrait study by the great painter, Clifford I. Addams.[6] For I am having the honor (and it is an honor, for it isn't just everyone who gets his portrait painted by a great and famous artist!) of having my portrait painted by Mr. Addams, one of the most distinguished living painters; an artist who studied abroad for years, under such masters as Whistler, the great American artist whose famous Paris studio was the mecca of all aspiring painters a generation ago.

Mr. Addams has been justly honored many times (see the list of his achievements in "Who's Who of America"), having been awarded, from time to time, more gold medals for distinguished work than he could pin on his breast! And as this distinguished painter is now preserving my humble likeness in the medium of his magic oils, perhaps for future generations of Art-lovers to look upon, I shall here take the liberty to sketch in words a brief description of him and his studio, which is located on historic old Washington Square, overlooking the famous Washington Arch, from which begins Fifth Avenue, in the Greenwich Village section of New York City.

Mr. Addams is a man of perhaps sixty, or thereabout (though by some secret of youth he scarcely looks half that); of medium stature, with a handsome English cast of features that suggest both strength and tenderness. The slight tinge of iron-grey hair about his temples, and the humorous twinkle in his penetrating but kindly eyes give him a sort of fraternal attractiveness that makes one wish to know and to be friends with him. He is one of those amazingly versatile and learned men who make one wonder how they ever find time to do much studying. And his career has been a most colorful and interesting one: He served as an officer in the British navy during the World War; and he seems to know personally most of the great personalities of his time (but this is easily understood when we consider his fame), and has a wealth of pleasant anecdotes with which he charmingly entertains, the few fortunate ones who can claim his friendship.

---

6. On Addams, see Chapter 1, Footnote 27.

For like most truly great persons, he is modest and shy amongst strangers, even almost to the point of appearing cool. But one look at him will convince any discerning person that here truly is a genuinely aristocratic and superior person, a real gentleman in the noble and proper sense of that much-abused word.

And now that I've given you a sort of thumbnail sketch of the great painter himself, I will briefly describe his studio for you.

His atelier or studio takes up an entire floor (the second story) of a good-sized building. And he possesses perhaps one of the most valuable and unique collections of heterogeneous art extant. He has originals—that is, original paintings, etc., by old masters—that are literally worth their weight in gold! He owns some of the most exquisitely beautiful antique objects in the world; things he has picked up here and there, as the fancy struck him, from most every country on earth. Huge old Oriental vases, that might have been among the originals used by Ali Baba and the forty thieves, stand beside monstrous-looking Chinese dragons that give one the shivers to look at. He possesses delicate and lovely old screens, precious handwrought things with their myriad artistic designs and indecipherable legends traced in the margins—rare, ancient creations that fairly scintillate with oriental splendor, and seem to sweep one away in a perfume of exotic dreams, to ages and places far removed from the prosaic and humdrum existence of us mortals of common clay. And, indeed, Mr. Addams himself seems to have imbibed or absorbed something of the patrician charm and princely hospitality of their former oriental owners; for, like the generous-natured Chinese gentle-folk of old, he is just apt to offer as a present any valuable object which his guest may particularly admire! And, it is rather embarrassing to be offered as a gift some rare and precious old object of art, for which its good-hearted owner may have journeyed half around the world and spent hundreds of dollars to possess.

Though this distinguished American is now enjoying the fruits of his hard-earned success, he has not always been thus, for, like most struggling geniuses, he, too, had his share of suffering, of misery and sad disappointments (as who hadn't!). But like the fabled phoenix, his unconquerable spirit seems to have had the happy knack of rising anew from the bitter ashes of failure and defeat which have so often dogged the footsteps of aspiring geniuses in the world.

As some of our readers might like to know just how a great painter goes about his work, I will here close our article with a few brief words of description.

Punctually, at 11 o'clock in the morning (for artists are apt to be temperamental folk, and will not brock delay), I enter the outer street door and push the button under his card in the vestibule. And presently the lock on the door will start clicking electrically, which means that I can then open it and come up. My gracious host, the painter, is waiting for me in his door at the head of the stairs on the second landing. After the friendly, welcoming handshake and the preliminary "social amenities" have been exchanged, the artist, in smoking jacket and house slippers or maybe already in his painter's smock, invites me to join him at a beautiful and valuable old table, a 16th century antique, where he serves an appetizing breakfast which he has prepared himself. Having thus breakfasted, we then chat for a while or glance over the morning paper and relax before beginning our work. I don a big, loose-sleeved red robe, suggestive of a Chinese Mandarin, and set relaxed reading a book on a rather regal-looking 15th century settee, with a huge vase behind me and a little gorgon-like dragon at my elbow, for about an hour one day each week, while the artist stands at his easel a few feet away, busy with his paints and brushes, producing a likeness of me on a life-size canvas that may hang on some museum wall for future generations of art-lovers to look upon, when these eyes and hands are but dust in some forgotten grave.

A Strange Place
June 26, 1939

New York, is unlike any other city in America, for, like London and Paris, it is truly a world metropolis. A seething bee-hive of a focal-point of all the earth's concentrated aspirations, dreams, plans, schemes, visions, comedies, dramas, farces, tragedies, hopes and, alas! Despair.

And here amid this Kaleidoscope, ever-shifting scene—for New York is always changing, ever growing; being constantly pulled down and built up, there being perhaps as many as a hundred big buildings going up here at any one time!—and here in the midst and center of all this rout and racket, hubbub and turmoil are to be found representative specimens of every race, clime and country on God's earth. And this is probably why New York has long been the mecca, the center and chief attraction of our artists, writers and other intellectually creative folk; they find so many engrossing subjects here to claim their time and attention, and upon which to exercise their talents.

New York is truly the Wonder City of the age. And New York, except for the cheap, ignorant foreign riff-raff—those Simian-like hordes of Jews and "Wops" who poured in here literally by the millions from the filthy ghettos and hell-holes of Europe—except for the agglomerated mass of worthless human trash, this scum of creation, New York is one of the politest, most humane and warm-hearted cities in the world.

Just let the slightest accident of misfortune befall one in the street, and almost instantly there will be a crowd of sympathetic and kind-hearted people gathered to proffer their commiseration, advice and aid, and especially their money, for the high-type New Yorkers are without doubt the most generous and warm-hearted people on earth. There are several reasons (but mostly economic and sociological in background) why this is so; but I should have to write an essay on social philosophy in order to fully explain and account for them.

It is not often that I write about New York in my articles. And perhaps some of our readers may wonder why I don't devote more time and attention to such an interesting scene and subject. There are several reasons why I do not concern myself more with this truly amazing, this strangely fascinating this mysteriously attractive cosmopolitan that is "Little Ole New York." ("Little" for sooth! There are ten million people here within a radius of twenty miles.) But to reiterate, there may be several reasons (for even we ourselves do not always know or understand all the hidden reasons for our acting and reacting as we do!)—there are, then, several reasons why I do not write more often about New York. But let one reason—an obvious one—suffice here: Practically all my life since adulthood I have lived away from home (for Alabama shall always be "home" to me!), and much of the time in large cities—such as Los Angeles, San Francisco, Seattle, Denver, Chicago, Detroit, Philadelphia, New York, etc.—and when one remains long in one environment, be it rural or urban, one becomes accustomed to it, takes it for granted, and thinks nothing about it.

But there is also another, a less obvious reason why one soon despairs of capturing the spirit of this modern Babylon, of describing its everchanging lights and shadows; its perplexing medley of odors and colors and tones; its motley of moods that range from the mad caprice, the empty-headed giddiness of its light and frivolous devotees of gaiety, to the black despair and melancholy sadness of those forlorn and wretched poor souls who are utterly without hope, being, as many of their despairing faces so eloquently attest, without home and friends, and in the fell clutches of misery, that unspeakable and fatal disease.

All this goes to make up the awe inspiring, the overwhelming New York which we know and yet know not; and it is simply too much for one to attempt to capture its manifold spirit within the limits of one brief article, or even a thousand long ones! There have, indeed, been literally hundreds of books written on

New York; and all of them interesting, yet none of them really comprehensive or giving a true and complete picture of this appallingly huge metropolis, this monstrous paradox that is at once the most wicked and the most saintly city in the world! For, verily, it would take a whole library of books to adequately describe and depict this exasperating, this too-big, too awful, too-impossible "Little Ole New York."

This New York that controls and governs our great country as completely and as surely as ever Athena ruled ancient Greece. For do not nearly all our books and art, our fads and fashions, our news and ideas, our theatrical and cinematic enterprises, our money market and commodity prices, and a thousand other influencing factors originate in or spread from this same New York?

This New York where the richest people in the world and the poorest ones live within a few city blocks of one another; and yet their respective worlds are as unlike as if they lived on different planets: Within half a mile of where hundreds of homeless men can be found sleeping in public parks a certain fabulously rich man, an eccentric money-lender, pays more than two hundred thousand dollars a year rent for his sumptuous living establishment alone, and lives entirely by himself!

This New York wherein from one to five poor mortals commit suicide every day in the year; while as many are murdered.

This New York with its sixteen thousand taxi-cabs and its twenty thousand policemen (and yet you can't find a single one of either when most wanted)!

This New York with its more restaurants and eating-places than you could ever live to dine in, even if you should take each meal at a different restaurant throughout a long life-time!

And now I've given you at least two of the reasons why I do not write more often about New York. There are also other reasons. But it's like an ocean—too big and too deep, too dreadfully mysterious and too fearfully repelling for one to tempt, or to hope to ever fathom—this Little Ole New York.

On Reaching Middle Age
July 5, 1939

Often, when hungrily scanning the too few and too short (!) columns of our cherished and indispensable old home paper, I am shocked to come across an item in the "Local and Personal" columns which tells me that so-and-so and his (or her) children were visiting their old home and friends here and there in the community.

Lord bless them! They themselves were scarcely more than children when last I saw them; and now I read that they are fathers and mothers. All of which brings home to me the unpleasant realization that Old Father Time, with his fateful scythe, is clipping the years from under my wayward feet at a rather uncomfortably brisk rate. Indeed, that unromantic period of life often respectfully referred to as "middle age" is stealing upon me with the dread inevitability of a Greek tragedy. To think that I, who have always thought of myself as the Eternal Youth, should actually live to be thirty-nine—well, that's a little too much! If vengeful old Dame Nature thinks she can pile her silly years upon my head, and carve her unsightly initials in funny little crow's feet around my eyes, she's sadly mistaken! I, who have never considered myself even quite old enough to get married, or to run for any public office or anything—why should this innocent, overgrown babe of a me, who hasn't as much as one wife in the whole world; why should I suddenly have to wake up and find myself walking around in the summer of my fortieth year, without even so much as ten years' notice to get ready for it? It simply isn't fair, and I'm writing this in hopes that somebody, some of my old school chums, or maybe one of my dear old teachers, will take it up with the proper authorities, and get something done about it. There certainly ought to be some way out of this dreadful situation? But just what it might be, I haven't the faintest notion, for nothing like this has ever happened to me before, positively never!

Of course I appreciate the fact and am not insensible to the possibility that there may even be a few of those exasperatingly cool and calm individuals who may be so unfeeling, so utterly devoid of sympathy as to think it a blessing to my readers and a good thing for my editor that I have finally discovered that I have reached the mature age of adulthood, and may (but this would be hoping too much!) start writing accordingly, instead of disporting myself, like the juvenile show— that I've too long been.

But I believe I started out to write a nice little piece about the preciousness of the home paper to those, who like myself, are far away and often homesick to see the familiar old places and faces that meant so much to us in childhood. And so, you see, the first thing that smug and despised old "middle age" has done for me is to make me spoil a perfectly good little piece about the home paper!

The Coming Struggle
May 8, 1940

As these lines are being written here in the office of a big New York newspaper, the reports and stories are being flashed in by cable and wireless from every capital in Europe. And every bit of rumor, every item of news adds its ominous burden of gloomy uncertainty to the terrible story that is now being written in blood on the various battlefields of the Old World, where the luring specter of death again stalks forth in ghastly horror and hideous wantonness. Truly, "War is hell," as General Sherman so tersely but sapiently observed. And it is so senseless, so futile, so often purposeless, as many of you who went "over there" scarcely a generation ago in order, as you thought, to "make the world safe for Democracy," well know.

A few years ago, I wrote in these columns what now seems to have been a prophetic article, one in which if you recall, I said that the coming "battle of Armageddon" would probably be fought out in our time, and that the chief-opponents in that dreadful struggle, that fearful conflagration would undoubtedly be England, France and the United States on one side, and probably Germany, Italy, Japan and Russia on the other. And the late Col. Lusk was so impressed upon reading that article that he sat down and wrote me a most interesting and cherished letter, one in which he agreed that the handwriting was plain to be seen upon the wall, and that, unless the world quickly changed its wicked ways, the human race would certainly suffer the martyrdom foreseen by the Prophet.[7] And though Col. Lusk—Lord rest his gracious soul—is now beyond the troublous vale, there are many thoughtful and enlightened men still living who think that we are now approaching those dark and awful days foretold by John the Revelator. Be that as it must, but even the blindest materialist, the crassest money-grabber must surely sense something ominous in the pretentious ways that things are shaping themselves? The last few years have seen the most extraordinary and amazing changes taking place right here in our midst; changes that the most sanguinely optimistic revolutionary could not have hoped for even a decade ago! And the beginning is not the beginning of the end.

For what it may be worth, I will here tell you a psychic dream (as contradistinguished from ordinary dreams, which are merely a continuation or

---

7. See Chapter 4, Footnote 6.

an elaboration of the usual cerebral processes) which I had some four years ago, and which so impressed my mind that it left me in a strangely sad and depressed mood for several days. I might add here, what some of you may have already guessed from some of my writings, that I am what is sometimes termed "psychic"—that is, sensitive to supersensory impressions. For instance, I possess the strange faculty of sometimes (but this happens rarely) being able to read parts of letters, sometimes several days before I receive them. And I have, being naturally of an inquiring mind, an often unknown "sixth sense" by making notes on certain characteristics of the writings such as letter formations, etc. and then comparing them with the real writing when the letter would arrive, for the letter always does arrive faithfully, as if to verify my mental pictures or "psychogram" of it. But I have absolutely no control whatever over this strange gift, for I have often tried, or rather very much wanted, to read the contents of letters or papers before they came, but got no results whatever for my pains! So, it is obviously nothing that I can consciously control.

But to return to the psychic dream. It seemed that I had been precipitated, I know not how, from California into some city in the Orient, but I did not know just where, only I had the "feeling" that it was not in Japan. And I further got the impression, somehow, that a great, a very grave and most awful world struggle had come to an end. And even in the dream I was shocked and distressed at the sudden realization that the Occidental world had been defeated, for I looked above (something, I knew not what, seemed to be directing my attention) the desolate city and saw a flag flying victoriously from a building. It was the flag of the rising sun—Japan. And then my attention was attracted to the street, and there I saw, very plainly and vividly, the satisfied and smiling faces of Japanese officers, and then the vision, if vision it was, vanished, and I awoke dreadfully depressed, much more so than any mere dream has ever influenced me.

What was it? Could it, perhaps, have been the Chinese-Japanese war I foresaw? I do not think so; for I distinctly had the impression that what I was being permitted to witness was something of a grave and stupendous order. Time may tell. Meanwhile I pray to God that the impression was not a true one, or that it did not mean what I feared it meant.

The Days of Reckoning
June 12, 1940

The "day of reckoning," so often referred to in those prophetic passages in the Bible, seems to have come with appalling and devastating suddenness upon both of the world's mightiest empires, Britain and France, as well as upon other and smaller ones—Belgium, Holland, Denmark, etc. Truly these are perilous times. Perhaps the gravest and most momentous period in all history is now transpiring on the bloody fields of France. Indeed, many wise and learned men believe that the world is now entering that awful time of sorrows and tribulations spoken of by so many of those inspired Prophets and writers in Holy Writ.

And in times of universal distress like the present, when people are seriously "searching their hearts" and secretly wondering as to their moral and spiritual conditions, should worse come to worse and we should have to lay down our earthly bodies and enter the spiritual realms or state of life; under such prevailing circumstances one desires to know just what it all means, and especially what the Bible and the Prophets have to say about it. What, then, does the Bible say about this ominous period of the world's existence? It says that never since time was upon earth have there been such truly awful, such frightful calamities as those that shall come upon the earth just before the end. Jesus, when asked by the disciples what would be the signs of His second coming to the earth and the end of the world, answered them in these cryptic words (Matthew 24: 3-8):

"For nation shall rise against nation, and kingdom against kingdom; and there shall be famines and pestilences and earthquakes, in divers places. And all of these are the beginning of sorrows."

And have not all of these ominous and portentous signs been appearing throughout the earth with unmistakable and convincing terribleness during these past few years? As witness those awful famines that have visited such desolation upon vast areas of China and Asia, plunging unnumbered millions of poor, helpless mortals into death by starvation. Witness the dreadful and mysterious dust storms which have wrought such havoc upon the great wheat-belt of the United States, rendering untold thousands of once-prosperous citizens homeless, to become hopeless wanderers up and down the highways and byways of the land, to become the piteous subject of such terrible books as "Grapes of Wrath," etc. Witness the terrible earthquakes that have shaken mighty cities to the ground, even since the last World War, in Japan, South America, Turkey,

California, etc. (I myself was in Santa Barbara, California, when that beautiful city was rent asunder by the great earthquake, some sixteen years ago.[8] So, I know what an earthquake is!)

Witness the amazing rise and spread of those vicious and damnable doctrines and philosophies of atheism and infidelity so assiduously and industriously propagated and advocated by the Communists, Fascists, Nazis, and other false prophets and misleaders of the world. Witness the colossal evils of racketeering which have spread terror and murder throughout our country these past few years, literally threatening the very foundations of society itself!

These things are truly signs, to those who have eyes to see, and who are wise enough to know the meaning thereof. Why, only last year, the God-fearing, law-abiding citizens of Brooklyn, here in New York, had to organize themselves into vigilance committees and form armed bands in order to be able to get to their churches on Sunday without being assaulted and robbed by murderous foreign-born thugs on the way! Even as these lines are being written, a gang of those underworld "gorillas" are being indicted in the New York courts for 52 murders! Shocking, outrageous.

Such conditions are almost beyond belief; and the fact that they could exist right here in the very heart of the most populous city in our country is in itself a sign that things are most certainly not what they ought to be, by a long, long shot. And what, you may well ask, is the explanation for this most deplorable, this utterly inexcusable state of affairs? Money, the Bible tells us, is the root of all evil. Of course, there are obviously other contributing factors but the inordinate love of wealth and the material things which wealth will buy is unquestionably the main or root cause of it all.

Our Savior, whose word cannot fall (for it is Truth), further tells us, concerning that awful time of sorrows and tribulations. (Luke 21: 25-26)— "Upon the earth distress of nations, with perplexity; . . . men's hearts failing them for fear, and for looking after those things which are coming on earth."

And how well does 2 Timothy 3: 1-5 describe the very conditions that prevail upon earth today, and which, we are forewarned, is a sure sign that we are living in that very time referred to in the following prophetic words: "This know also, that in the last days perilous times shall come. For men shall be lovers of their own selves, covetous, boasters, proud, blasphemers, disobedient to parents, unthankful, unholy, without natural affection, truthbreakers (as

---

8. On June 29, 1925, Santa Barbara, California experienced a 6.8 earthquake. Scott Harrison, "From the Archives: The 1925 Santa Barbara Earthquake," *Los Angeles Times*, June 28, 2019.

witness Hitler and Stalin!), false accusers, incontinent, fierce, despisers of those that are good, traitors, heady, high-minded lovers of pleasures more than lovers of God; having a form of godliness but denying the power thereof . . ."

Who, indeed, can read these words today without immediately recognizing the unmistakable application to our present time? And as regards the time of tribulations and sorrows which has descended upon the two mightiest empires of the world—the Bible plainly tells us that those to whom much is given, much shall be demanded of them. And what have the British and French empires really done, to justify the mighty and incalculable resources for goodness and right which were committed to their care and stewardship? One must answer, in all candor, very little indeed: Those old empire systems have been cruel and ruthless oppression, disease, ignorance and unspeakable poverty for the great masses of the people; while a little clique of the ruling class have had the audacity to sit themselves up as "lords" of creation! And though they refuse flatly to repay their just and honest war debts, they nevertheless are getting in the habit of howling for us Americans to come fight their eternal wars for them! It is a well-known fact that the poor people of England are by all odds the most miserable poor creatures on the face of God's earth! It is even said that one reason King Edward resigned his throne was because he, being a true humanitarian at heart, wanted to do something really constructive by way of alleviating the terrible suffering and misery of the millions of poor mining families in England and Wales; but the ruling clique of moneybags that really control the empire simply laughed him out of court!

But with all their faults—and they are many—one cannot but prefer the old exploiting empire system to the inhuman and monstrous ironheel methods of the atheistic dictators, who would have the peoples of all the earth, including, of course, ourselves, goose-stepping to their barked commands and reduced to the pitiful status of bond-slaves.

In closing this article, I will relate, in connection with the war now raging in Europe, some visions which I have had lately, leaving it to you to interpret them for yourself. But I will say here that I know, positively KNOW that the invisible Power which so graciously permits me to see these things—I seem to see them as if I were looking at a motion picture being unreeled before me—this unseen force is much, much higher and holier and wiser than my humble self can ever hope to be, here or hereafter. And I am most humbly grateful for the honor and privilege which has thus been bestowed upon my unworthy self, and I consider it a sacred duty to let these things be known, for whatever they may mean.

Late the other night, as I sat reading the Prophet Isaiah, I was suddenly, it seemed, carried to a fearfully high place, which seemed to be a very old and deserted city. And from the great, massive arches and other architectural characteristics I "felt" that it was a spiritual representation of Rome in which I thus found myself. (But do not misunderstand me: The streets of that city seemed as real to me as do the streets of New York normally.) I came to a place that looked something like the entrance to a wired enclosure, and which might have been the entrance to a concentration camp, or something on that order. And as I stood looking into that wired enclosure, the guard on duty motioned me to look behind me. And when I turned to look, my heart almost froze in my breast! For there, far, far below me, so far down that it made me dizzy to look, and I held on to the iron post to keep from falling—for there in the yawning chasm below I saw the bluest body of water that I have ever seen, and at a certain point that projected out into the blue water there appeared to be a great fort or something of that kind, and around this were anchored a great number of ships, which I distinctly saw from my great height. I seemed to have the feeling that something would descend upon those ships from a great height. Then the vision vanished and I found myself again sitting at the little table with my Bible. Now the only interpretation I can put on that vision is this: The Mediterranean Sea is a very blue body of water, and something is going to transpire there that may have profound historical significance for the world?

A night or two later, when I had put out the light and retired, I suddenly saw, as if marching through a street somewhere, what looked to be a column of boy scouts with a great number of small American flags, and before these very young marchers there went a great number of grey-headed men in soldiers' uniforms. Just what this may signify, I do not know, unless it meant that both old and young shall have to go before our next war is over?

And last evening, as I sat composing a poem, I was suddenly shown, in that strange, mysterious spiritual light which the seers have so often spoken of, a man (for it was a man's hands) was reading out of a very big book, one that looked like a huge record book, or something of that kind. I could not see the man's face, nor his body, except his hands and the huge book. And as the vision vanished (I saw it in a flash), I seemed to hear as if in a whisper, (But not with my physical ears) the word "Stalin." And I thus concluded that maybe Russia's Godless hordes would play some sort of important role in the coming struggle? But one thing is certain: These visions which I'm being permitted to witness are most definitely not mere "hallucinations," and they have nothing whatever to do with my mental imagination. But then even these things are also a very part of the fulfilling of prophecy; for we are told that in the last days "Old men shall dream dreams and young men shall see visions."

———•·•———

No Peace
June 26, 1940

"They will cry 'peace, peace,' but there shall be no peace."
—The Bible

In the logically thought-out and well-written article on peace which appeared in last issue of this paper, Myragene Huckaby (who, I presume, is a lady for the name sounds feminine?) says some things which are very timely and to the point, and that should provoke serious discussions upon this profoundly important question.[9] For there can be no doubt whatever that we are headed straight for war—a war the hellish likes of which the world has never seen before.

That Roosevelt has ambitions to be a war president, is obvious, even to a blind man. And it certainly bodes no good to the country that he is surrounded and naturally influenced by a clique of internationally-minded individuals who are more interested in avenging their grievances on Hitler than they are in guarding the real, bona fide interests of America. This is most unfortunate, but it is deplorably true; alas, I fear, tragically true.

Now Miss Huckaby (for I am sure that the writer is a "miss") is absolutely correct in noting that President Wilson was treacherously double-crossed by the gang of plotting intriguers who were in the saddle at that time of the alleged "peace conference" which so selfishly and so (as it turns out) shortsightedly attempted to reduce a proud and ingenious people to a state of object servitude.

But the tables are, for the time at least, now turned: It is now France's time to be lashed to the whipping post and all but denuded. And for what? As Miss Huckaby thoughtfully points out, the days of wars of conquest are definitely past. For imperialistic ventures no longer settle even the very problems they raise. The world has, indeed, by the grace of modern inventions (which, after all, is only an expression of the wise workings of Providence?) and the advancement in mass education and communication—what with all these things, the

---

9. The editor found no information on a Myragene Huckaby although there were Huckabys in Guntersville, Alabama.

world today is becoming one big community, with Shelley's ideal of "the brotherhood of man" in the process of becoming fact?

No. What the world needs is not war with its horrible train of calamities, its monstrous maladjustments and disastrous subsidiary evils; what the world needs is rather the Christ spirit brotherliness and a heeding of that profoundly wise injunction to "love thy neighbor as thyself." And those superficial cynics and smart-alec scoffers who reason erroneously from analogy that mankind can never progress to that state of intellectual and moral elevation enjoined by the Master; such shallow pates do not stop the truly amazing progress which the world has made in even one century—the last one. At the beginning of the last century the staid citizenry of the great commonwealth of Massachusetts were still persecuting the few delicately sensitive souls (now called "mediums" but then declared to be "witches") who were attuned to higher vibrations than those compassed within the range of the (ordinary) five senses; and the one-gallus nit-wits who were debating, in words of one-syllable amongst themselves the grave question of whether women were really entitled to the same civil privileges as were the men—namely the right to vote. These and such like imbecilities were agitating the minds (if they could be called minds?) of our citizens that know enough to come in out of the rain, who can say that humanity does not progress, or that we shall never, as a species, reach that stage in our evolutionary journey through the Cosmos where we can govern ourselves without having to resort to cave-man tactics and stratagems so universally employed today? The club, the garrote, the dagger, the bullet, the various gases and the other lethal contrivances and contraptions now invoked to exterminate those who do not see things precisely as we do; these and all such like childish tomfooleries and hideous monkey-shines will have been laid aside in shuddering and blushful shame, when our race shall have come of age, mentally and morally.

But in closing this Jeremiad, I would beg to dissent from Miss Huckaby's closely reasoned peace thesis by pointing out, what she, I fear, has overlooked, namely: the very patent fact that the Germanic peoples, of all the peoples on earth, are obviously the least fitted what with their congenital arrogance, their ruthless iron heel, goose-stepping idiocy; their harsh and vindictive methods of dealing with those vanquished people who are hopelessly at their mercy; considering all these things, one cannot but shudder at the fate that awaits mankind should the inhuman "blitzkrieg" tactics of the Third Reich succeed in breaking the power of the British Empire. For, whether we like it or not, we Americans are essentially Anglo-Saxons in origin and tastes, etc., and the pan-European

"Kultures" and customs which the ruthless hordes of victorious Germans and Russians would impose on the rest of the world would most certainly be a bitter pill for us to swallow—and swallow we would, by force!

No, our interests, as a Democracy, lie irretrievably, inevitably with the so-called world-democracies, even to the extent of war. But please remember: I say "our interests as a democracy." Democracy, however, is not necessarily synonymous with life, or the inalienable rights of the people, though it is, as I see it, the best way of life yet constitutionally devised or conceived. But I am unalterably opposed to war, all war—for "war is hell," nothing else. Hell means disharmony. What the world needs is more HARMONY.

A Sad Christmas
December 11, 1940

How far afield our modern world has strayed from moral and ethical and social and religious precepts and truths so beautifully and simply taught by the divine and holy Christ whose (earthly) natal day the so-called Christian world will soon be celebrating again! With tens of millions of the sons of earth now under arms, and countless other millions of our fellow beings reduced to virtual slavery, our need not be a prophet to perceive that something, yea, much has gone wrong with us? With all the energy, ingenuity, and determination of a billion people absorbed in mad pursuit of war, or the intense and hectic preparation therefor, what else can we expect?

Tragedy, disaster and destruction have been visited upon the helpless heads of millions and millions of innocent people, and sorrow and sadness too deep for words, and all because of power and mere material things, and the love and worship thereof by those mad, world-wrecking dictators who are urged and egged on and lashed to fury by their evil geniuses, the invisible powers of darkness, who are now their absolute masters. And if you are inclined to doubt that these world-leaders and men of great power are controlled by discarnate intelligence from the invisible world of spirit, then let me suggest that you read the works of the ancient Hebrew historian Josephus and especially that part of his history that refers to Alexander the Great, who conquered the world and then wept because there were no more worlds for him to conquer. Josephus, who as a contemporary of St. Paul, tells us that it was because of the advice and encouragement which he received in a dream that caused Alexander the Great to enter upon his predestined activities. And after he had conquered the world, this same young Alexander the Great, was led by his invisible creator to Jerusalem, where he met the old Hebrew patriarch and holy man whom he had previously seen in the dream; and at sight of the old priest, Alexander the Great fell upon his knees and would have worshipped him had not the old patriarch forbidden it. How truly mysterious and inscrutable are the ways of God!

Our modern mis-educated scoffers and materialistic infidels who go to our institutions of so-called "higher learning," and among whom it is considered fashionable and "smart" to laugh out of the corner of their mouths in superior condescension at such "old-fogey relics of the caveman age" as disembodied intelligence and spiritual phenomena of all classes and kinds—the ambitious wordlings will one day come to bitterly regret their noisy and vainglorious conceits, and then the laugh will be out of the other side of their mouth! But to get back to our subject—war and Christmas.

I had tea one evening last week with a most charming and cultured little Southern lady, an Alabamian by the way who incidentally, is an aunt of our Senator Lister Hill, of Alabama. This cultured little lady has lived abroad mostly in France, I believe, for many years. And she was in France when Hitler's legions came swarming in like locusts to strip and despoil the country of all that the people held dear, even destroying or taking away the great and prized masterpieces of art and statuary, which had been the pride and glory of France, and had so eloquently testified to the culture and civilization and genius of this great and ancient nation. And, worst of all, the awful misery and destitution, which swept over the countless tens of thousands of homeless victims of war—the aged and crippled and blind, and pregnant mothers and babies in arms, all tramping the muddy, shell-torn, corpse strewn roads of France, poor, starving, roofless outcasts with no place to go, no friends to turn to, with no government to look after them, and utterly without hope.

Thousands upon thousands of them perished of hunger and cold and disease and fright, in the desolate fields and along those pitiful, terror-haunted roads. Starving babies clinging like little pathetic skeletons to the dry breasts of mothers who were likewise starving and too weak to move farther. Many of these poor souls fell from sheer exhaustion in the road where they marched, and were ground into the very earth by the pitiless treads of Hitler's iron tanks!

Yes, Sherman was right; War is hell. And what else could it be but hell? For wars are instigated by the forces and powers of evil, whose seat and center are literally hell itself. And out of evil nothing but evil can come. And this old, mysterious world of ours would indeed be utterly without hope and a very hell to live in were it not for Him whose birthday we shall now in a few days be remembering. And if I may have sounded too much like the preacher in this article, I can only plead extenuation, with Wordsworth, that "The world is too much with us soon and late." And in such times as these it may behoove us to get in the habit of occasionally taking our minds from the empty shells and shadow illusions of this material world in which we are temporarily imprisoned, and turn our thoughts and attentions toward that eternal world of reality and spirit, that timeless realm where decay and corruption are not, and death is a mere fiction. For there begins our Real Life, for which this, our present molecular world, is the mere kindergarten and preparatory school. Yes, this will be a sad yuletide for many of earth's inhabitants: but to those who are reassured in the blessed knowledge that life continues beyond the grave, and that God is truly the just and holy and merciful Father we have been taught to believe Him to be, life can hold no cross too hard, nor death no terror that can daunt us.

What I Saw I Hell (Part I)
March 19, 1941

By way of preface to this and the articles that will follow, permit me to try to explain as much as it's possible for one to "explain" such things to those who perhaps know but little or nothing about them, from either reading or personal experience—allow me to say just this by way of introduction to these psychic or spiritual experiences of mine—surely the strangest, perhaps, that you have ever heard or read of: That they are plain, simple statements of fact, and in no way colored or distorted by my own everyday physical imagination, at least not to my conscious knowledge. And if you find it difficult to bring yourself to believe such things are true, then do not condemn yourself as being unduly skeptical, for your skepticism is only natural and logical, for, until our spiritual faculties have become developed to the point where they are capable of receiving spiritual truth—in other words, until we become psychically sensitive to the degree that we are susceptible to the supernormal or super-sensual impressions and contacts, we simply cannot comprehend or appreciate the great fact and holy truth of spiritual communication between the two worlds, the so-called "living" and the so-called "dead." And I hope and pray that there will come the time, while you are still in the flesh, that you will know for a certainty, as I now do, that there really and truly is no death. For when, and if, you finally realize this great central truth of life, then Death will no longer hold any terrors or fears or grim forebodings for you.

Death is simply the terminal point of the crisis in which the living spirit must go through in shedding the earthly body, this faithful old fleshly mask or exact counterpart of the real person within. And it is that real you (the spirit-body) that shall go right on living and knowing and doing, long after—yes, forever after—your present body of flesh and blood and bones has returned back to dust or to the earth whence it came; while the spirit goes to the place it has prepared for itself by the way it lived and the life it led while on earth. This is the simple and holy truth.

And this brings us now to the experience which I shall truthfully describe, just as I was permitted to see them as they actually are and exist in the spirit-world. But just let me repeat, for the benefit of those who may not be familiar with my previous writings on the subject, that of late years I seem to have been chosen as perhaps the instrument or messenger through whom to reveal certain spiritual truths to those who may not care to know them. And I can say in all sincerity that, while I do not consider myself worthy of such high honor and consideration on the part of my unseen superiors, I nevertheless am most humbly grateful to the Powers that be, and I shall, to the best of my limited ability and feeble talents, comply with their wishes; for I know for a certainty that my spiritual "guide" or "guardian angel" is a high and noble and true servant of God, and not a disguised agent, as some might think, of the Powers of Darkness. And how do I know this? How do you know a person's true character, except by his acts, his deeds, his general philosophy, and philosophy of life? And, too, evil spirits cannot deceive other spirits in the spiritland, for in that world they are seen and known for just exactly what they are. And though it's true that they can, and do, deceive people who are still in the flesh and thus unable to see them spiritually; yet it should be remembered that when I'm taken into the spirit realms I go as a spirit, though other spirits seem to know, somehow, that I have not yet entered their world forever, but only temporarily. How they know this I cannot yet tell, unless they can see something of the material earth still about me? To myself, I look just as I always do.

Our Savior tells us to "Ask and ye shall receive; knock and it shall be opened unto you; search and ye shall find." And knowing what I now do about both worlds—the spiritual and the material—I can only say to those who would know something of these things for themselves, then let them begin by preparing themselves for any and every service they may be called upon to perform, without thought of renumeration or compensation and only for the love of their fellow man and the greater love of their God. You must prepare yourself by living very simply, even humbly, and, above all things, righteously. You must learn to meditate and to pray with your whole soul and heart and spirit; and this does not mean praying with your speaking voice in the public or the churches, but rather, as St. Paul advised, pray in secret, in your closet. Have no fears that your secret prayers and thoughts will not be heard, for they will, and ever are heard in the spirit world, whether they're answered or not. That depends upon other things, whether, for instance, it serves the Divine will and purpose to answer your prayers. Never pray for anything that you do not absolutely need in order to make a better person out of you. Never, for instance, ask the Lord to do anything you or someone else, can do for you, even if you should have to struggle for long years to do it. For by struggling you learn patience, fortitude, and many, many other things which schoolbooks did not teach you! You must learn to have faith—faith in yourself, in your fellow man, and above all, in your creator. Remember Christ's rebuke, to even his very own disciples: "O, ye of little faith!" And how He went on to tell them that if they but had the faith of a mustard-seed they could even command mountains to vanish! And why did our Savior choose the mustard-seed in order to illustrate his teachings? Because a grain of seed in the cold ground must have sublime faith to keep its vital energies together until the voice of Nature, which is the servant of God, bids it awaken from its cold, wet bed of dirt and come forth to life and leafage and beauty. "O, ye of little faith!"

Before describing my visits to the hells (I say "the hells" for there are many and varying degrees of them), let me say merely that hells are simply mental prisons, and some of them (the milder ones) are somewhat similar to such penal institutions on earth. And it was not until I had been taken to some of these milder ones that I was taken to some of the—well, not so mild ones; which, let me emphasize, is a masterpiece of understatement! For truly there are things in the spirit-world which it is not lawful to utter . . .

And now I will tell you something about my "spirit-guide" or guardian angel who so kindly and graciously condescends to take me—literally he seems to lead me by the hand, though I do not see him, but I do hear his voice and he answers my questions most civilly and fatherly—and thus away we go, seeming to distant regions, and we travel with speed of thought, which is even faster than the electricity in your reading lamp! Yes, I mean this literally. And why do I not see my Guide or Guardian Angel? When I myself asked him this very question, he replied simply and I know truthfully, that I could not yet see him because I could not bear it—in other words, his rate of spiritual vibrations is so much superior to my own, so to speak, embryo earthly one that he is entirely invisible to even my spirit-eyes, just as the spokes in a fast-moving wheel become invisible to the human eye. But maybe I do not quite succeed in making myself clear? But he did once show me a spirit-picture of himself as he was during his last years on earth. And I could compare to nothing as much as a tall and stately and dignified and intellectually and morally highly developed English statesman or poet or perhaps man of letters. His hair was silvery in color and fell in a gentle silken cascade down about his manly, erect shoulders. He wore a large wide-brimmed brown hat, and seemed to have an Inverness cape or some sort of flowing robe that fell in straight folds from his shoulders. This is the way he looked when on earth in flesh. Permit me to say that he is entirely too modest and self-effacing to even as much as discuss himself. And you can imagine how a person of so small consequence and ability as I must feel when in the holy presence of such exalted personage who yet is so sweetly humble as regards himself! And he has very great powers, I have learned from decidedly personal experiences. Truly he has power over "hell and the grave," for I have seen, as later you shall hear, how not only the evil human spirits in the spirit prisons fell on their faces in obsequious homage before him, but the very demons—yes, I mean demons, infernal creatures with evil human faces but with horns on their heads and claws on their feet (speak the truth)—I have seen even these fiends and demons bow down before my Guardian angel, and appear to become immovable, as if transfixed with paralyzing fear, before him. Thus, I know he is truly a very high and exalted personage.

In the succeeding articles I shall describe things that "mortal eye hath not seen nor ear heard" (for I did not see them with these mortal eyes that are constructed only for the cruder rate vibrations of the material world, but with the spiritual eyes). And I must ask you, who know me as your county historian and man of letters, to please believe me when I candidly vouch for the veracity and literal truth of that which hereinafter follows. And, in concluding this our introductory article, I cannot emphasize enough the serious meaning and importance they hold for us, who are shortly to be faced with the most crucial and trying times in the history of the world. And as some of us may soon, while all of us must ultimately, be ushered into that other world, it cannot do us any harm, and may be of help to us, to know much as we possibly can learn or in anywise find out about that sphere of existence and the conditions that obtain there. For that world is, after all, the one that's to be our long home; this one is merely a sort of preparatory way-station on the road to Eternity.

[**Editors' note:** Although this was to be the first of a series, no further parts were published.]

The Old Folks at Home
August 20, 1941

The leaves on the earlier and less hardy varieties of trees in Central Park here in New York City have begun to turn yellow and to thin out, a true sign that another long and peaceful summer is drawing to a close.

Though this has been one of the hottest summers on record here in the city, I have not, strangely enough, been in the parks a half-dozen times the whole season. And only lately I stroll up to the "Mall" in Central Park occasionally on an evening to hear the famous out-door band there give their wonderful free concerts, which are quite as fine as any that one could hear in the expensive concert halls in the metropolis. And it is good, so to speak, to lose oneself now and then in the transporting raptures of glorious music, and to thus get away from and forget the sad and depressing news of war and all its attendant horrors and destruction. And, too, I occasionally like to wander off deep into the unbroken quietude of woodland, to find some serene and tranquil spot of wild loveliness, and there to meditate and think, to commune with the real me that is deep down beneath this conventional exterior and mask of worldly sophistication. And at such cherished and rare moments one can truly appreciate the simple truth of Wordsworth's oft-quoted and famous lines about the world's being "too much with us, soon and late."

But what has all this to do with the old folks at home? Well, it's just that one sometimes feels in the mood to be, as it were, sort of homesick, especially when one has been so far from home for so many years.

One likes to recall the old familiar faces and scenes of the dear old long ago; to live over again the precious moments in life that meant so much to one, and to cherish as earth's rarest possession the kindly words of encouragement from true friends, the friendly greetings and mutual exchanges of sincere fellowship with one's old reliable and always dependable neighbors; and, above all those whispered and secret little words of love that went straight from heart to heart—little treasures that time cannot blight nor the passing of years erase . . .

It is perhaps not inappropriate that these sentimental lines, called up by the feeling and mood of nostalgia, which, with me, is always most poignant and acutely felt in the late summer or early autumn; as I say, it is keeping with the cultural, poetic, and gentile atmosphere that pervades, yea, that fairly exudes from every blessed inch of this revered and famous old New York landmark. For these lines are being scribbled over my coffee here at a little table in a corner of this cozy little "coffee shop" in Washington Irving's old home. Directly across the street, opposite this little old-fashioned red-brick, two-story house, stands the great ten-story Washington Irving High School, with its huge bronze bust of the beloved author looking benignly down from his stately pedestal upon Father Knickerbocker's teeming millions of hurrying sons and daughter.

Coming up Fifth Avenue from my humble lodgings to this little literary rendezvous, I passed Mark Twain's old home at the southeast corner of Fifth Avenue and Ninth Street, and it occurred to me how much alike those two great American geniuses were: They were both gentle by nature and possessed sympathetic and understanding souls; both were kindly and wise in their relations and attitudes toward life and their fellow beings; both were endowed with deep and penetrating minds, which were richly stored with knowledge, and each of them had a sense of humor, so kindly and pronounced that it left its mark on their memory forever.

But the American writer who so masterfully and perfectly expressed the feeling of poignant nostalgia (homesickness) that all must feel, more or less, who are long away from their homes, was that uniquely and divinely gifted poet and composer Stephen Foster, who composed the most hauntingly beautiful and soul-stirring melodies that America possesses, and are now being sung and played the wide world over. Such incomparably lovely old folk-songs as "Old Black Joe," "My Old Kentucky Home," "Swanee River," etc. never grow old or monotonous by repetition. Many writers and critics have been puzzled to account for the seemingly mysterious phenomenon of Stephen Foster's perennial and everlasting popularity. But it is really not a mystery at all: The songs simply came from the heart; and the human heart is so constituted that it always recognizes its own, regardless of who expresses it.

Stephen Foster, by the way, spent his last days in the place where I am now living.

Humble Poet: A Sampling

What sadder end could Fate devise
than this that bows his head
to inferiors who despise
him while throwing him his bread?
—William Nabors

Life's Mystery
November 10, 1937

What everlasting wonder here,
These tides of night and day
That ebb and flow from year to year
And bring and take our lives away?

Light and shadow, time and space,
And man, upon his little isle
Buffeted from place to place
And living here such little while!

Yet the spirit of his race,
The special hunger of his kind,
Seeks this mystery to trace,
Hopes the answer yet to find.

From what far-off unknown shore
Come these vital emanations,
Vibrant visitants that pour
Their blessings are like revelations?

What the purpose, what the Cause
Of this wondrous visitation?
Who the Author of its Laws?
What or where its destination?

Transient little shadows, we,
Of all that's come and gone before;
Future man we cannot see—
Only the wish, nothing more.

Enveloped here its little hour
In mortal flesh, the human soul
Rejects its mundane limitations
For a yet diviner goal.

Like a moth our little flight,
And ever higher leads the way,
Back to Oneness and to Light,
Of the tides of night and day.

———•◦•———

The Road We Take
December 8, 1937

It's not so much the life we live—
Whether it's high or low,
But rather the service that we give
As through this life we go.

It's not so much the success we make
In the eyes of other men;

It's more the road in life we take,
And the spirit we take it in.

Some there are of station and wealth,
Others have talent or beauty;
But more important far than these
Are those who do their duty!

Whether we dine from plate of gold
In some resplendent room
Or sup from tin in hovel cold
And barren and in gloom—

A failure may sit at the plate of gold,
A success at the plate of tin,
Depending upon the codes we hold,
And the spirit that we hold them in.

———•·•———

There is No Death
April 10, 1940

There is no death
Dear grieving friend,
To rob thee of affection,
For the change of form
Is not the end,
But the beginning of perfection.
Remember the words,
Of that beautiful story
About "sown in dishonor,
Raised in glory."

So, dry thy tears
Dear grieving one;
They only sadden
Him you mourn,

For though his labor here is done,
The spiritself is merely sorn
To another realm of life—
To its God-appointed sphere,
Wherein to witness the fruition
Of the thoughts most cherished here.

A P P E N D I X

Historical figures whom William Nabors professed to have known

Addams, Clifford (painter)
Adimari, Ralph (literary critic)
Bevans, Homer (sculptor)
Bodenheim, Maxwell (novelist)
Bryan, Jr., William Jennings (lawyer)
Cardozo, Benjamin (Associate Supreme Court Justice)
Denisevich, Anna (widow of novelist Leonid Andreyev)
Dressler, Marie (actress)
Grey, Zane (novelist)
Hunt, George W.P. (Governor of Arizona)
Lindsay, Vachel (poet)
Markham, Edwin (poet)
Masters, Edgar Lee (poet)
O'Brien, Dan (Hobo King)
Pickering, Simeon H. (painter)
Wells, H.G. (writer)

Bibliography

Newspapers

Advertiser-Gleam (Guntersville, AL)
Algona Upper Des Moines
Birmingham News
Bowery News
Brooklyn Daily Eagle
Brooklyn Times Union
Chicago Tribune
Columbia Spectator
Davis County Clipper (Bountiful, UT)
Greenville News (Greenville, SC)
Guntersville Advertiser (Guntersville, AL)
Guntersville Democrat (Guntersville, AL)
Guntersville Gleam (Guntersville, AL)
Los Angeles Times
Miami News
New York Times
Salt Lake Tribune
San Francisco Examiner
St. Louis Post-Dispatch
Times Record (New York, NY)
Times (Munster, IN)

Books, Journals, and Websites

Ackroyd, Peter. *Blake: A Biography*. New York: Alfred A. Knopf, 1996.
Ady, Julia Mary Cartwright. *Jean François Millet, His Life and Letters*. London: Swan Sonnenschein & Co., 1902.
Barnard, Harry. *Independent Man: The Life of Senator James Couzens*. Detroit: Wayne State University Press, 2002.
Beasley, Norman. *Frank Knox, American: A Short Biography*. New York: Doubleday, 1936.

Bennett, James R. and Karen R. Utz. *Iron and Steel: A Guide to the Birmingham Area Industrial Heritage*. Tuscaloosa: University of Alabama Press, 2010.

Berman, David R. *George Hunt: Arizona's Crusading Seven-Term Governor*. Tucson: University of Arizona Press, 2015.

Blackorby, Edward. *Prairie Rebel: The Public Life of William Lemke*. Lincoln: University of Nebraska Press, 1963.

Bodenheim, Maxwell. *My Life and Loves in Greenwich Village*. New York City: Belmont, 1961.

Brooks, ed., Van Wyck. *The Journal of Gamaliel Bradford, 1883–1932*. Boston: Houghton Mifflin Co., 1933.

Burton, Hal. *The Morro Castle: Tragedy at Sea*. New York: Viking, 1973.

Calhoun, Janet, ed. *Trails & Traces, People & Places*. Albertville, AL: Creative Printers, 1994.

Cannadine, David. *Mellon: An American Life*. New York: Vintage, 2008.

Carter, Dan T. *Scottsboro: A Tragedy of the American South*. Baton Rouge: Louisiana State University Press, 2007.

Conrow, Robert. *Field Day: The Life, Times & Reputation of Eugene Field*. New York: Charles Scribner's Sons, 1974.

Coodley, Lauren. *Upton Sinclair: California Socialist, Celebrity Intellectual*. Lincoln: Bison Books, 2013.

Craig, Douglas B. *Progressives at War: William G. McAdoo and Newton D. Baker, 1863–1941*. Baltimore: Johns Hopkins University Press, 2013.

Daugherty, Greg. "Odd McIntyre: The Man Who Taught America about New York." *Smithsonian Magazine*. Accessed April 8, 2020. https://www.smithsonianmag.com/history/odd-mcintyre-the-man-who-taught-america-about-new-york-2317241/.

Davis, Roderick. "John Allan Wyeth." *Encyclopedia of Alabama*. Accessed April 7, 2020. http://www.encyclopediaofalabama.org/article/h-3522.

Dempsey, Jack. *Dempsey*. New York: Harper & Row, 1977.

Denver Post. *Denver Memories*. Pediment Publishing, 2017.

———. *Denver Memories II*: The Early Years and the 1940s. Pediment Publishing, 2018.

Dickson, Foster. "Andrew Lytle." *Encyclopedia of Alabama*. Accessed April 8, 2020. http://www.encyclopediaofalabama.org/article/h-3943.

Dowling, William C. *Oliver Wendell Holmes in Paris: Medicine, Theology, and the Autocrat of the Breakfast Table*. Lebanon, NH: University of New Hampshire Press, 2006.

Downs, Matthew L. *Transforming the South: Federal Development in the Tennessee Valley, 1915–1960*. Baton Rouge: Louisiana State University Press, 2014.

Duberman, Martin B. *James Russell Lowell: Poet, Critic, Editor, Teacher, Diplomat*. Boston: Houghton Mifflin, Co., 1966.

Duncan, Katherine and Larry Smith. *The History of Marshall County*. Albertville, AL: Thompson Printing Co., 1969.

Dunlap, Annette B. *Charles Gates Dawes: A Life*. Evanston, IL: Northwestern University Press, 2016.

DeVillo, Stephen Paul. *The Bowery: The Strange History of New York's Oldest Street*. New York: Skyhorse Publishing, 2017.

Fairbanks, Robert B. *For the City as a Whole: Planning, Politics, and the Public Interest in Dallas, Texas, 1900–1965*. Columbus: Ohio State University Press, 1998.

Fausold, Martin L. *James W. Wadsworth, Jr.: The Gentleman from New York*. Syracuse: Syracuse University Press, 1975.

Ferrara, Eric. *The Bowery: A History of Grit, Graft, and Grandeur*. Charleston, SC: The History Press, 2011.

Filler, Louis. *The Unknown Edwin Markham: His Mystery and Its Significance*. Kent, OH: Kent State University Press, 1966.

Fisher, O.C. *Cactus Jack: A Biography of John Nance Garner*. Waco: Texian Press, 1978.

Gallagher, Thomas. *Fire at Sea: The Mysterious Tragedy of the Morro Castle*. Guilford, CT: Lyons Press, 2003.

"Gerald Lyman Kenneth Smith." *Encyclopedia of Arkansas*. Accessed April 8, 2020. https://encyclopediaofarkansas.net/entries/gerald-lyman-kenneth-smith-1767/.

Gill, Gillian. *Mary Baker Eddy*. Boston: De Capo Press, 1998.

Goodman, James. *Stories of Scottsboro*. New York: Vintage Books, 1994.

Griffith, Sally Foreman. *Home Town News: William Allen White and the Emporia Gazette*. New York: Oxford University Press, 1989.

Hair, William Ivy. *The Kingfish and His Realm: The Life and Times of Huey P. Long*. Baton Rouge: Louisiana State University Press, 1991.

Harbaugh, William. *Lawyers' Lawyer: The Life of John W. Davis*. New York: Oxford University Press, 1973.

Hare, Richard. *Maxim Gorky: Romantic Realist and Conservative Revolutionary*. New York: Oxford University Press, 1962.

Hargrove, Erwin C. *Prisoners of Myth: The Leadership of the Tennessee Valley Authority, 1933–1990*. Princeton: Princeton University Press, 1994.

Harris, Mark. *City of Discontent: An Interpretive Biography of Vachel Lindsay, Being also the Story of Springfield for that City, that State, and that Nation*. Second Chance Press, 1990.

Hessen, Robert. *Steel Titan: The Life of Charles M. Schwab*. Pittsburgh: University of Pittsburgh Press, 1990.

Hill, Patricia Evridge. *Dallas: The Making of a Modern City*. Austin: University of Texas Press, 1996.

Holroyd, Michael. *Bernard Shaw: The One-Volume Definitive Edition*. New York: Random House, 1998.

"James Alexander Reed." Biographical Directory of the United States Congress, 1774–Present. Accessed April 6, 2020. https://bioguideretro.congress.gov/ Home /MemberDetails?memIndex=r000118.

Jeansonne, Glen. *Gerald L.K. Smith: Minister of Hate*. Baton Rouge: Louisiana State University Press, 1997.

Kaun, Alexander. *Leonid Andreyev: A Critical Study*. New York: B.W. Huebsch, Inc., 1924.

Lagos, Taso G. *American Zeus: The Life of Alexander Pantages, Theater Mogul*. Jefferson, NC: McFarland, 2018.

Lake, Inez Hollander. *The Road from Pompey's Head: The Life and Works of Hamilton Basso*. Baton Rouge: Louisiana State University Press, 1999.

Langford, Gerald. *Alias O. Henry: A Biography of William Sidney Porter*. New York: Macmillan, 1957.

Larson, Edward J. *Summer of the Gods: The Scopes Trial and America's Continuing Debate over Science and Religion*. New York: Basic Books, 2020.

Lee, Betty. *Marie Dressler: The Unlikeliest Star*. Lexington: University Press of Kentucky, 1997.

Lowitt, Richard. *George W. Norris: The Triumph of a Progressive, 1933–1944*. Chicago: University of Illinois Press, 1978.

MacDonald, Edgar E. *James Branch Cabell and Richmond-In-Virginia*. Jackson: University Press of Mississippi, 1993.

MacLean, Nancy K. *Behind the Mask of Chivalry: The Making of the Second Ku Klux Klan*. New York: Oxford University Press, 1995.

Maddox, Robert James. *William E. Borah and American Foreign Policy*. Baton Rouge: Louisiana State University Press, 1970.

May, Stephen J. *Zane Grey: Romancing the West*. Athens: Ohio University Press, 1997.

McDaniel, George William. *Smith Wildman Brookhart: Iowa's Renegade Republican*. Iowa City: Iowa State Press, 1995.

McGann, Jerome. *The Poet Edgar Allan Poe: Alien Angel*. Cambridge: Harvard University Press, 1994.

Mitchell, Ruth. *My Brother Bill: A Biography of General "Billy" Mitchell*. New York City: Harcourt Brace, 1953.

Moore, Jack B. *Maxwell Bodenheim*. New York City: Twayne Publishers, 1970.

Murray, Paul. *A Fantastic Journey: The Life and Literature of Lafcadio Hearn*. Ann Arbor: University of Michigan Press, 1997.

"Murray, William Henry David." Oklahoma Historical Society. Accessed April 7, 2020. https://www.okhistory.org/publications/enc/entry.php?entry=MU014.

Newcombe, Josephine. *Leonid Andreyev*. Ungar, 1973.

Nowell, Elizabeth. *Thomas Wolfe: A Biography*. Praeger, 1973.

"The Ocean Liner Leviathan." National Museum of American History. Accessed April 10, 2020. https://americanhistory.si.edu/collections/object-groups/the-ocean-liner-leviathan.

Ohl, John Kennedy. *Hugh S. Johnson and the New Deal*. DeKalb: Northern Illinois University Press, 1985.

Palmer, Frederick. *This Man Landon: The Record and Career of Governor Alfred M. Landon of Kansas*. New York: Dodd, Mead & Co., 1936.

Pauly, Thomas H. *Zane Grey: His Life, His Adventures, His Women*. Chicago: University of Illinois Press, 2005.

Posner, Richard A. *Cardozo: A Study in Reputation*. Chicago: University of Illinois Press, 1990.

Proctor, Ben. *William Randolph Hearst: The Later Years, 1911–1951*. New York: Oxford University Press, 2007.

Rapaport, Brooke Kamin. *Houdini: Art and Magic*. New Haven: Yale University Press, 2010.

Rawlings, William. *The Second Coming of the Invisible Empire: The Ku Klux Klan of the 1920s*. Macon: Mercer University Press, 2017.

Roberts, Adam. *H.G. Wells: A Literary Life*. New York: Palgrave Macmillan, 2019.

Roberts, Randy. *Jack Dempsey, the Manassa Mauler*. Chicago: University of Illinois Press, 2003.

Russell, Herbert K. *Edgar Lee Masters: A Biography*. Chicago: University of Illinois Press, 2001.

Slayton, Robert A. *Empire Statesman: The Rise and Redemption of Al Smith*. New York: Simon and Schuster, 2007.

Smith, Larry, ed. *Guntersville Remembered*. Albertville, AL: Creative Publishers, 2001.

Snow, Whitney A. and Barbara J. Snow. *Lake Guntersville*. Mount Pleasant, SC: The History Press, 2018.

Snow, Whitney A. and Barbara J. Snow. *Wyeth City: Alabama's Model Industrial Experiment*. Birmingham, AL: Banner Digital Printing and Publishing, 2019.

Squires, Radcliffe. *Allen Tate: A Literary Biography*. Pegasus, 1971.

"Stark Young." *Mississippi Encyclopedia*. Accessed April 8, 2020. https://mississippi encyclopedia.org/entries/stark-young/

Strouse, Jean. *Morgan: American Financier*. New York: Random House, 1999.

Stuart, David. *O. Henry: A Biography of William Sydney Porter*. New York: Stein & Day, 1990.

Szasz, Ferenc M. "T. DeWitt Talmage: Spiritual Tycoon of the Gilded Age." *Journal of Presbyterian History* 59, no. 1 (Spring 1981): 18–32.

Talmage, T. De Witt. *T. De Witt Talmage: As I Knew Him*. New York: E.P. Dutton and Co., 1912.

Tarbell, Ida M. *The Life of Elbert H. Gary: The Story of Steel*. New York: D. Appleton and Co., 1925.

Teachout, Terry. *The Skeptic: A Life of H.L. Mencken*. New York: HarperCollins Publishers, 2002.

Von der Goltz, Anna. *Hindenburg: Power, Myth, and the Rise of the Nazis*. New York: Oxford University Press, 2009.

Walsh, Michael T. *Baltimore Prohibition: Wet and Dry in the Free State*. Mount Pleasant, SC: The History Press, 2017.

Ware, Caroline F. *Greenwich Village, 1920–1930*. Berkeley: University of California Press, 1994.

Warren, Donald. *Radio Priest: Charles Coughlin, The Father of Hate Radio*. New York: Free Press, 1996.

Watson, Elbert L. "J. Thomas Heflin." *Encyclopedia of Alabama*. Accessed April 7. 2020. http://www.encyclopediaofalabama.org/article/h-2952.

Welsch, Tricia. *Gloria Swanson: Ready for her Close-Up*. Jackson: University Press of Mississippi, 2013.

Wendt, Lloyd and Herman Kogan. *Big Bill of Chicago*. Evanston, IL: Northwestern University Press, 2005.

Williams, Benjamin Buford. "Samuel Peck." *Encyclopedia of Alabama*. Accessed April 4, 2020. http://www.encyclopediaofalabama.org/article/h-2550.

Wolfskill, George. *The Revolt of the Conservatives: A History of the American Liberty League, 1934–1940*. Boston: Houghton Mifflin Co., 1962.

York, Maurice. *Ralph Waldo Emerson: The Infinitude of the Private Man*. Chicago: Wrightwood Press, 1994.

Zimmer, Amy. *Lost Denver*. Pavilion, 2016.

Index

Index

www.ingramcontent.com/pod-product-compliance
Lightning Source LLC
Chambersburg PA
CBHW021354090426
42742CB00009B/849